Frommer's®

Portable
Puerto Vallarta, Manzanillo & Guadalajara

7th Edition

by David Baird & Shane Christensen

WILEY
Wiley Publishing, Inc.

Published by:

WILEY PUBLISHING, INC.

111 River St.
Hoboken, NJ 07030-5774

ISBN 978-0-470-48722-8

Editor: Jennifer Polland
Production Editor: Jana Stefanciosa
Cartographer: Nick Trotter
Photo Editor: Richard Fox
Production by Wiley Indianapolis Composition Services

Front cover photo: Church of Guadalupe above Puerto Vallarta in Jalisco
State © Chad Ehlers / Alamy Images

For information on our other products and services or to obtain technical
support, please contact our Customer Care Department within the U.S. at
877/762-2974, outside the U.S. at 317/572-3993 or fax 317/572-4002.

Wiley also publishes its books in a variety of electronic formats. Some content that appears in print may not be available in electronic formats.

Manufactured in the United States of America

5   4   3   2   1

CONTENTS

LIST OF MAPS

ABOUT THE AUTHORS

A writer, editor, and translator, **David Baird** has lived several years in different parts of Mexico. Now based in Austin, Texas, he spends as much time in Mexico as possible.

A former resident of Mexico City, **Shane Christensen** has written extensively for Frommer's throughout Mexico, and is also the author of *Frommer's Dubai* and *Frommer's Grand Canyon*. He resides in New York, and goes back to Mexico at every chance he gets.

HOW TO CONTACT US

In researching this book, we discovered many wonderful places—hotels, restaurants, shops, and more. We're sure you'll find others. Please tell us about them, so we can share the information with your fellow travelers in upcoming editions. If you were disappointed with a recommendation, we'd love to know that, too. Please write to:

Frommer's Portable Puerto Vallarta, Manzanillo & Guadalajara, 7th Edition
Wiley Publishing, Inc. • 111 River St. • Hoboken, NJ 07030-5774

AN ADDITIONAL NOTE

Please be advised that travel information is subject to change at any time—and this is especially true of prices. We therefore suggest that you write or call ahead for confirmation when making your travel plans. The authors, editors, and publisher cannot be held responsible for the experiences of readers while traveling. Your safety is important to us, however, so we encourage you to stay alert and be aware of your surroundings. Keep a close eye on cameras, purses, and wallets, all favorite targets of thieves and pickpockets.

FROMMER'S STAR RATINGS, ICONS & ABBREVIATIONS

Every hotel, restaurant, and attraction listing in this guide has been ranked for quality, value, service, amenities, and special features using a star-rating system. In country, state, and regional guides, we also rate towns and regions to help you narrow down your choices and budget your time accordingly. Hotels and restaurants are rated on a scale of zero (recommended) to three stars (exceptional). Attractions, shopping, nightlife, towns, and regions are rated according to the following scale: zero stars (recommended), one star (highly recommended), two stars (very highly recommended), and three stars (must-see).

In addition to the star-rating system, we also use **eight feature icons** that point you to the great deals, in-the-know advice, and unique experiences that separate travelers from tourists. Throughout the book, look for:

(Finds)	Special finds—those places only insiders know about
(Fun Facts)	Fun facts—details that make travelers more informed and their trips more fun
(Kids)	Best bets for kids, and advice for the whole family
(Moments)	Special moments—those experiences that memories are made of
(Overrated)	Places or experiences not worth your time or money
(Tips)	Insider tips—great ways to save time and money
(Value)	Great values—where to get the best deals
(Warning!)	Warning—traveler's advisories are usually in effect

The following **abbreviations** are used for credit cards:

AE	American Express	**DISC**	Discover	**V**	Visa
DC	Diners Club	**MC**	MasterCard		

TRAVEL RESOURCES AT FROMMERS.COM

Frommer's travel resources don't end with this guide. Frommer's website, **www.frommers.com**, has travel information on more than 4,000 destinations. We update features regularly, giving you access to the most current trip-planning information and the best airfare, lodging, and car-rental bargains. You can also listen to podcasts, connect with other Frommers.com members through our active-reader forums, share your travel photos, read blogs from guidebook editors and fellow travelers, and much more.

Planning Your Trip to Mid-Pacific Mexico

by Shane Christensen

Along the Pacific coast of Mexico, palm-studded jungles sweep down to meet the deep blue of the Pacific Ocean, providing spectacular backdrops for three modern resort cities, as well as smaller coastal villages. This lovely stretch of coastline, which extends from Puerto Vallarta down to Manzanillo, is known as the Mexican Riviera. Modern hotels, easy air access, and a growing array of activities and adventure tourism attractions have transformed this region into one of Mexico's premier resort areas. And for those who would like to explore the inland region, the bustling city of Guadalajara, home to some of Mexico's greatest artisans and mariachis, is only a few hours' drive away.

Travelers to Mexico should be aware of security concerns in certain parts of the country and take precautions to maximize their safety. For the most part, Mexico is safe for travelers who steer clear of drugs and those who sell them, but visitors should still exercise caution in unfamiliar areas and remain aware of their surroundings at all times. See "Safety," below, for more details; and visit the U.S. State Department's website, www.travel.state.gov, for up-to-date information on travel to Mexico.

For additional help in planning your trip and for more on-the-ground resources in Mid-Pacific Mexico, please turn to "Fast Facts," on p. 160.

1 THE REGION IN BRIEF

Puerto Vallarta, with its traditional Mexican architecture and gold-sand beaches bordered by jungle-covered mountains, is one of the most visited resort cities in Mexico. Although it has grown rapidly in recent years, Vallarta (as the locals refer to it) still maintains a small-town charm despite sophisticated hotels, great restaurants, a thriving arts community, an active nightlife, and a growing variety of ecotourism attractions. **Manzanillo** is surprisingly relaxed, even though it's one of Mexico's most active commercial ports; it also offers great fishing and golf. And along the **Costa Alegre,** between Puerto Vallarta and Manzanillo, pristine coves are home to unique luxury and value-priced resorts that cater to travelers seeking seclusion and privacy. Just north of Puerto Vallarta is **Punta Mita,** home of the first Four Seasons resort in Latin America and a Jack Nicklaus golf course. For a more essentially Mexican experience, head inland over the mountains to **Guadalajara,** Mexico's second-largest city and the birthplace of many of the country's traditions.

International airports at Puerto Vallarta, Manzanillo, and Guadalajara make getting to each easier; Guadalajara and Puerto Vallarta have the most frequent connections. Distances in the region are easily managed by car and the roads are in generally good condition. **Barra de Navidad,** for example, is so close to Manzanillo that it's easy to combine several days there with a stay in Manzanillo. From Puerto Vallarta, **Bucerías, Yelapa, San Sebastian,** and **Sayulita** all offer a change of pace and scenery. Hotelito Desconocido and Las Alamandas are both closer to Puerto Vallarta, with the remainder of the luxury coastal resorts between Manzanillo and Puerto Vallarta, nearer to Manzanillo. More frequent flights fly to and from Puerto Vallarta, and many people find that Puerto Vallarta provides the best access to the coastal area.

2 WHEN TO GO

SEASONS

Mexico has two principal travel seasons: high and low. High season begins around December 20 and continues through Easter, although in some places high season can begin as early as mid-November. Low season begins the day after Easter and continues through mid-December; during low season, prices may drop 20% to 50%. In beach destinations, the prices may also increase during the months of July and August, the traditional national summer vacation period. Prices in inland cities, such as Guadalajara, seldom fluctuate from high to low season, but may rise dramatically during Easter and Christmas weeks.

CLIMATE

From Puerto Vallarta south, all the way to Huatulco, Mexico offers one of the world's most perfect winter climates—dry and balmy with temperatures ranging from the 80s during the day to the 60s at night.

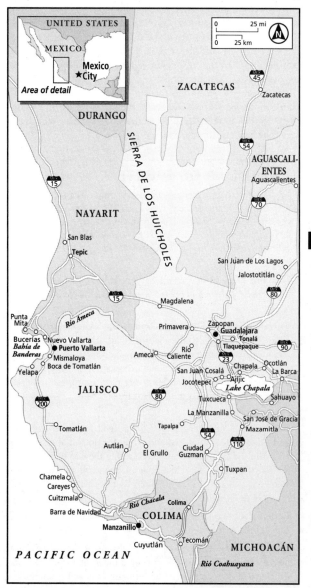

From Puerto Vallarta on south, you can swim year-round. High mountains shield Pacific beaches from *nortes* (northerns—freezing blasts out of Canada via the Texas Panhandle).

Summers are hot and sunny, with an increase in humidity during the rainy season, between May and October. Rains come almost every afternoon in June and July, and are usually brief but strong—just enough to cool off the air for evening activities. In September, heat and humidity are least comfortable and rains heaviest.

The climate in inland Guadalajara is mostly mild. During the winter, it's a good idea to carry a sweater when going out in the evenings. The city also receives summer afternoon showers, although the rest of the day is usually hot and dry.

CALENDAR OF EVENTS

For an exhaustive list of events beyond those listed here, check http://events.frommers.com, where you'll find a searchable, up-to-the-minute roster of what's happening in cities all over the world. During national holidays, Mexican banks and governmental offices—including immigration—are closed.

JANUARY

New Year's Day (Año Nuevo). National holiday. Parades, religious observances, parties, and fireworks welcome in the New Year everywhere. January 1.

Three Kings Day (Día de los Reyes). Commemorates the Three Kings' bringing of gifts to the Christ Child. Children receive gifts, and friends and families gather to share the *Rosca de Reyes,* a special cake. Inside the cake is a small doll representing the Christ Child; whoever receives the doll in his or her piece must host a tamales and atole party the next month. January 6.

FEBRUARY

Candlemas. Music, dances, processions, food, and other festivities lead up to a blessing of seed and candles, a ritual that mixes pre-Hispanic and European traditions marking the end of winter. All those who attended the Three Kings' Celebration reunite to share atole and tamales at a party hosted by the recipient of the doll found in the Rosca. February 2.

Carnaval. Carnaval takes place the 3 days preceding Ash Wednesday and the start of Lent.

Ash Wednesday. The start of Lent and time of abstinence. It's a day of reverence nationwide, but some towns honor it with folk dancing and fairs. Lent begins on February 17 in 2010, and March 9 in 2011.

MARCH

Benito Juárez's Birthday. National holiday. March 21.

APRIL

Holy Week. Celebrates the last week in the life of Christ, from Palm Sunday to Easter Sunday, with somber religious processions almost nightly, spoofings of Judas, and reenactments of specific biblical events, plus food and craft fairs. Businesses close during this week of Mexican national vacations.

If you plan on traveling to or around Mexico during Holy Week, make your reservations early. Airline seats on flights in and out of the country are reserved months in advance. Buses to almost anywhere in Mexico will be full, so try arriving on the Wednesday or Thursday before Good Friday. Easter Sunday is quiet.

MAY

Labor Day (May Day). Nationwide parades; everything closes. May 1.

Holy Cross Day (Día de la Santa Cruz). Workers place a cross on top of unfinished buildings and celebrate with food, bands, folk dancing, and fireworks around the work site. May 3.

Cinco de Mayo. A national holiday that celebrates the defeat of the French in the Battle of Puebla. May 5.

JUNE

National Ceramics Fair and Fiesta, Tlaquepaque, Jalisco. This pottery center outside Guadalajara hosts crafts demonstrations and contests, mariachis, dancers, and parades. June 14.

Día de San Pedro (St. Peter and St. Paul's Day). Celebrated wherever St. Peter is the patron saint, and honors anyone named Pedro or Peter. It's especially festive at San Pedro Tlaquepaque, near Guadalajara, with numerous mariachi bands, folk dancers, and parades with floats. In Mexcatitlan, Nayarit, shrimpers hold a regatta to celebrate the season opening. June 29.

SEPTEMBER

Mariachi Festival, Guadalajara, Jalisco. Public mariachi concerts, with groups from around the world (even Japan!). Workshops and lectures are given on the history, culture, and music of the mariachi. Plans for an extension of this festival in Puerto Vallarta are being worked out—call © **800-44-MEXICO** [800/446-3942] or click on www.mariachi-jalisco.com.mx to confirm dates and performance schedules. August 29 to September 5.

Independence Day. Celebrates Mexico's independence from Spain. A day of parades, picnics, and family reunions throughout the country. At 11pm on September 15, the president of Mexico gives the famous independence *grito* (shout) from the National Palace in Mexico City, which is duplicated by every *presidente municipal* (mayor) in every town plaza in Mexico. Both Guadalajara and Puerto Vallarta have great parties in the town plaza on the nights of September 15 and 16.

OCTOBER

Fiestas de Octubre (October Festivals), Guadalajara. This "most Mexican of cities" celebrates for a whole month with its mariachi music trademark. A bountiful display of popular culture and fine arts, and a spectacular spread of traditional foods, Mexican beers, and wines all add to the celebration. All month.

NOVEMBER

Day of the Dead. The Day of the Dead is actually 2 days, All Saints' Day (honoring saints and deceased children) and All Souls' Day (honoring deceased adults). Relatives gather at cemeteries carrying candles and food, and often spend the night beside the graves of loved ones. Weeks before, bakers begin producing bread shaped like mummies or round loaves decorated with bread "bones." Decorated sugar skulls emblazoned with glittery names are sold everywhere. Many days ahead, homes and churches erect special altars laden with Day of the Dead bread, fruit, flowers, candles, and favorite foods and photographs of saints and of the deceased. Children, dressed in costumes and masks, carry mock coffins and pumpkin lanterns through the streets at night, expecting people to drop money in them. November 1 and 2.

Gourmet Festival. Puerto Vallarta, Jalisco. In this culinary capital of Mexico, chefs from around the world join local restaurateurs to create special menus, as well as host wine and tequila tastings, cooking classes, gourmet food expos, and other special events. Dates vary; contact the Tourism Board (© **888/384-6822** in the U.S.; www.festivalgourmet.com) for a schedule. Late November.

Revolution Day. Commemorates the start of the Mexican Revolution in 1910 with parades, speeches, rodeos, and patriotic events. November 20.

DECEMBER

The Puerto Vallarta Film Festival, Puerto Vallarta, Jalisco. Featuring a wide range of North American independent and Latin American productions, this elaborate showcase includes galas, art expos, and concerts, with celebrity attendees. Check local calendars; call © **800/44-MEXICO** or go to www.vallartafilmfestival.com for details. First week of December.

Feast of the Virgin of Guadalupe. Throughout the country, the patroness of Mexico is honored with religious processions, street fairs, dancing, fireworks, and Masses. It is one of Mexico's most moving and beautiful displays of traditional culture. The Virgin of Guadalupe appeared to a young man, Juan Diego, in December 1531, on a hill near Mexico City. He convinced the bishop that he had seen the apparition by revealing his cloak, upon which the Virgin was emblazoned. Children dress up as Juan Diego, wearing mustaches and red bandannas. December 12.

In Puerto Vallarta, the celebration begins on December 1 and extends through December 12, with traditional processions to the church for a brief *misa* (Mass) and blessing. Businesses, neighborhoods, associations, and groups make pilgrimages (called *peregrinaciones*) to the church, where they exchange offerings for a brief blessing by the priest. In the final days, the processions and festivities take place around the clock, with many of the processions featuring floats, mariachis, Aztec dancers, and fireworks. Hotels frequently invite guests to participate in the walk to the church. The central plaza is filled with street vendors and a festive atmosphere, and a major fireworks exhibition takes place on December 12 at 11pm.

Christmas Posadas. On each of the 9 nights before Christmas, it's customary to reenact the Holy Family's search for an inn, with door-to-door candlelit processions in cities and villages nationwide. Most business and community organizations host them in place of the northern tradition of a Christmas party. December 15 to December 24.

Christmas. Mexicans extend this celebration, often starting 2 weeks before Christmas, through New Year's. Many businesses close, and resorts and hotels fill up. December 24 and 25.

New Year's Eve. As in the rest of the world, New Year's Eve is celebrated with parties and fireworks.

3 ENTRY REQUIREMENTS

PASSPORTS

All travelers to Mexico are required to present **photo identification** and **proof of citizenship,** such as a valid passport, naturalization papers, or an original birth certificate with a raised seal, along with a driver's license or official ID, such as a state or military-issued ID. Driver's licenses and permits, voter registration cards, affidavits, and similar documents are not sufficient to prove citizenship for readmission into the United States. If the last name on the birth certificate is different from your current name, bring a photo identification card *and* legal proof of the name change, such as the original marriage license or certificate. *Note:* Photocopies are *not* acceptable.

Virtually every air traveler **entering the U.S.** is required to show a passport. As of January 23, 2007, all U.S. and Canadian citizens traveling by **air** to Mexico are required to present a valid passport or other valid travel document to enter or reenter the United States. In addition, effective June 1, 2009, all travelers, including U.S. and Canadian citizens, attempting to enter the United States by **land** or **sea** must have a valid passport or other WHTI compliant document.

Other valid travel documents (known as WHTI-compliant documents; visit www.travel.state.gov for more information) include the new **Passport Card** and SENTRI, NEXUS, FAST, and the U.S. Coast Guard Mariner Document. Members of the U.S. Armed Forces on active duty traveling on orders are exempt from the passport requirement. U.S. citizens may apply for the new, limited-use, wallet-size Passport Card. The card is valid only for land and sea travel between the U.S. and Canada, Mexico, the Caribbean region, and Bermuda.

From our perspective, it's easiest just to travel with a valid passport. Safeguard your passport in an inconspicuous, inaccessible place, like a money belt, and keep a copy of the critical pages with your passport number in a separate place. If you lose your passport, visit the nearest consulate of your native country as soon as possible for a replacement.

For information on how to get a passport, see p. 162 in "Fast Facts."

VISAS

For detailed information regarding visas to Mexico, visit the **National Immigration Institute** at www.inm.gob.mx.

American and Canadian tourists are not required to have a visa or a tourist card for stays of 72 hours or less within the border zone (20–30km/12–19 miles from the U. S. border).

For travel to Mexico beyond the border zone, all travelers must be in possession of a tourist card, also called **Tourist Migration Form** (FMTTV: Migration Form for Tourists, Transmigrants, Visiting Businesspersons or Visiting Consultants). This document is provided by airlines or by immigration authorities at the country's points of entry. If you enter Mexico by land, it is your responsibility to stop at the immigration module located at the border.

Authorities can demand to see your tourist card at any time. You must therefore carry the original or a copy at all times and must surrender the original upon leaving Mexico. Failure to do so will result in a fine and/or expulsion.

In order to obtain a tourist card, travelers are required to present a valid passport or valid official photo identification (such as a passport or driver's license) and proof of citizenship (such as a passport, birth certificate, or citizenship card).

Your tourist card is stamped on arrival. If traveling by bus or car, ensure you obtain such a card and have it stamped by immigration authorities at the border. If you do not receive a stamped tourist card at the border, ensure that, when you arrive at your destination within Mexico, you immediately go to the closest National Institute of Immigration office, present your bus ticket, and request a tourist card. Travelers who fail to have their tourist card stamped may be fined, detained, or expelled from the country.

The FMT can be issued for up to 180 days. Do not assume that you will be granted the full 180 days. Sometimes officials don't ask but just stamp a time limit, so be sure to tell them you're going to stay 6 months, or at least twice as long as you intend to stay. An extension of your stay can be requested for a fee at the National Institute of Immigration of the Ministry of the Interior or its local offices.

If you plan to enter Mexico by car, please read the vehicle importation requirements on p. 12.

For information on obtaining a visa, please visit "Fast Facts," on p. 164.

TOURISM TAX

Mexican authorities impose a tourism tax (approx. $20) for all visitors to Mexico. This fee is normally included in airline ticket prices. Visitors arriving by road (car or bus) will be asked to pay this fee at any bank in Mexico (there is a bank representative at every port of entry). The bank will stamp your tourist card. Visitors to the northern border zone (20–30km/12–19 miles from the U. S. border) and those going to Mexico on cruise ships are exempt.

For travelers entering Mexico by car at the border of Baja California, note that FMTs are issued only in Tijuana, Tecate, and Mexicali, as well as in Ensenada and Guerrero Negro. If you travel anywhere beyond the frontier zone without the FMT, you will be fined $40. Permits for driving a foreign-plated car in Mexico are available only in Tijuana, Ensenada, Tecate, Mexicali, and La Paz.

Note on travel of minors: Mexican law requires that any non-Mexican citizen under the age of 18 departing Mexico without both parents must carry notarized written permission from the parent or guardian who is not traveling with the child to or from Mexico. This permission must include the name of the parent, the name of the child, the name of anyone traveling with the child, and the notarized signature(s) of the absent parent(s). The U.S. Department of State recommends that permission include travel dates, destinations, airlines, and a summary of the circumstances surrounding the travel. The child must be carrying the original letter (not a facsimile or scanned copy), and proof of the parent/child relationship (usually a birth certificate or court document), and an original custody decree, if applicable. Travelers should contact the Mexican Embassy or closest Mexican Consulate for current information.

CUSTOMS

Mexican Customs inspection has been streamlined. At most points of entry, tourists are requested to press a button in front of what looks like a traffic signal, which alternates on touch between red and green. Green light and you go through without inspection; red light and your luggage or car may be inspected. If you have an unusual amount of luggage or an oversized piece, you may be subject to inspection anyway.

What You Can Bring into Mexico

When you enter Mexico, Customs officials will be tolerant if you are not carrying illegal drugs or firearms. Tourists are allowed to bring in their personal effects duty-free. A laptop, camera equipment, and sports equipment that could feasibly be used during your stay are also allowed. The underlying guideline is: Don't bring anything that looks as if it's meant to be resold in Mexico. **U.S. citizens** entering Mexico by the land border can bring in gifts worth up to $50 duty-free, except for alcohol and tobacco products. Those entering Mexico by air or sea can bring in gifts worth a value of up to $300 duty-free. The website for Mexican Customs ("Aduanas") is **www.aduanas.gob.mx/aduana_mexico/2008/pasajeros/139_10134.html**.

What You Can Take Home from Mexico

For information on what you're allowed to bring home, contact one of the following agencies:

U.S. Citizens: U.S. Customs & Border Protection (CBP), 1300 Pennsylvania Ave., NW, Washington, DC 20229 (© **877/287-8667;** www.cbp.gov).

Canadian Citizens: Canada Border Services Agency (© **800/461-9999** in Canada, or 204/983-3500; www.cbsa-asfc.gc.ca).

U.K. Citizens: HM Customs & Excise (© **0845/010-9000,** or 020/8929-0152 from outside the U.K.; www.hmce.gov.uk).

Australian Citizens: Australian Customs Service (© **1300/363-263;** www.customs.gov.au).

MEDICAL REQUIREMENTS

No special vaccinations are required for entry into Mexico. For other medical requirements and health-related recommendations, see "Health," p. 21.

---

4 GETTING THERE & GETTING AROUND

GETTING TO MID-PACIFIC MEXICO
By Plane

Mexico has dozens of international and domestic airports. Among the airports in the mid-Pacific coast are Puerto Vallarta (PVR), Manzanillo (ZLO), and Mazatlán (MZT). The other major airport in Jalisco is in Guadalajara (GDL).

The main departure points in North America for international airlines are Atlanta, Chicago, Dallas/Fort Worth, Denver, Houston, Las Vegas, Los Angeles, Miami, New York, Orlando, Philadelphia, Phoenix, Raleigh/Durham, San Antonio, San Francisco, Seattle, Toronto, and Washington, D.C.

To find out which airlines travel to mid-Pacific Mexico, please see "Airline, Hotel & Car Rental Websites," p. 165.

By Car

Driving is not the cheapest way to get to Mexico. While driving is a convenient way to see the country, you may think twice about taking your own car south of the border once you've pondered the bureaucracy involved. One option is to rent a car once you arrive and tour around a specific region. The mid-Pacific coast is a great place to do this. Rental cars in Mexico generally are clean and well maintained, although they are often smaller than rentals in the U.S., may have manual rather than automatic transmission, and are comparatively expensive due to pricey mandatory insurance. Discounts are often available for rentals of a week or longer, especially when you make arrangements in advance online or from the United States. Be careful about estimated online rates, which often fail to include the price of the mandatory insurance. (See "Car Rentals," later in this chapter, for more details.)

> **(Tips) Carrying Car Documents**
>
> You must carry your temporary car-importation permit, tourist permit (see "Entry Requirements," earlier in this chapter), and, if you purchased it, your proof of Mexican car insurance (see below) in the car at all times. The temporary car-importation permit papers are valid for 6 months to a year, while the tourist permit is usually issued for 30 days. It's a good idea to overestimate the time you'll spend in Mexico so if you have to (or want to) stay longer, you'll avoid the hassle of getting your papers extended. Whatever you do, don't overstay either permit. Doing so invites heavy fines, confiscation of your vehicle (which will not be returned), or both. Also remember that 6 months does not necessarily equal 180 days—be sure that you return before the earlier expiration date.

If, after reading the section that follows, you have additional questions or you want to confirm the current rules, call your nearest Mexican consulate or the Mexican Government Tourist Office. Although travel insurance companies generally are helpful, they may not have the most accurate information. To check on road conditions or to get help with any travel emergency while in Mexico, call ✆ **01-800/482-9832,** or 55/5089-7500 in Mexico City. English-speaking operators staff both numbers.

In addition, check with the **U.S. Department of State** (see "Safety," later in this chapter) for warnings about dangerous driving areas.

Car Documents

To drive your car into Mexico, you'll need a **temporary car-importation permit,** which is granted after you provide a required list of documents (see below). The permit can be obtained through Banco del Ejército (Banjercito) officials at the *aduana* (Mexican Customs) building after you cross the border into Mexico.

The following requirements for border crossing were accurate at press time:

- **A valid driver's license,** issued outside of Mexico.
- **Current, original car registration and a copy of the original car title.** If the registration or title is in more than one name and not all the named people are traveling with you, a notarized letter from the absent person(s) authorizing use of the vehicle for the trip is required; have it ready. The registration and your credit card (see below) must be in the same name.

- **Original immigration documentation.** This is either your tourist permit (FMT) or the original immigration booklet, FM2 or FM3, if you hold more permanent status.
- **Processing fee and posting of a bond.** With an international credit card, you are required to pay a $27 car-importation fee. The credit card must be in the same name as the car registration. Mexican law also requires the posting of a bond at a Banjercito office to guarantee the export of the car from Mexico within a time period determined at the time of the application. For this purpose, American Express, Visa, or MasterCard credit card holders will be asked to provide credit card information; others will need to make a cash deposit of $200 to $400, depending on the make/model/year of the vehicle. In order to recover this bond or avoid credit card charges, travelers must go to any Mexican Customs office immediately before leaving Mexico.

If you receive your documentation at the border, Mexican officials will make two copies of everything and charge you for the copies. For up-to-the-minute information, a great source is the Customs office in Nuevo Laredo, or *Módulo de Importación Temporal de Automóviles, Aduana Nuevo Laredo* (*©* **867/712-2071**).

Important reminder: Someone else may drive, but the person (or relative of the person) whose name appears on the car-importation permit must *always* be in the car. (If stopped by police, a nonregistered family member driving without the registered driver must be prepared to prove familial relationship to the registered driver—no joke.) Violation of this rule subjects the car to impoundment and the driver to imprisonment, a fine, or both. You can drive a car with foreign license plates only if you have a foreign (non-Mexican) driver's license.

Mexican Auto Insurance (Seguros de Auto)

Liability auto insurance is legally required in Mexico. U.S. insurance is invalid; to be insured in Mexico, you must purchase Mexican insurance. Any party involved in an accident who has no insurance may be sent to jail and have his or her car impounded until all claims are settled. This is true even if you just drive across the border to spend the day. U.S. companies that broker Mexican insurance are commonly found at the border crossing, and several quote daily rates.

You can also buy car insurance through **Sanborn's Mexico Insurance,** P.O. Box 52840, 2009 S. 10th, McAllen, TX (*©* **800/222-0158;** fax 800/222-0158 or 956/686-0732; www.sanbornsinsurance.com). The company has offices at all U.S. border crossings. Its policies cost the same as the competition's do, but you get legal coverage (attorney and bail bonds if needed) and a detailed mile-by-mile guide for your proposed route. Most of the Sanborn's border offices are open Monday through Friday; a few are staffed on Saturday and Sunday. **AAA** auto club (www.aaa.com) also sells insurance.

Returning to the U.S. with Your Car
You *must* return the car documents you obtained when you entered Mexico when you cross back with your car, or within 180 days of your return. (You can cross as many times as you wish within the 180 days.) If the documents aren't returned, heavy fines are imposed ($250 for each 15 days you're late), your car may be impounded and confiscated, or you may be jailed if you return to Mexico. You can return the car documents only to a Banjercito official on duty at the Mexican *aduana* building *before* you cross back into the United States. Some border cities have Banjercito officials on duty 24 hours a day, but others do not; some do not have Sunday hours.

By Ship
Numerous cruise lines serve Mexico. Some (such as Carnival and Royal Caribbean) cruise to Puerto Vallarta with likely stops in Cabo San Lucas and Mazatlán. Others travel to Manzanillo, Ixtapa/Zihuatanejo, and Acapulco. Several cruise-tour specialists sometimes offer last-minute discounts on unsold cabins. One such company is **CruisesOnly** (© 800/278-4737; www.cruisesonly.com).

By Bus
Greyhound-Trailways (or its affiliates) offers service from around the United States to the Mexican border, where passengers disembark, cross the border, and buy a ticket for travel into Mexico. Many border crossings have scheduled buses from the U.S. bus station to the Mexican bus station.

In each applicable section in this book, we've listed bus arrival information.

GETTING AROUND
By Plane
Mexico has two large private national carriers: **Mexicana** (© 800/531-7921; www.mexicana.com) and **AeroMéxico** (© 866/275-6419; www.aeromexico.com), in addition to several up-and-coming low-cost carriers. Mexicana and AeroMéxico offer extensive connections to the United States as well as within Mexico.

Up-and-coming low-cost carriers include **Aviacsa** (www.aviacsa.com), **Click Mexicana** (www.click.com.mx), **InterJet** (www.interjet.com.mx), and **Volaris** (www.volaris.com.mx). Regional carriers include **Aerovega** (www.oaxaca-mio.com/aerovega.htm), **Aero Tucán** (www.aero-tucan.com), and **AeroMéxico Connect** (www.amconnect.com).

The regional carriers can be expensive, but they go to difficult-to-reach places. In each applicable section of this book, we've mentioned regional carriers with all pertinent telephone numbers.

Because major airlines may book some regional carriers, check your ticket to see if your connecting flight is on one of these smaller carriers—they may use a different airport or a different counter.

AIRPORT TAXES   Mexico charges an airport tax on all departures. Passengers leaving the country on international flights pay about $24 in dollars or the peso equivalent. It has become a common practice to include this departure tax in your ticket price. Taxes on each domestic departure within Mexico are around $17, unless you're on a connecting flight and have already paid at the start of the flight.

RECONFIRMING FLIGHTS   Although Mexican airlines say it's not necessary to reconfirm a flight, it's still a good idea. To avoid getting bumped on popular, possibly overbooked flights, check in for an international flight $1^1/_2$ hours in advance of travel.

By Car

Most Mexican roads are not up to U.S. standards of smoothness, hardness, width of curve, grade of hill, or safety markings. Driving at night is dangerous—the roads are rarely lit; trucks, carts, pedestrians, and bicycles usually have no lights; and you can hit potholes, animals, rocks, dead ends, or uncrossable bridges without warning.

The spirited style of Mexican driving sometimes requires keen vision and reflexes. Be prepared for new customs, as when a truck driver flips on his left turn signal when there's not a crossroad for many kilometers. He's probably telling you the road's clear ahead for you to pass. Another custom that's very important to respect is turning left. Never turn left by stopping in the middle of a highway with your left-turn signal on. Instead, pull onto the right shoulder, wait for traffic to clear, and then proceed across the road.

GASOLINE   There's one government-owned brand of gas and one gasoline station name throughout the country—**Pemex** (Petroleras Mexicanas). There are two types of gas in Mexico: *magna,* 87-octane unleaded gas, and *premio* 93 octane. In Mexico, fuel and oil are sold by the liter, which is slightly more than a quart (1 gal. equals about 3.8L). Many franchise Pemex stations have restroom facilities and convenience stores—a great improvement over the old ones. Gas stations accept both credit and debit cards for gas purchases.

TOLL ROADS   Mexico charges some of the highest tolls in the world for its network of new toll roads, so they are rarely used. Generally, though, using toll roads cuts travel time. Older toll-free roads are generally in good condition, but travel times tend to be longer.

BREAKDOWNS   If your car breaks down on the road, help might already be on the way. Radio-equipped green repair trucks, run by uniformed English-speaking officers, patrol major highways during daylight hours. These **"Green Angels"** perform minor repairs and adjustments free, but you pay for parts and materials.

Your best guide to repair shops is the Yellow Pages. For repairs, look under *Automóviles y Camiones: Talleres de Reparación y Servicio;* auto-parts stores are under *Refacciones y Accesorios para Automóviles.* To find a mechanic on the road, look for the sign TALLER MECÁNICO.

Places called *vulcanizadora* or *llantera* repair flat tires, and it is common to find them open 24 hours a day on the most traveled highways.

MINOR ACCIDENTS   When possible, many Mexicans drive away from minor accidents, or try to make an immediate settlement, to avoid involving the police. If the police arrive while the involved persons are still at the scene, the cars will likely be confiscated and both parties will likely have to appear in court. Both parties may also be taken into custody until liability is determined. Foreigners who don't speak fluent Spanish are at a distinct disadvantage when trying to explain their version of the event. Three steps may help the foreigner who doesn't wish to do as the Mexicans do: If you were in your own car, notify your Mexican insurance company, whose job it is to intervene on your behalf. If you were in a rental car, notify the rental company immediately and ask how to contact the nearest adjuster. (You did buy insurance with the rental, right?) Finally, if all else fails, ask to contact the nearest Green Angel, who may be able to explain to officials that you are covered by insurance. See also "Mexican Auto Insurance," in "Getting to Mid-Pacific Mexico," earlier in this chapter.

CAR RENTALS   You'll get the best price if you reserve a car at least a week in advance in the United States. For a list of car-rental firms operating in this region, turn to "Airline, Hotel & Car Rental Websites," p. 165.

Cars are easy to rent if you are 25 or older and have a major credit card, valid driver's license, and passport with you. Without a credit card, you must leave a cash deposit—usually a big one. One-way rentals are usually simple to arrange, but they are more costly.

Car-rental costs are high in Mexico because cars are more expensive. The condition of rental cars has improved greatly over the years, and clean new cars are the norm. You will pay the least for a manual car without air-conditioning. Prices may be considerably higher if you rent around a major holiday. Also double-check charges for insurance—some companies will increase the insurance rate after several days. Always ask for detailed information about all charges you will be responsible for.

| ⓘWarning! | **Bus Hijackings** |

The U.S. Department of State notes that bandits target long-distance buses traveling at night, but daylight robberies have occurred as well. First-class buses on toll *(cuota)* roads sustain a markedly lower crime rate than second-class and third-class buses that travel the less secure "free" *(libre)* highways.

Car-rental companies usually write credit card charges in U.S. dollars.

Deductibles   Be careful—these vary greatly; some are as high as $2,500, which comes out of your pocket immediately in case of damage.

Insurance   Insurance is offered in two parts: **Collision and damage** insurance covers your car and others if the accident is your fault, and **personal accident** insurance covers you and anyone in your car. Read the fine print on the back of your rental agreement and note that insurance may be invalid if you have an accident while driving on an unpaved road.

Damage   Inspect your car carefully and note every damaged or missing item, no matter how minute, on your rental agreement, or you may be charged.

By Taxi

Taxis are the preferred way to get around almost all of Mexico's resort areas, and around Mexico City. Fares for short trips within towns are generally preset by zone and are quite reasonable compared with U.S. rates. (Los Cabos is one exception; another is taxi service to the north side of the bay from Puerto Vallarta. Travelers are better off renting a car than paying these exorbitant taxi fares—about $100 for a one-way trip to Punta Mita.) For longer trips or excursions to nearby cities, taxis can generally be hired for around $15 to $20 per hour, or for a negotiated daily rate. A negotiated one-way price is usually much less than the cost of a rental car for a day, and a taxi travels much faster than a bus. For anyone who is uncomfortable driving in Mexico, this is a convenient, comfortable alternative. A bonus is that you have a Spanish-speaking person with you in case you run into trouble. Many taxi drivers speak at least some English. Your hotel can assist you with the arrangements.

By Bus

Mexican buses run frequently, are readily accessible, and can transport you almost anywhere you want to go. Taking the bus is much more common in Mexico than in the U.S., and the executive and first-class coaches can be as comfortable as business class on an airline. Buses are often the only way to get from large cities to other nearby cities and small villages. Don't hesitate to ask questions if you're confused about anything, but note that little English is spoken in bus stations.

Dozens of Mexican companies operate large, air-conditioned, Greyhound-type buses between most cities. Classes are *segunda* (second), *primera* (first), and *ejecutiva* (deluxe), which goes by a variety of names. Deluxe buses often have fewer seats than regular buses, show video movies, are air-conditioned, and make few stops. Many run express from point to point. They are well worth the few dollars more. In rural areas, buses are often of the school-bus variety, with lots of local color.

Whenever possible, it's best to buy your reserved-seat ticket, often using a computerized system, a day in advance on long-distance routes and especially before holidays.

5 MONEY & COSTS

The Value of the Mexican Peso vs. Other Popular Currencies

Peso	US$	Can$	UK£	Euro€	Aus$	NZ$
100	$7.55	C$8.90	£4.98	€5.60	A$10.09	NZ$12.92

Frommer's lists exact prices in the local currency. The currency conversions quoted above were correct at press time. However, rates fluctuate, so before departing consult a currency exchange website such as **www.oanda.com/convert/classic** to check up-to-the-minute rates.

In general, Mexico is considerably cheaper than most U.S. and European destinations, although prices vary significantly depending on the specific location. The most expensive destinations are those with the largest number of foreign visitors, such as Puerto Vallarta. The least expensive are those off the beaten path and in small rural villages. In the major cities, prices vary greatly depending on the neighborhood. As you might imagine, tourist zones tend to be much more expensive than local areas.

The currency in Mexico is the **peso.** Paper currency comes in denominations of 20, 50, 100, 200, and 500 pesos. Coins come in denominations of 1, 2, 5, 10, and 20 pesos, and 20 and 50 **centavos** (100 centavos = 1 peso). The current exchange rate for the U.S. dollar, and the one used in this book, is 13 pesos; at that rate, an item that costs 13 pesos would be equivalent to US$1.

Money Matters

The **universal currency sign ($)** is used to indicate pesos in Mexico. The use of this symbol in this book, however, denotes U.S. currency.

Many establishments that deal with tourists, especially in coastal resort areas, quote prices in dollars. To avoid confusion, they use the abbreviations "Dlls." for dollars and "M.N." (*moneda nacional,* or national currency) for pesos. ***Note:*** Establishments that quote their prices primarily in U.S. dollars are listed in this guide with U.S. dollars. Prices in this book are listed in the currency advertised by the establishment.

Getting **change** is a problem. Small-denomination bills and coins are hard to come by, so start collecting them early in your trip. Shopkeepers and taxi drivers everywhere always seem to be out of change and small bills; that's doubly true in markets. There seems to be an expectation that the customer should provide appropriate change, rather than the other way around.

Don't forget to have enough pesos to carry you over a weekend or Mexican holiday, when banks are closed. In general, avoid carrying the U.S. $100 bill, the bill most commonly counterfeited in Mexico and therefore the most difficult to exchange, especially in smaller towns. Because small bills and coins in pesos are hard to come by in Mexico, the $1 bill is very useful for tipping. ***Note:*** A tip of U.S. coins, which cannot be exchanged into Mexican currency, is of no value to the service provider.

Casas de cambio (exchange houses) are generally more convenient than banks for money exchange because they have more locations and longer hours; the rate of exchange may be the same as at a bank or slightly lower. Before leaving a bank or exchange-house window, count your change in front of the teller before the next client steps up.

Large airports have currency-exchange counters that often stay open whenever flights are operating. Though convenient, they generally do not offer the most favorable rates.

A hotel's exchange desk commonly pays less favorable rates than banks; however, when the currency is in a state of flux, higher-priced hotels are known to pay higher rates than banks, in an effort to attract dollars. ***Note:*** In almost all cases, you receive a better rate by changing money first, then paying.

The bottom line on exchanging money: Ask first, and shop around. Banks generally pay the top rates.

(Tips) A Few Words About Prices

Most hotels in Mexico—except places that receive little foreign tourism—quote prices in U.S. dollars. Thus, currency fluctuations are unlikely to affect the prices most hotels charge.

Mexico has a **value-added tax** of 15% (*Impuesto de Valor Agregado*, or IVA; pronounced "*ee*-bah") on most everything, including restaurant meals, bus tickets, and souvenirs. (Exceptions are Cancún, Cozumel, and Los Cabos, where the IVA is 10%; as ports of entry, they receive a break on taxes.) Hotels charge the usual 15% IVA, plus a locally administered bed tax of 2% (in most areas), for a total of 17%. In Cancún, Los Cabos, and Cozumel, hotels charge the 10% IVA plus 2% room tax. The prices quoted by hotels and restaurants do not necessarily include IVA. You may find that upper-end properties (three or more stars) quote prices without IVA included, while lower-priced hotels include IVA. Ask to see a printed price sheet and ask if the tax is included.

Banks in Mexico are rapidly expanding and improving services. They tend to be open weekdays from 9am until 5pm, and often for at least a half-day on Saturday. In larger resorts and cities, they can generally accommodate the exchange of dollars (which used to stop at noon) anytime during business hours. Some, but not all, banks charge a 1% fee to exchange traveler's checks. But you can pay for most purchases directly with traveler's checks at the establishment's stated exchange rate. Don't even bother with personal checks drawn on a U.S. bank—the bank will wait for your check to clear, which can take weeks, before giving you your money.

Travelers to Mexico can easily withdraw money from **ATMs** in most major cities and resort areas. The U.S. Department of State recommends caution when you're using ATMs in Mexico, stating that they should be used only during business hours and in large protected facilities, but this pertains primarily to Mexico City, where crime remains a significant problem. In most resorts in Mexico, the use of ATMs is perfectly safe—just use the same precautions you would at any ATM. Universal bank cards (such as the Cirrus and PLUS systems) can be used. The exchange rate is generally more favorable than at *casas de cambio*. Most machines offer Spanish/English menus and dispense pesos, but some offer the option of withdrawing dollars. *Note:* Many banks impose a fee every time you use a card at another bank's ATM, and that fee can be higher for international transactions (although seldom more than $2 in Mexico) than for domestic ones. In addition, the bank from which you withdraw cash may charge its own fee. For international withdrawal fees, ask your bank.

In Mexico, Visa, MasterCard, and American Express are the most accepted credit cards. You'll be able to charge most hotel, restaurant, and store purchases, as well as almost all airline tickets, on your credit card. Pemex gas stations have begun to accept credit card purchases for gasoline, though this option may not be available everywhere and often not at night—check before you pump. You can get cash advances of several hundred dollars on your card, but there may be a wait of 20 minutes to 2 hours. Charges will be made in pesos, then converted into dollars by the bank issuing the credit card. Generally you receive the favorable bank rate when paying by credit card. However, be aware that some establishments in Mexico add a 5% to 7% surcharge when you pay with a credit card. This is especially true when using American Express. Many times, advertised discounts will not apply if you pay with a credit card.

6 HEALTH

As of July 3, 2009, the WHO had reported nearly 90,000 A(H1N1) ("swine flu") cases around the world, including 382 deaths, with Mexico among the most heavily affected countries. The number of cases continued to rise worldwide, and it was too early to tell how far or for how long the virus would spread. The **World Health Organization (WHO)** pandemic alert reached level 6 at press time, signaling pandemic, although with moderate severity. According to the **Centers for Disease Control and Prevention (CDC),** the symptoms of this contagious virus are similar to those of seasonal flu and include fever, cough, sore throat, runny or stuffy nose, body aches, headache, chills, and fatigue. Many people who have been infected with this virus also reported diarrhea and vomiting. Like seasonal flu, severe symptoms and death have occurred as a result of illness associated with this virus. It is important to note, however, that most cases of influenza are not the A(H1N1) virus. For the latest information regarding the risks of swine flu when traveling to Mexico, and what to do if you get sick, please consult the **U.S. State Department**'s website at www.travel. state.gov, the **CDC** website at www.cdc.gov, or the website of the **World Health Organization** at www.who.int.

GENERAL AVAILABILITY OF HEALTH CARE

In most of Mexico's resort destinations, you can usually find health care that meets U.S. standards. Care in more remote areas is limited.

(Tips) Treating & Avoiding Digestive Trouble

It's called "travelers' diarrhea" or *turista,* the Spanish word for "tourist": persistent diarrhea, often accompanied by fever, nausea, and vomiting, that used to attack many travelers to Mexico. (Some in the U.S. call this "Montezuma's revenge," but you won't hear it called that in Mexico.) Widespread improvements in infrastructure, sanitation, and education have practically eliminated this ailment, especially in well-developed resort areas such as Puerto Vallarta. Most travelers make a habit of drinking only bottled water, which also helps to protect against unfamiliar bacteria. In resort areas, and generally throughout Mexico, only purified ice is used. If you do come down with this ailment, nothing beats Pepto-Bismol, readily available in Mexico. Imodium is also available in Mexico and is used by many travelers for a quick fix. A good high-potency (or "therapeutic") vitamin supplement and even extra vitamin C can help; active-culture yogurt is good for healthy digestion.

Since dehydration can quickly become life threatening, the Public Health Service advises that you be careful to replace fluids and electrolytes (potassium, sodium, and the like) during a bout of diarrhea. Drink Pedialyte, a rehydration solution available at most Mexican pharmacies, or natural fruit juice, such as guava or apple (stay away from orange juice, which has laxative properties), with a pinch of salt added.

How to Prevent It: The U.S. Public Health Service recommends the following measures for preventing travelers' diarrhea: **Drink only purified water** (boiled water, canned or bottled beverages, beer, or wine). **Choose food carefully.** In general, avoid salads (except in first-class restaurants), uncooked vegetables, undercooked protein, and unpasteurized milk or milk products, including cheese. Choose food that is freshly cooked and still hot. In addition, something as simple as **clean hands** can go a long way toward preventing *turista.*

Standards of medical training, patient care, and business practices vary greatly among medical facilities in beach resorts throughout Mexico. Puerto Vallarta has first-rate hospitals, for example, but health care in other cities may not be of the same quality. In recent years, some U.S. citizens have complained that certain health-care facilities in beach resorts have taken advantage of them by overcharging or providing unnecessary medical care.

Prescription medicine is broadly available at Mexico pharmacies; however, be aware that you may need a copy of your prescription or need to obtain a prescription from a local doctor.

COMMON AILMENTS

SUN EXPOSURE Mexico is synonymous with sunshine; most of the country is bathed in intense sunshine for much of the year. Avoid excessive exposure, especially in the tropics where UV rays are more dangerous. The hottest months in Mexico's south are April and May, but the sun is intense most of the year.

DIETARY RED FLAGS Travelers' diarrhea—persistent **diarrhea**, often accompanied by fever, nausea, and vomiting—used to attack many travelers to Mexico. Widespread improvements in infrastructure, sanitation, and education have greatly diminished this ailment, but visitors should still take precautions to avoid this ailment, such as drinking only bottled water and purified ice, and regularly washing your hands. See "Treating & Avoiding Digestive Trouble," above, for more information on this ailment.

BUGS, BITES & OTHER WILDLIFE CONCERNS Mosquitoes are prevalent along the coast. *Repelente contra insectos* (insect repellent) is a must, and it's not always available in Mexico. If you'll be in these areas and are prone to bites, bring along a repellent that contains the active ingredient DEET. Avon's Skin So Soft also works extremely well. Another good remedy to keep the mosquitoes away is to mix citronella essential oil with basil, clove, and lavender essential oils. If you're sensitive to bites, pick up some antihistamine cream from a drugstore at home.

Most readers won't ever see an *alacrán* (scorpion). But if one stings you, go immediately to a doctor. The one lethal scorpion found in some parts of Mexico is the *Centruroides,* part of the Buthidae family,

---

(Tips) Over-the-Counter Drugs in Mexico

Antibiotics and other drugs that you'd need a prescription to buy in the States are often available over the counter in Mexican pharmacies. Mexican pharmacies also carry a limited selection of common over-the-counter cold, sinus, and allergy remedies.

characterized by a thin body, thick tail, and triangular-shaped sternum. Most deaths from these scorpions result within 24 hours of the sting as a result of respiratory or cardiovascular failure, with children and elderly people most at risk. Scorpions are not aggressive (they don't hunt for prey), but they may sting if touched, especially in their hiding places. In Mexico, you can buy scorpion toxin antidote at any drugstore. It is an injection, and it costs around $25. This is a good idea if you plan to camp in a remote area, where medical assistance can be several hours away.

TROPICAL ILLNESSES   You shouldn't be overly concerned about tropical diseases if you stay on the normal tourist routes and don't eat street food. However, both dengue fever and cholera have appeared in Mexico in recent years. Talk to your doctor or to a medical specialist in tropical diseases about precautions you should take. You can protect yourself by taking some simple precautions: Watch what you eat and drink; don't swim in stagnant water (ponds, slow-moving rivers, or wells); and avoid mosquito bites by covering up, using repellent, and sleeping under netting. The most dangerous areas seem to be on Mexico's west coast, away from the big resorts.

WHAT TO DO IF YOU GET SICK AWAY FROM HOME

Any English-speaking embassy or consulate staff in Mexico can provide a list of area doctors who speak English. The U.S. Embassy's consular section, for example, keeps a list of reliable English-speaking doctors. If you get sick in Mexico, consider asking your hotel concierge to recommend a local doctor—even his or her own. You can also try the emergency room at a local hospital or urgent care facility. Many hospitals also have walk-in clinics for emergency cases that are not life-threatening; you may not get immediate attention, but you won't pay emergency room prices.

For travel to Mexico, you may have to pay all medical costs upfront and be reimbursed later. Medicare and Medicaid do not provide coverage for medical costs outside the U.S. (that means neither Medicare nor Medicaid reimburses for emergency health care in Mexico, either). Before leaving home, find out what medical services your health insurance covers. To protect yourself, consider buying medical travel insurance.

Very few health insurance plans pay for medical evacuation back to the U.S. (which can cost $10,000 and more). A number of companies offer global medical evacuation services. If you're ever hospitalized more than 150 miles from home, **MedjetAssist** (© **800/527-7478;** www.medjetassist.com) will pick you up and fly you to the hospital of your choice, virtually anywhere, in a medically equipped and staffed

(Tips) Smoke-Free Mexico?

In early 2008, the Mexican president signed into law a nationwide smoking ban in workplaces and public buildings, and on public transportation. Under this groundbreaking law, private businesses are permitted to allow public smoking only in enclosed ventilated areas. Hotels may maintain up to 25% of guest rooms for smokers. Violators face stiff fines, and smokers refusing to comply could receive up to 36-hour jail sentences. Despite some uncertainty over how thoroughly the legislation is being followed and enforced throughout different parts of the country, they place Mexico—where a significant percentage of the population smokes—at the forefront of efforts to curb smoking and improve public health in Latin America. So before you light up, be sure to ask about the application of local laws in Mexican public places and businesses you visit.

aircraft—24 hours a day, 7 days a week. Annual memberships are $250 individual, $385 family; you can also purchase short-term memberships.

It is generally less expensive and more reliable to contract a U.S.-based company for a medical evacuation from Mexico to the U.S. than to contract a Mexican-based company. Contact the consular affairs section of the U.S. Embassy in Mexico City or nearest consulate for suggestions.

I list additional **emergency numbers** in "Fast Facts," p. 162.

7 SAFETY

Although the vast majority of visitors to Mexico return home unharmed, it should be noted that taxi robberies, kidnappings, highway carjackings, and other crimes have beset tourists as well as locals in recent years. And in border regions and some other parts of Mexico, drug-related violence and organized crime have escalated significantly.

That said, this stretch of the Mexican Pacific Coast is one of the safer regions of Mexico. Precautions are necessary, but travelers should be realistic. You can generally trust a person whom you approach for help or directions, but be wary of anyone who approaches you offering the same. The more insistent the person is, the more cautious you should be.

Exercise caution when you're in unfamiliar areas, and be aware of your surroundings at all times. Leave valuables and irreplaceable items in a safe place, or don't bring them at all. A significant number of pickpocket incidents, purse snatchings, and hotel-room thefts do occur. Use hotel safes when available. And remember that public transportation is a popular place for wallet thefts and purse snatchings.

Enjoy the ocean, but don't swim alone in isolated beach areas because of strong currents and powerful waves. Try to swim where a lifeguard is present. All beaches in Mexico are public by law, and it is best not to be out on the beaches at night.

Before you travel to any notable hot spots in Mexico (see below), consult **www.travel.state.gov** for the U.S. Department of State's country specific information and travel alerts.

CRIME IN RESORT TOWNS

A number of rapes have been reported in resort areas, usually at night or in the early morning. Armed street crime is a serious problem in all the major cities. Some bars and nightclubs can be havens for drug dealers and petty criminals.

CRIME NATIONWIDE
Kidnappings

Kidnapping—including the kidnapping of non-Mexicans—continues at alarming rates. The U.S. Department of State Travel Alert for Mexico states the following, which applies to all travelers: "In recent years, dozens of U.S. citizens have been kidnapped across Mexico and many cases remain unresolved. U.S. citizens who believe they are being targeted for kidnapping or other crimes should notify Mexican officials and the nearest American consulate or the Embassy as soon as possible. U.S. citizens should make every attempt to travel on main roads during daylight hours, particularly the toll *(cuota)* roads, which are generally more secure. U.S. citizens are encouraged to stay in well-known tourist destinations and tourist areas of the cities with more adequate security, and provide an itinerary to a friend or family member not traveling with them. U.S. citizens should avoid traveling alone, and should carry a GSM-enabled cellphone that functions internationally."

So-called "express kidnappings"—an attempt to get quick cash in exchange for the release of an individual—have occurred in almost all the large cities in Mexico and appear to target not only the wealthy, but the middle class. Car theft and carjackings are also a common occurrence.

Highway Safety

Travelers should exercise caution while traveling Mexican highways, avoiding travel at night, and using toll *(cuota)* roads rather than the less secure free *(libre)* roads whenever possible. It is also advised that you should not hike alone in backcountry areas nor walk alone on less-frequented beaches, ruins, or trails.

Travelers are advised to cooperate with official checkpoints when traveling on Mexican highways. Avoid driving along coastal roads at night, and try not to drive alone.

Bus travel should take place during daylight hours on first-class conveyances. Although bus hijackings and robberies have occurred on toll roads, buses on toll roads have a markedly lower rate of incidents than second-class and third-class buses that travel the less secure "free" highways.

Bribes & Scams

As is the case around the world, there are occasional bribes and scams in Mexico, targeted at people believed to be naive, such as telltale tourists. For years, Mexico was known as a place where bribes—called *mordidas* (bites)—were expected; however, the country is rapidly changing. Frequently, offering a bribe today, especially to a police officer, is considered an insult, and it can land you in deeper trouble.

When you are crossing the border, should the person who inspects your car ask for a tip, you can ignore this request—but understand that the official may suddenly decide that a complete search of your belongings is in order. If you sense you're being asked for a bribe, understand that although it may be common, offering a bribe to a public official to avoid a ticket or other penalty is officially a crime in Mexico.

Many tourists have the impression that everything works better in Mexico if you "tip"; however, in reality, this only perpetuates the *mordida* tradition. If you are pleased with a service, feel free to tip. But you shouldn't tip simply to attempt to get away with something illegal or inappropriate—whether it is evading a ticket that's deserved or a car inspection as you're crossing the border.

Whatever you do, **avoid impoliteness;** you won't do yourself any favors if you insult a Mexican official. Extreme politeness, even in the face of adversity, rules Mexico. In Mexico, *gringos* have a reputation for being loud and demanding. By adopting the local custom of excessive courtesy, you'll have greater success in negotiations of any kind. Stand your ground, but do it politely.

As you travel in Mexico, you may encounter several types of **scams,** which are typical throughout the world. One involves some kind of a **distraction** or feigned commotion. While your attention is diverted, for example, a pickpocket makes a grab for your wallet. In another common scam, an **unaccompanied child** pretends to be lost and frightened and takes your hand for safety. Meanwhile the child or an accomplice plunders your pockets. A third involves **confusing currency.** A shoeshine boy, street musician, guide, or other individual might offer you a service for a price that seems reasonable—in pesos. When it comes time to pay, he or she tells you the price is in dollars, not pesos. Be very clear on the price and currency when services are involved.

8 SPECIALIZED TRAVEL RESOURCES

In addition to the destination-specific resources listed below, please visit Frommers.com for additional specialized travel resources.

GAY & LESBIAN TRAVELERS

Mexico is a conservative country, with deeply rooted Catholic religious traditions. Public displays of same-sex affection are rare and still considered shocking for men, especially outside of urban or resort areas. Women in Mexico frequently walk hand in hand, but anything more would cross the boundary of acceptability. However, gay and lesbian travelers are generally treated with respect and should not experience harassment, assuming they give the appropriate regard to local customs.

While much of Mexico is socially conservative, Puerto Vallarta is not. Popular with many gay travelers, Puerto Vallarta offers gay-friendly accommodations, bars, clubs, and activities. For more information, visit **MexGay Vacations** at www.mexgay.com.

TRAVELERS WITH DISABILITIES

Mexico may seem like one giant obstacle course to travelers in wheelchairs or on crutches. At airports, you may encounter steep stairs before finding a well-hidden elevator or escalator—if one exists. Airlines will often arrange wheelchair assistance to the baggage area. Porters are generally available to help with luggage at airports and large bus stations, once you've cleared baggage claim.

Mexican airports are upgrading their services, but it is not uncommon to board from a remote position, meaning you either descend stairs to a bus that ferries you to the plane, which you board by climbing stairs, or you walk across the tarmac to your plane and ascend the stairs. Deplaning presents the same problem in reverse.

Escalators (and there aren't many in the country) are often out of order. Stairs without handrails abound. Few restrooms are equipped for travelers with disabilities; when one is available, access to it may be through a narrow passage that won't accommodate a wheelchair or a person on crutches. Many deluxe hotels (the most expensive) now have rooms with bathrooms designed for people with disabilities. Those traveling on a budget should stick with one-story hotels or hotels with elevators. Even so, there will probably still be obstacles somewhere. Generally speaking, no matter where you are, someone will lend a hand, although you may have to ask for it.

However, Puerto Vallarta is an exception, as it is becoming more and more accessible to travelers with disabilities. The city renovated the majority of its downtown sidewalks and plazas with ramps that accommodate wheelchairs (as well as baby strollers). Even the airport has ramps adjacent to all stairways, and special wheelchair lifts. A local citizen with disabilities deserves the credit for this impressive task—hopefully setting the stage for greater accessibility in other towns and resorts.

FAMILY TRAVEL

If you have trouble getting your kids out of the house in the morning, dragging them to a foreign country may seem like an insurmountable challenge. But family travel can be immensely rewarding, giving you new ways of seeing the world through the eyes of children.

Children are considered the national treasure of Mexico, and Mexicans will warmly welcome and cater to your children. Many parents were reluctant to bring young children into Mexico in the past, primarily due to health concerns, but I can't think of a better place to introduce children to the exciting adventure of exploring a different culture. Some of the best family destinations include Puerto Vallarta and Manzanillo. Hotels can often arrange for a babysitter.

Before leaving, ask your doctor which medications to take along. Disposable diapers cost about the same in Mexico but are of poorer quality. You can get Huggies Supreme and Pampers identical to the ones sold in the United States, but at a higher price. Many stores sell Gerber's baby foods. Dry cereals, powdered formulas, baby bottles, and purified water are easily available in midsize and large cities or resorts.

Cribs may present a problem; only the largest and most luxurious hotels provide them. However, rollaway beds are often available. Child seats or highchairs at restaurants are common.

Consider bringing your own car seat; they are not readily available for rent in Mexico.

Every country's regulations differ, but in general, children traveling abroad should have plenty of documentation on hand, particularly if they're traveling with someone other than their own parents (in which case, a notarized form letter from a parent is often required). For details on entry requirements for children traveling abroad, turn to p. 9.

To locate accommodations, restaurants, and attractions that are particularly kid-friendly, refer to the "Kids" icon throughout this guide.

WOMEN TRAVELERS

Mexicans in general, and men in particular, are nosy about single travelers, especially women. If a taxi driver or anyone else with whom you don't want to become friendly asks about your marital status, family, and so forth, my advice is to make up a set of answers (regardless of the truth): "I'm married, traveling with friends, and I have three children." Saying you are single and traveling alone may send the wrong message. U.S. television—widely viewed now in Mexico—has given many Mexican men the image of American single women as being sexually promiscuous.

SENIOR TRAVEL

Mexico is a popular country for retirees. This is particularly the case in Puerto Vallarta and Mazatlán. For decades, North Americans have been living indefinitely in Mexico by returning to the border and re-crossing with a new tourist permit every 6 months. Mexican immigration officials have caught on, and now limit the maximum time in the country to 6 months within any year. This is to encourage even partial residents to acquire proper documentation.

Some of the most popular places for long-term stays are Guadalajara, Lake Chapala, Ajijic, and Puerto Vallarta—all in the state of Jalisco.

AIM-Adventures in Mexico, Apartado Postal 31–70, 45050 Guadalajara, Jalisco, is a well-written, informative newsletter for prospective retirees. Subscriptions are $29 to the United States.

Sanborn Tours, 2015 S. 10th St., P.O. Drawer 519, McAllen, TX 78505-0519 (© **800/395-8482;** www.sanborns.com), offers a "Retire in Mexico" orientation tour.

STUDENT TRAVEL

Because Mexicans consider higher education a luxury rather than a birthright, there is no formal network of student discounts and programs. Most Mexican students travel with their families rather than with other students, so student discount cards are not commonly recognized.

However, more hostels have entered the student travel scene. **www.hostels.com/mx.html** offers a list of hostels in Puerto Vallarta, Manzanillo, Guadalajara, and many other cities throughout Mexico.

9 SUSTAINABLE TOURISM

The diverse geography of the Mexican Riviera and its wealth of eco- and adventure-tour options have made it a natural favorite of travelers interested in ecotourism. From Mazatlán to Manzanillo, this stretch of Mexico's Pacific Coast presents one of the country's most ecologically stunning landscapes. The Costa Alegre, extending between Puerto Vallarta and Manzanillo, has been designated an "Ecological Tourism Corridor" by the state of Jalisco. This largely undeveloped coastline includes the spectacular beaches, jungles, and surrounding mountains of Barra de Navidad Bay, Tenacatita Bay, Careyes Coast, Chamela Bay, and the Majahuas Coast, and is home to an ecological reserve protecting the region's land and marine life. The Hotel Desconocido (p. 102), located along this coast, is one of Mexico's most prominent ecotourism resorts.

For hands-on activities with local sea life while in Puerto Vallarta, consider **Dolphin Adventure** (p. 74). Hiking, boating, snorkeling, and scuba diving are all popular activities in Puerto Vallarta and the nearby resorts.

AMTAVE (Asociación Mexicana de Turismo de Aventura y Ecoturismo, A.C.) is an active association in Mexico of eco- and adventure-tour operators dedicated to the operation and promotion of ecotourism and adventure travel in Mexico. They publish an annual catalog of participating firms and their offerings, all of which must meet certain criteria for security, and for quality and training of the guides, as well as for sustainability of natural and cultural environments. For more information, contact AMTAVE (© **800/509-7678;** www.amtave.org).

ANIMAL-RIGHTS ISSUES

The Pacific Coast presents many opportunities to swim with dolphins. The capture of wild dolphins was outlawed in Mexico in 2002. The only dolphins added to the country's dolphin swim programs since then were born in captivity. This law may have eased concerns about the death and implications of capturing wild dolphins, but the controversy is not over. Marine biologists who run the dolphin swim programs say the mammals are thriving and that the programs provide a forum for research, conservation, education, and rescue operations. Animal rights advocates maintain that keeping these intelligent

General Resources for Green Travel

In addition to the resources for Mid-Pacific Mexico listed above, the following websites provide valuable wide-ranging information on sustainable travel. For a list of even more sustainable resources, as well as tips and explanations on how to travel greener, visit www.frommers.com/planning.

- **Responsible Travel** (www.responsibletravel.com) is a great source of sustainable travel ideas; the site is run by a spokesperson for ethical tourism in the travel industry. **Sustainable Travel International** (www.sustainabletravel international.org) promotes ethical tourism practices, and manages an extensive directory of sustainable properties and tour operators around the world.

- In the U.K., **Tourism Concern** (www.tourismconcern.org. uk) works to reduce social and environmental problems connected to tourism. The **Association of Independent Tour Operators** (**AITO;** www.aito.co.uk) is a group of specialist operators leading the field in making holidays sustainable.

- In Canada, **www.greenlivingonline.com** offers extensive content on how to travel sustainably, including a travel and transport section and profiles of the best green shops and services in Toronto, Vancouver, and Calgary.

- In Australia, the national body which sets guidelines and standards for ecotourism is **Ecotourism Australia** (www. ecotourism.org.au). **The Green Directory** (www.thegreen directory.com.au), **Green Pages** (www.thegreenpages.com. au), and **Eco Directory** (www.ecodirectory.com.au) offer sustainable travel tips and directories of green businesses.

mammals in captivity is nothing more than exploitation. Their argument is that these private dolphin programs don't qualify as "public display" under the Marine Mammal Protection Act because the entry fees bar most of the public from participating.

Visit the website of the **Whale and Dolphin Conservation Society** at www.wdcs.org or the **American Cetacean Society,** www. acsonline.org, for further discussion on the topic.

Bullfighting is considered an important part of Latin culture, but before you attend a *correo,* you should know that, in all likelihood, the

- **Carbonfund** (www.carbonfund.org), **TerraPass** (www.terrapass.org), and **Carbon Neutral** (www.carbonneutral.org) provide info on "carbon offsetting," or offsetting the greenhouse gas emitted during flights.
- **Greenhotels** (www.greenhotels.com) recommends green-rated member hotels around the world that fulfill the company's stringent environmental requirements. **Environmentally Friendly Hotels** (www.environmentally friendlyhotels.com) offers more green accommodations ratings. The **Hotel Association of Canada** (www.hacgreen hotels.com) has a Green Key Eco-Rating Program, which audits the environmental performance of Canadian hotels, motels, and resorts.
- **Sustain Lane** (www.sustainlane.com) lists sustainable eating and drinking choices around the U.S.; also visit **www.eatwellguide.org** for tips on eating sustainably in the U.S. and Canada.
- For information on animal-friendly issues throughout the world, visit **Tread Lightly** (www.treadlightly.org). For information about the ethics of swimming with dolphins, visit the **Whale and Dolphin Conservation Society** (www.wdcs.org).
- **Volunteer International** (www.volunteerinternational. org) has a list of questions to help you determine the intentions and the nature of a volunteer program. For general info on volunteer travel, visit **www.volunteer abroad.org** and **www.idealist.org**.

bulls (at least four) will undergo torture, shed lots of blood, and die before a team of horses drags their carcasses unceremoniously out of the ring. That said, a bullfight is a portal into understanding Mexico's Spanish colonial past, and traditional machismo is on full display. Bullfights take place in towns as different as Tijuana and Puerto Vallarta, and they afford a colorful spectacle like no other, with a brass band playing; the costumed matador's macho stare; men shaking their heads at less-than-perfect swipes of the cape; and overly made-up, bloodthirsty women chanting *"Ole,"* waving their white hankies, and throwing roses, jackets, and hats at the matador's feet. There is also the extremely miniscule chance that, if the bull puts up a good enough fight or pierces his horn through the matador's leg, he will be spared for breeding purposes. It does happen, if only rarely. To read more about the implications of attending a bullfight, visit **www.peta. org**, the website of People for the Ethical Treatment of Animals (PETA).

For information on animal-friendly issues throughout the world, visit **Tread Lightly** (www.treadlightly.org).

10 SPECIAL-INTEREST TRIPS

ACADEMIC TRIPS & LANGUAGE CLASSES

For Spanish-language instruction, **IMAC** (© **866/306-5040;** www. spanish-school.com.mx) offers programs in Guadalajara, Puerto Vallarta, and Playa del Carmen. For information about studying Spanish in conjunction with a local university in Puerto Vallarta, visit **Spanish Abroad** (© **888/722-7623;** www.spanishabroad.com/puertovallarta).

To explore your inner Frida or Diego while in Mexico, look into **Mexico Art Tours,** 1233 E. Baker Dr., Tempe, AZ 85282 (© **888/ 783-1331** or 480/730-1764; www.mexicanarttours.com). Typically led by Jean Grimm, a specialist in the arts and cultures of Mexico, these unique tours feature compelling speakers who are themselves respected scholars and artists. Itineraries include visits to Chiapas, Guadalajara, Guanajuato, Puebla, Puerto Vallarta, Mexico City, San Miguel de Allende, and Veracruz—and other cities. Special tours involve archaeology, architecture, interior design, and culture—such as a Day of the Dead tour.

The **Archaeological Conservancy,** 5301 Central Ave. NE, Ste. 402, Albuquerque, NM 87108 (© **505/266-1540;** www.american archaeology.com), presents various trips each year, led by an expert, usually an archaeologist. The trips change from year to year and space is limited; make reservations early.

ADVENTURE & WELLNESS TRIPS

AMTAVE (Asociación Mexicana de Turismo de Aventura y Ecoturismo, A.C.) is an active association of ecotourism and adventure tour operators. It publishes an annual catalog of participating firms and their offerings, all of which must meet certain criteria for security, quality, and training of the guides, as well as for sustainability of natural and cultural environments. For more information, contact AMTAVE (© **55/5688-3883;** www.amtave.org).

FOOD & WINE TRIPS

If you're looking to eat your way through Mexico, sign up with **Culinary Adventures,** 6023 Reid Dr. NW, Gig Harbor, WA 98335 (© **253/851-7676;** fax 253/851-9532; www.marilyntausend.com). It runs a short but select list of cooking tours in Mexico. Culinary Adventures features well-known cooks, with travel to regions known for excellent cuisine. Destinations vary each year. The owner, Marilyn Tausend, is the author of *Cocinas de la Familia* (Family Kitchens), *Savoring Mexico,* and *Mexican,* and co-author of *Mexico the Beautiful Cookbook.*

VOLUNTEER & WORKING TRIPS

For numerous links to volunteer and internship programs throughout Mexico involving teaching, caring for children, providing health care, feeding the homeless, and doing other community and public service, visit **www.volunteerabroad.com**.

---

11 STAYING CONNECTED

TELEPHONES

Mexico's telephone system is slowly but surely catching up with modern times. Most telephone numbers have 10 digits. Every city and town that has telephone access has a two-digit (Mexico City, Monterrey, and Guadalajara) or three-digit (everywhere else) area code. In Mexico City, Monterrey, and Guadalajara, local numbers have eight digits; elsewhere, local numbers have seven digits. To place a local call, you do not need to dial the area code. Many fax numbers are also regular phone numbers; ask whoever answers for the fax tone *("me da tono de fax, por favor").*

The **country code** for Mexico is **52.**

To call Mexico: If you're calling Mexico from the United States:

1. Dial the international access code: 011 from the U.S.; 00 from the U.K., Ireland, or New Zealand; or 0011 from Australia.
2. Dial the country code: 52.
3. Dial the two- or three-digit area code, then the eight- or seven-digit number. For example, if you wanted to dial the U.S. Embassy in Mexico City, the entire number would be 011-52-55-5209-9100.

To make international calls: To make international calls from Mexico, dial 00, then the country code (U.S. or Canada 1, U.K. 44,

Ireland 353, Australia 61, New Zealand 64). Next, dial the area code and number. For example, to call the British Embassy in Washington, you would dial 00-1-202-588-7800.

For directory assistance: Dial ✆ **040** if you're looking for a number inside Mexico. *Note:* Listings usually appear under the owner's name, not the name of the business, and your chances to find an English-speaking operator are slim.

For operator assistance: If you need operator assistance in making a call, dial ✆ **090** to make an international call, and ✆ **020** to call a number in Mexico.

Toll-free numbers: Numbers beginning with 800 within Mexico are toll-free, but calling a U.S. toll-free number from Mexico costs the same as an overseas call. To call an 800 number in the U.S., dial 001-880 and the last seven digits of the toll-free number. To call an 888 number in the U.S., dial 001-881 and the last seven digits of the toll-free number. For a number with an 887 prefix, dial 882; for 866, dial 883.

CELLPHONES

Telcel is Mexico's expensive, primary cellphone provider. It has upgraded its systems to GSM and offers good coverage in much of the country, including the major cities and resorts. Most Mexicans buy their cellphones without a specific coverage plan, and then pay as they go or purchase pre-paid cards with set amounts of air-time credit. These cellphone cards with scratch-off PINs can be purchased in Telcel stores as well as many newspaper stands and convenience stores.

Many U.S. and European cellphone companies offer networks with roaming coverage in Mexico. Rates can be very high, so check with your provider before committing to making calls this way. An increasing number of Mexicans, particularly among the younger generation, prefer the less expensive rates of **Nextel** (www. xtel.com. mx), which features push-to-talk service. **Cellular Abroad** (www. cellularabroad.com) offers cellphone rentals and purchases as well as SIM cards for travel abroad. Whether you rent or purchase the cellphone, you need to purchase a SIM card that is specific for Mexico.

To call a Mexican cellular number in the same area code, dial 044 and then the number. To dial the cellular phone from anywhere else in Mexico, first dial 01, and then the three-digit area code and the seven-digit number. To place an international call to a cellphone (for example, from the U.S.), you now must add a "1" after the country code; for example, 011-52-1 + 10-digit number.

INTERNET & E-MAIL

Wireless Internet access is increasingly common in Mexico's major cities and resorts. Mexico's largest airports offer Wi-Fi access provided for a fee by Telcel's Prodigy Internet service. Most five-star hotels now offer Wi-Fi in the guest rooms, although you will need to check in advance whether this service is free or for a fee. Hotel lobbies often have Wi-Fi, as well. To find public Wi-Fi hotspots in Mexico, go to **www.jiwire.com**; its Hotspot Finder holds the world's largest directory of public wireless hotspots.

Many large Mexican airports have **Internet kiosks,** and quality Mexican hotels usually have business centers with Internet access. You can also check out such copy stores as **FedEx Office** (formerly Kinko's) or **OfficeMax,** which offer computer stations with fully loaded software (as well as Wi-Fi).

12 TIPS ON ACCOMMODATIONS

MEXICO'S HOTEL RATING SYSTEM

The hotel rating system in Mexico is called "Stars and Diamonds." Hotels may qualify to earn one to five stars or diamonds. Many hotels that have excellent standards are not certified, but all rated hotels adhere to strict standards. The guidelines relate to service, facilities, and hygiene more than to prices.

Five-diamond hotels meet the highest requirements for rating: The beds are comfortable, bathrooms are in excellent working order, all facilities are renovated regularly, infrastructure is top-tier, and services and hygiene meet the highest international standards.

Five-star hotels usually offer similar quality, but with lower levels of service and detail in the rooms. For example, a five-star hotel may have less luxurious linens or, perhaps, room service during limited hours rather than 24 hours.

Four-star hotels are less expensive and more basic, but they still guarantee cleanliness and basic services such as hot water and purified drinking water. Three-, two-, and one-star hotels are at least working to adhere to certain standards: Bathrooms are cleaned and linens are washed daily, and you can expect a minimum standard of service. Two- and one-star hotels generally provide bottled water rather than purified water.

The nonprofit organization Calidad Mexicana Certificada, A.C., known as **Calmecac** (www.calmecac.com.mx), is responsible for hotel ratings; visit their website for additional details about the rating system.

In addition to the major international chains, you'll run across a number of less-familiar brands as you plan your trip to Mexico. They include:

- **Brisas Hotels & Resorts** (www.brisas.com.mx): These were the hotels that originally attracted jet-set travelers to Mexico. Spectacular in a retro way, these properties offer the laid-back luxury that makes a Mexican vacation so unique. Manzanillo has a Las Brisas property, Las Hadas Manzanillo.

- **Fiesta Americana** and **Fiesta Inn** (www.posadas.com): Part of the Mexican-owned Grupo Posadas company, these hotels set the country's midrange standard for facilities and services. They generally offer comfortable, spacious rooms and traditional Mexican hospitality. Fiesta Americana hotels offer excellent beach-resort packages. Fiesta Inn hotels are usually more business oriented. Grupo Posadas also owns the more luxurious Caesar Park hotels and the eco-oriented Explorean hotels. Mid-Pacific Mexico's offerings include Fiesta Americana Grand Guadalajara Country Club, the Fiesta Americana Guadalajara, the Fiesta Inn Guadalajara, and the Fiesta Americana Puerto Vallarta.

- **Hoteles Camino Real** (www.caminoreal.com): Once known as the premier Mexican hotel chain, Camino Real still maintains a high standard of service at its properties, although the company was sold in 2005, and many of the hotels that once formed a part of it have been sold off or have become independent. Its beach hotels are traditionally located on the best beaches in the area. This chain also focuses on the business market. The hotels are famous for their vivid and contrasting colors. In mid-Pacific Mexico, Camino Real has 3 hotels: the Camino Real Guadalajara, Camino Real Guadalajara Expo, and the Camino Real Manzanillo.

- **NH Hoteles** (www.nh-hotels.com): The NH hotels are noted for their family-friendly facilities and quality standards. The beach properties' signature feature is a pool, framed by columns, overlooking the sea. NH Hoteles has only one property in mid-Pacific Mexico, the NH Krystal Puerto Vallarta.

- **Quinta Real Grand Class Hotels and Resorts** (www.quintareal.com): These hotels, owned by Summit Hotels and Resorts, are noted for architectural and cultural details that reflect their individual regions. At these luxury properties, attention to detail and excellent service are the rule. Quinta Real is the top line Mexican hotel brand. The only Quinta Real hotel on the mid-Pacific coast is the Quinta Real Guadalajara.

(Finds) **Boutique Lodgings**

Mexico lends itself beautifully to the concept of small, private hotels in idyllic settings. They vary in style from grandiose estate to palm-thatched bungalow. **Mexico Boutique Hotels** (www.mexicoboutiquehotels.com) specializes in smaller places to stay with a high level of personal attention and service. Most options have less than 50 rooms, and the accommodations consist of entire villas, *casitas,* bungalows, or a combination.

HOUSE RENTALS & SWAPS

House and villa rentals and swaps are becoming more common in Mexico, but no single recognized agency or business provides this service exclusively for Mexico. In the chapters that follow, I have provided information on independent services that I have found to be reputable.

You'll find the most extensive inventory of homes at **Vacation Rentals by Owner (VRBO;** www.vrbo.com). They have more than 33,000 homes and condominiums worldwide, including a large selection in Mexico. Another good option is **VacationSpot** (© **888/903-7768;** www.vacationspot.com), owned by Expedia and a part of its sister company, Hotels.com. It has fewer choices, but the company's criteria for adding inventory is much more selective and often includes on-site inspections. They also offer toll-free phone support.

Settling into Puerto Vallarta

by Shane Christensen

No matter how extensively I travel in Mexico, Puerto Vallarta remains my favorite part of this colorful country, for its unrivaled combination of Mexican warmth, international diversity, and artistic charm. Beyond the cobblestone streets, graceful cathedral, and welcoming atmosphere, Puerto Vallarta offers a wealth of natural beauty and man-made pleasures, including hotels of all classes and prices, more than 250 restaurants, a sizzling nightlife, and enough shops and galleries to tempt even jaded consumers.

Vallarta (as locals refer to it) was never a "sleepy little fishing village," as is often claimed. It began as a port for processing silver brought down from mines in the Sierra Madre—then was forever transformed by a movie director and two star-crossed lovers. In 1963, John Huston brought stars Ava Gardner and Richard Burton here to film the Tennessee Williams play *Night of the Iguana.* Burton's new love, Elizabeth Taylor, came along to ensure the romance remained in full bloom—even though both were married to others at the time. Titillated, the international paparazzi arrived, and when they weren't photographing the famous couple—or Gardner water-skiing back from the set, surrounded by a bevy of beach boys—they shot the beauty of Puerto Vallarta.

Luxury hotels and shopping centers have sprung up north and south of the original town, allowing Vallarta to grow into a city of 400,000 without sacrificing its small-town charms. With the services and infrastructure—and, unfortunately, now the traffic—of a modern city, it still retains the authenticity of a colonial Mexican village.

Cool breezes flow down from the mountains along the Río Cuale, which runs through the center of town. Fanciful public sculptures grace the *malecón* (boardwalk), which is bordered by lively restaurants, shops, and nightclubs. The *malecón* is a magnet for both residents and visitors, who stroll the main walkway to take in an ocean breeze, a multihued sunset, or a moonlit, perfect wave.

SETTLING INTO PUERTO VALLARTA

To Bucerias, and Punta Mita

MARINA VALLARTA

Playa de Oro

Terminal Marítima (Cruise Pier)

Vista Vallarta Golf Course

area of inset

Plaza Peninsula

Puerto Vallarta

JALISCO

PACIFIC OCEAN

MICHOACÁN

Mexico City

| 0 | 200 mi |
| 0 | 200 km |

Marina Vallarta Accommodations & Dining

Airport

Albatros

Gaviota

Pelícano

Garzas

Garros

Bocanegra

Flamingos

Paseo de la Marina

Mástil

Timón

Ancla

Popa

Proa

Vallarta Adventures

Plaza Neptuno

Paseo de la Marina Norte

Paseo de la Vela

Paseo de la Marina Sur

Playa de Oro

Playa Las Glorias

Bahía de Banderas

Avenida de México

Ave. Francisco M. Ascencio

Playa Camarones

EL CENTRO

See "Downtown Puerta Vallarta" Map

Río Cuale

Playa Olas Altas

Playa Los Muertos

Playa Punta Negra

Playa Garza Blanca

Playa Gemelas

Los Arcos

Playa Mismaloya

To Yelapa and Tomatlán

To Manzanillo and El Eden Chino's

Bullring

ACCOMMODATIONS ■
Casa Tres Vidas **10**
Casa Velas **2**
Dreams Puerto Vallarta
  Resort & Spa **12**
Fiesta Americana Puerto
  Vallarta **6**
Hacienda San Angel **8**
Hotel Playa Los Arcos **9**
Marriott CasaMagna
  Resort & Spa **1**
Quinta María Cortez **11**
Villa Premiere Puerto Vallarta
  Hotel & Spa **7**
Westin Resort & Spa
  Puerto Vallarta **5**

DINING ◆
Benitto's **4**
Porto Bello **3**

2

1 PUERTO VALLARTA ESSENTIALS

GETTING THERE & DEPARTING

BY PLANE Puerto Vallarta's International Airport, **Gustavo Diaz Ordaz International Airport** (PVR), is about 10km (6¼ miles) north of Puerto Vallarta. Local numbers of some international carriers serving Puerto Vallarta are **Alaska Airlines** (✆ **322/221-1350**), **American Airlines** (✆ **322/221-1799**), **US Airways** (✆ **322/221-2936**), **Continental** (✆ **322/221-1025**), **Delta** (✆ **322/221-2425**), **Frontier** (✆ **800/432-1359**), and **United** (✆ **800/225-5833** in the U.S.).

AeroMéxico (✆ **322/221-1204,** -1030) flies from Los Angeles, San Diego, Aguascalientes, Guadalajara, La Paz, León, Mexico City, Morelia, and Tijuana. **Mexicana** (✆ **322/224-8900** or 221-1266) has direct or nonstop flights from Chicago, Los Angeles, Guadalajara, Mazatlán, and Mexico City.

For a list of international carriers serving Mexico, see "Airline, Hotel & Car Rental Websites," p. 165.

Major car-rental agencies have counters at the airport, including **Alamo** (✆ **322/221-1228**), **Avis** (✆ **322/221-1657**), **Budget** (✆ **322/221-1210**), **Dollar** (✆ **322/223-1354**), **Hertz** (✆ **322/221-1473**), and **National** (✆ **322/221-1226**), and are open after flight arrivals. After registering, they will send a shuttle to take you to the nearby car-rental lots. Daily rates run $40 to $80.

BY CAR The coastal Hwy. 200 is the only choice from Mazatlán (6 hr. north) or Manzanillo (3½–4 hr. south). Hwy. 15 from Guadalajara to Tepic takes 6 hours; to save as much as 2 hours, take Hwy. 15A from Chapalilla to Compostela, bypassing Tepic, then continue south on Hwy. 200 to Puerto Vallarta.

BY BUS The bus station, **Central Camionera de Puerto Vallarta,** is just north of the airport, approximately 11km (6¾ miles) from downtown. It offers overnight guarded parking and baggage storage. Most major first-class bus lines operate from here, including TAP, Pacifico, Futura, Turistar, Elite, Primera Plus, and ETN, with transportation to points throughout Mexico, including Mazatlán ($34), Manzanillo ($23), Guadalajara ($200), Barra de Navidad ($18), and Mexico City ($86). Taxis into town cost approximately $10 and are readily available; public buses operate from 7am to 11pm and regularly stop in front of the arrivals hall.

ARRIVING BY PLANE The airport is close to the north end of town near the Marina Vallarta, about 10km (6¼ miles) from downtown. **Transportes Terrestres** minivans and **Aeromovil** taxis make the trip. They use a zone pricing system, with fares clearly posted at the ticket booths. Fares start at $16 for a ride to Marina Vallarta and go up to $28 for the south shore hotels. Federally licensed airport taxis exclusively provide transportation from the airport, and their fares are more than three times as high as city (yellow) taxi fares. A trip to downtown Puerto Vallarta costs $25, whereas a return trip using a city taxi costs only $10. Only airport cabs may pick up passengers leaving the airport. You can also buy a ticket for a *colectivo* (a shuttle van that goes every 30 min.) at the official taxi stand which, at only $9 to downtown, is the cheapest option.

VISITOR INFORMATION Prior to arrival, a great source of general information is the **Puerto Vallarta Tourism Board** (© 888/384-6822 in the U.S., © 322/224-1175 in Mexico; www.visitpuerto vallarta.com). The office is located in the Hotel Canto del Sol in the Zona Comercial Las Glorias. If you have further questions after you arrive, visit the **Municipal Tourism Office** at Juárez and Independencia (© **322/226-8080,** ext. 230), in a corner of the white Presidencia Municipal building on the northwest end of the main square. In addition to offering a listing of current events and promotional brochures, the employees can assist with specific questions—there's usually an English speaker on staff. This is also the office of the tourist police. It's open Monday through Saturday from 8am to 8pm, Sunday from 10am to 6pm.

The **State Tourism Office,** Plaza Marina L 144, 2nd Floor (© **322/221-2676,** -2677, or -2678; fax 322/221-2680), also offers brochures and can assist with specific questions about Puerto Vallarta and other points in the state of Jalisco, including Guadalajara, Costa Alegre, the town of Tequila, and the program that promotes stays in authentic rural haciendas. It's open Monday through Friday from 9am to 5pm.

CITY LAYOUT The seaside promenade, the *malecón,* is a common reference point for giving directions. It's next to **Paseo Díaz Ordaz** and runs north–south through the central downtown area. From the waterfront, the town stretches back into the hills a half-dozen blocks. The areas bordering the **Río Cuale** are the oldest parts of town—the original Puerto Vallarta. The area immediately south of the river, called **Olas Altas** after its main street (and sometimes Los Muertos after the beach of the same name), is home to a growing selection of sidewalk cafes, fine restaurants, espresso bars, and hip nightclubs. In the center of town, nearly everything is within walking distance both north and south of the river. **Bridges** on Insurgentes (northbound traffic) and Ignacio Vallarta (southbound traffic) link the two sections of downtown.

AREA LAYOUT   Beyond downtown, Puerto Vallarta has grown along the beach to the north and south. Linking downtown to the airport is **Avenida Francisco Medina Ascencio,** home of many high-rise hotels (in an area called the **Zona Hotelera,** or Hotel Zone), plus several shopping centers with a variety of dining options.

Marina Vallarta, a resort city within a city, lies at the northern edge of the Hotel Zone not far from the airport. It boasts modern luxury hotels, condominiums, and homes; a huge marina with 450 yacht slips; a golf course; restaurants and bars; and several shopping plazas. Because it was originally a swamp, the beaches are somewhat less desirable, with darker sand and seasonal inflows of cobblestones. The Marina Vallarta peninsula faces the bay and looks south to the town of Puerto Vallarta.

Nuevo Vallarta is a booming planned resort north of the airport, across the Ameca River in the state of Nayarit (about 13km/8 miles north of downtown). It also has hotels, condominiums, and a yacht marina, with a growing selection of restaurants and shopping, including the new Paradise Plaza mall. Most hotels there are all-inclusive, with some of the finest beaches in the bay, but guests usually travel into Puerto Vallarta (about $21 a cab ride) for anything other than poolside or beach action. Regularly scheduled public bus service costs about $1.50 and runs until 10pm.

Bucerías, a small beachside village of cobblestone streets, villas, and small hotels, is farther north along Banderas Bay, 30km (19 miles) beyond the airport. Past Bucerías, following the curved coastline of Banderas Bay, you'll find **La Cruz de Huanaxcle,** a new megamarina project, but still an authentic, colorful seaside town. Continue to the end of the road and you'll reach **Punta Mita.** Once a rustic fishing village, it has been artfully developed as a luxury destination. In the works are a total of four exclusive luxury boutique resorts, private villas, and two golf courses. The site of an ancient celestial observatory, it is an exquisite setting, with white-sand beaches and clear waters. The northern shore of Banderas Bay is emerging as the area's most exclusive address for luxury villas and accommodations.

In the other direction from downtown is the southern coastal highway, home to more luxury hotels. Immediately south of town lies the exclusive residential and rental district of **Conchas Chinas.** Ten kilometers (6¼ miles) south, on **Playa Mismaloya** (where *Night of*

> ## (Tips) Don't Let Taxi Drivers Steer You Wrong
>
> Beware of restaurant and shopping recommendations from taxi drivers—many receive a commission from establishments where they bring passengers.

the Iguana was filmed), lies the Barceló La Jolla de Mismaloya resort. There's no road on the southern shoreline of Banderas Bay, but three small coastal villages are popular attractions for visitors to Puerto Vallarta: **Las Animas, Quimixto,** and **Yelapa,** all accessible only by boat. The tiny, pristine cove of **Caletas,** site of John Huston's former home, is a popular day- or nighttime excursion.

GETTING AROUND   By Taxi   Taxis are plentiful and relatively inexpensive. Most trips from downtown to the northern Hotel Zone and Marina Vallarta cost $5.50 to $10; to or from Marina Vallarta to Mismaloya Beach (to the south) costs $13 to $17. Rates are charged by zone and are generally posted in the lobbies of hotels. Taxis can also be hired by the hour or day for longer trips. Rates run $18 to $22 per hour, with discounts available for full-day rates—consider this an alternative to renting a car.

By Car   Rental cars are readily available at the airport, through travel agencies, and through the most popular U.S. car-rental services, but unless you're planning a distant side trip, don't bother. Car rentals are expensive, especially because of insurance rates, and parking around town is very challenging, unless you opt for one of the two new parking garages constructed on either end of the *malecón* zone (at Park Hidalgo to the north, and adjacent to the northern border of the Cuale River to the south). If you see a sign for a cheap car or Jeep rental, be aware that these are lures to get folks to attend timeshare presentations. Unless you are interested in a timeshare, stopping to inquire will be a (possibly annoying) waste of your time.

By Bus   City buses, easy to navigate and inexpensive, will serve just about all your transportation needs. They run from the airport through the Hotel Zone along Morelos Street (1 block inland from the *malecón*), across the Río Cuale, and inland on Vallarta, looping back through the downtown hotel and restaurant districts on Insurgentes and several other downtown streets. To get to the northern hotel strip from old Puerto Vallarta, take the ZONA HOTELES, IXTAPA, or LAS JUNTAS bus. These buses may also post the names of hotels they pass, such as Krystal, Sheraton, and others. Buses marked MARINA VALLARTA travel inside this area, stopping at the major hotels there.

Other buses operate every 10 to 15 minutes south to either Mismaloya Beach or Boca de Tomatlán (a sign in the front window indicates the destination) from Constitución and Basilio Badillo, a few blocks south of the river. Buses run generally from 6am to 11pm, and it's rare to wait more than a few minutes for one. The fare is about 50¢. You do not have to have exact change; the driver will make change.

By Boat The *muelle* (cruise-ship pier), also called Terminal Marítima, is where **excursion boats** to Yelapa, Las Animas, Quimixto, and the Marietas Islands depart. It's north of town near the airport, an inexpensive taxi or bus ride from town. Just take any bus marked IXTAPA, LAS JUNTAS, PITILLAL, or AURORA and tell the driver to let you off at the Terminal Marítima. *Note:* Oddly enough, you must pay a $1.50 federal tax to gain access to the pier—and your departing excursion boat.

Water taxis to Yelapa, Las Animas, and Quimixto leave at 10:30 and 11am from the pier at Los Muertos Beach (south of downtown), on Rodolfo Rodríguez next to the Hotel Marsol. Another water taxi departs around 11:30am from the beachside pier at the northern edge of the *malecón*. A round-trip ticket to Yelapa (the farthest point, which takes about 45 min. each way) costs $22. Return trips usually depart between 3 and 5pm, but confirm the pickup time with your water taxi captain. Other water taxis depart from Boca de Tomatlán, about 30 minutes south of town by public bus. These water taxis are the better option if you want more flexible departure and return times from the southern beaches. Generally, they leave on the hour for the southern shore destinations, or more frequently if there is traffic. Prices run about $15 round-trip, with rates clearly posted on a sign on the beach. A private water taxi costs $60 to $120, depending on your destination, and allows you to choose your own return time. They'll take up to eight people for that price, so often people band together at the beach to hire one.

Fast Facts **Puerto Vallarta**

Area Code The telephone area code is **322.**

Climate It's warm all year, with tropical temperatures; however, evenings and early mornings in the winter can turn quite cool. Summers are sunny, with an increase in humidity during the rainy season, between May and October. Rains come almost every afternoon in June and July, and are usually brief but strong—just enough to cool off the air for evening activities. In September, heat and humidity are least comfortable and rains heaviest.

Currency Exchange Banks are found throughout downtown and in the other prime shopping areas. Most banks are open Monday through Friday from 9am to 4pm, with shorter hours on Saturday. ATMs are common throughout Vallarta, including the central plaza downtown. They are becoming the most favorable way to exchange currency, with bank rates plus 24-hour convenience. *Casas de cambio* (money-exchange houses), located throughout town, offer longer hours than the banks, with only slightly lower exchange rates.

Drugstores **CMQ Farmacia,** Basilio Badillo 365 (© **322/222-1330**), is open 24 hours and makes free deliveries to hotels between 11am and 10pm with a minimum purchase of $20. **Farmacias Guadalajara,** Emiliano Zapata 232 (© **322/224-1811**), is also open 24 hours.

Embassies & Consulates The **U.S. Consular Agency** office (© **322/222-0069;** fax 322/223-0074; 24 hr. a day for emergencies) is located in Nuevo Vallarta, in the Paradise Plaza, Local L-7, on the second floor. It's open Monday through Friday from 8:30am to 12:30pm. The **Canadian Consulate** (© **322/293-0099,** -0098; 24-hr. emergency line 01-800/706-2900 in Mexico) is located in Plaza Las Glorias, 1951 Blvd. Francisco Medina Ascencio, Edificio Obelisco, Loc. 108 (you'll see the Canadian flag hanging from the balcony). It's open Monday through Friday from 9am to 3pm.

Emergencies **Police** emergency, © **060;** local police, © **322/290-0513,** -0512; intensive care **ambulance,** © **322/225-0386** (*Note:* English-speaking assistance is not always available at this number); **Cruz Roja (Red Cross),** © **322/222-1533; Global Life Ambulance Service** (provides both ground and air ambulance service), © **322/226-1010,** ext. 304.

Hospitals The following offer U.S.-standards service and are available 24 hours: **Ameri-Med Urgent Care,** Avenida Francisco Medina Ascencio at Plaza Neptuno, Loc. D-1, Marina Vallarta (© **322/226-2080;** fax 322/226-2060; www.amerimed-hospitals. com); **San Javier Marina Hospital,** Av. Francisco Medina Ascencio 2760, Zona Hotelera (© **322/226-1010**); and **Cornerstone Hospital,** Av. los Tules 136 (behind Plaza Caracol; © **322/224-9400**).

Newspapers & Magazines Vallarta Today, a daily English-language newspaper (✆ **322/225-3323** or 224-2829), is a good source for local information and upcoming events. The bilingual quarterly city magazine *Vallarta Lifestyles* (✆ **322/ 221-0106**) is also very popular. Both are for sale at area newsstands and hotel gift shops. The weekly English-language *Vallarta Tribune* (✆ **322/223-0585;** www.vallartatribune. com) is distributed free throughout town and offers an objective local viewpoint. *PVMirror* (**www.pvmirror.com**) is another English-language city paper and online site that offers local news and visitor information.

Post Office The *correo* is at Colombia Street, behind Hidalgo park, and is open Monday through Friday from 9am to 6pm, Saturday from 9am to 1pm.

Safety Puerto Vallarta enjoys a very low crime rate. Public transportation is safe to use, and Tourist Police (dressed in white safari uniforms with white hats) are available to answer questions, give directions, and offer assistance. Most encounters with the police are linked to using or purchasing drugs—so don't (see chapter 1). *Note:* The tourist police conduct random personal searches for drugs. Although there is some question about their right to do this, the best course of action if they want to frisk you is to comply—objecting will likely result in a free tour of the local jail. However, you are within your rights to request the name of the officer. Report any unusual incidents to the local consular office.

2 WHERE TO STAY

Beyond a varied selection of hotels and resorts, Puerto Vallarta offers many alternative accommodations. Oceanfront or marina-view condominiums and elegant private villas can offer families and small groups a better value and more ample space than a hotel. For short-term rentals, check out **www.costavallartaboutiquevillas.com**, ✆ **800/728-9098** in the U.S. and Canada, or 322/221-2277. Office hours are Monday through Friday 8am to 7pm, Saturday 9am to 2pm. Prices start at $99 a night for nonbeachside condos and go to $3,000 for penthouse condos or private villas. Susan Weisman's **Bayside Properties,** Francisco Rodríguez 160, corner of Olas Altas (✆ **322/222-8148;** www.baysidepropertiespv.com), rents condos, villas, and hotels for individuals and large groups, including gay-friendly accommodations. Another reputable full-service travel agency is **Holland Travel Companies** (© 415/704-0455; www.puerto vallartavillas.com). For the ultimate, indulge in a Punta Mita Villa rental within this exclusive resort. Contact **Mita Residential** (© 877/561-2893 in the U.S., or 329/291-5300; www.mitaresidential.com).

This section lists hotels from the airport south along Banderas Bay.

MARINA VALLARTA

Marina Vallarta is the most modern and deluxe area of hotel development in Puerto Vallarta. Located immediately south of the airport and just north of the cruise ship terminal, it's a planned development whose centerpiece is a 450-slip modern marina.

The hotels reviewed below are on the beachfront of the peninsula. The beaches here are somewhat less attractive than beaches in other parts of the bay; the sand is darker, firmly packed, and, during certain times of the year, quite rocky. These hotels compensate with oversize pool areas and exotic landscaping. This area suits families and those looking for lots of centralized activity. Marina Vallarta is also home to an 18-hole **golf course** designed by Joe Finger.

In addition to the hotels reviewed below, an excellent choice is **Casa Velas,** on the golf course at Pelícanos 311 (© 866/529-8813 in the U.S., or 322/226-6688; www.hotelcasavelas.com). The elegant, boutique-style hotel has extra large rooms, an on-site spa, and a lovely pool. Although it is not located on the beach, it has a stunning beach club with food and beverage service, a pool, and sun chairs, with shuttle service for guests. High-season rates start at $250 per person, all inclusive. Due to traffic, a taxi from the Marina to downtown can take 20 to 30 minutes.

Marriott CasaMagna Resort & Spa ★★ (Kids) Set on a lovely stretch of beach in Marina Vallarta, the family-friendly CasaMagna underwent a $10.7-million renovation in 2008. Guest rooms, all of which are accessed through open-air hallways, have been upgraded with contemporary Mexican styling, marble floors, and flower accents, and bougainvillea hangs from each balcony overlooking the pool and bay. Pool activities and beach watersports are offered throughout the day, and there's a luxurious yet reasonably priced spa. Among the many diversions for children is a turtle-preservation program that runs from June to November and provides guests the chance to release baby turtles into the sea. The resort houses four restaurants, including the teppanyaki-style (cook at your table) Mikado, as well as the colonial-designed Mexican La Estancia. The head chef offers interactive cooking classes ($90 per person), beginning with a tour of the hotel's own chili, herb, and cactus garden. Service in the hotel, which has wonderful energy, is first rate.

Paseo de la Marina 5, Marina Vallarta, 48354 Puerto Vallarta, Jal. ℭ **800/223-6388** in the U.S., or 322/226-0000. Fax 322/226-0060. www.puertovallartamarriott.com. 433 units. High season $279–$309 double, $459–$479 suite; low season $179–$199 double, $359–$389 suite. AE, DC, MC, V. Free parking. **Amenities:** 4 restaurants; deli; 3 bars, including lobby bar and pool bar; kids' club; concierge; golf privileges at Marina Vallarta Golf Club; state-of-the-art fitness center and spa w/ classes (fee), sauna, steam room, and whirlpool; oceanside pool; room service; 2 lighted grass tennis courts. *In room:* A/C, flatscreen TV, iHome audio player and alarm clock, hair dryer, minibar, Wi-Fi.

Westin Resort & Spa Puerto Vallarta ★★   Stunning architecture and vibrant colors are the hallmarks of this award-winning property. Although the grounds are large—over 8 hectares (20 acres) with 260m (853 ft.) of beachfront—the warm service creates the feeling of an intimate resort. Hammocks are strung between the palms closest to the beach, where there are also private beach cabañas. All rooms have balconies with ocean views and are contemporary in style, with oversize wood furnishings, tile floors, original art, and tub/showers. Rooms on the 5th to 14th floors were redecorated in 2008, and a certain number of them have been designated as "Westin Workout rooms." Eight junior suites and some double rooms have Jacuzzis, and the five grand suites consist of two levels, with spacious living areas. Two floors of rooms make up the Royal Beach Club with VIP services, including a private lounge with continental breakfast and evening drinks included. The fitness center is modern and well equipped, with scheduled spinning and yoga classes.

Paseo de la Marina Sur 205, Marina Vallarta, 48354 Puerto Vallarta, Jal. ℭ **800/228-3000** in the U.S., or 322/226-1100. Fax 322/226-1144. www.starwoodhotels.com/westin. 280 units. High season $309–$539 double, $555–$839 suite; low season $150–$400 double, $440–$700 suite. AE, DC, MC, V. Free parking. **Amenities:** 2 restaurants; beach bar; lobby bar; poolside bar; kids' club; golf privileges at Marina Vallarta Golf Club; state-of-the-art health club w/treadmills, Stairmasters, resistance equipment, sauna, and steam room; room service; 3 lighted grass tennis courts. *In room:* A/C, TV, hair dryer, minibar, Wi-Fi (fee).

THE HOTEL ZONE

The main street running between the airport and town is Avenida Francisco Medina Ascencio. The hotels here offer excellent wide beachfronts with generally tranquil waters for swimming. From here it's a quick taxi or bus ride to downtown.

Fiesta Americana Puerto Vallarta ★★ **(Kids)**   The Fiesta Americana's towering, three-story, thatched *palapa* lobby is a landmark in the Hotel Zone, and the hotel is known for its excellent beach and friendly service. An abundance of plants, splashing fountains, constant breezes, and comfortable seating areas in the lobby create a casual South Seas ambience. The nine-story terra-cotta building embraces a large plaza with a pool facing the beach. Marble-trimmed rooms in neutral tones with pastel accents contain carved headboards and comfortable rattan and wicker furniture. All have private balconies with ocean and pool views. Beachside massages are given from morning to sunset, and pool activities take place throughout the day. The hotel is especially popular with Mexican and North American families.

Av. Francisco Medina Ascencio Km 2.5, 48300 Puerto Vallarta, Jal. ✆ **322/226-2100.** Fax 322/224-2108. www.fiestaamericana.com. 291 units. High season $200–$400 double; low season $145–$250 double; year-round $400 and up suite. AE, DC, MC, V. Limited free parking. **Amenities:** 2 restaurants; lobby bar w/live music weekends; large pool w/activities and children's activities in high season; room service. *In room:* A/C, TV, hair dryer, minibar.

Villa Premiere Puerto Vallarta Hotel & Spa ★★ Located just a few blocks north of the start of Puerto Vallarta's *malecón,* the Premiere lies within walking distance of downtown restaurants, shops, galleries, and clubs. With a first-rate spa and a policy that restricts guests to ages 16 and older, it's a place that caters to relaxation. Four types of rooms are available, but all are decorated in warm colors with tile floors and light-wood furnishings. Deluxe rooms have ocean views, a small seating area with comfortable chairs, and a sizable private balcony. Spa suites offer Jacuzzis in the bedrooms. The stunning bi-level spa is the real attraction of this hotel—scented with aromatherapy and glowing with candlelight, it uses top-notch, 100% natural products, most based on Mexico's natural treasures like coconut, aloe, and papaya. The Premiere also offers an all-inclusive option, with all meals and drinks included.

San Salvador 117, behind the Buenaventura Hotel, Col. 5 de Diciembre, 48350 Puerto Vallarta, Jal. ✆ **877/886-9176** in the U.S., or 322/226-7001 or -7040. Fax 322/226-7043. www.premiereonline.com.mx. 83 units. Room only: High season $185–$430 double; low season $135–$370 double. All-inclusive: High season $335–$560 per person, based on double occupancy; low season $185–$360 per person, double. AE, MC, V. Limited street parking. No children younger than 16 accepted. **Amenities:** 3 restaurants; fitness center; yoga classes and meditation workshops; 2 small outdoor pools; room service; full spa. *In room:* A/C, TV, hair dryer, minibar.

DOWNTOWN TO LOS MUERTOS BEACH

This part of town has undergone a renaissance; economical hotels and good-value guesthouses dominate. Several blocks off the beach, you can find numerous budget inns offering clean, simply furnished rooms; most offer discounts for long-term stays.

Hacienda San Angel ★★ Finds This is Puerto Vallarta's most upscale boutique hotel, with a more formal feel than most Vallarta accommodations. Although it's not on the beach, you'll hardly miss the surf since the hotel offers beautiful vistas of the city and Bay of Banderas. Once the home of Richard Burton, it lies just behind Puerto Vallarta's famed church and, in fact, looks somewhat like a church itself. The Hacienda consists of five rustic colonial villas; the first two are joined to the third villa by a path that winds through a lovely terraced tropical garden with statuary and a fountain. The heated pool and deck lie adjacent to the elegant open-air restaurant, and a second sun deck with Jacuzzi overlooks the church and water beyond. Each morning, continental breakfast is served outside your suite at the hour you request. Hacienda San Angel is open for dinner to nonguests (see "Where to Dine," below).

Miramar 336, Col. Centro, 48300 Puerto Vallarta, Jal. ℂ **415/738-8220** or 322/222-2692. www.haciendasanangel.com. 10 units. High season $320–$680 double; low season $285–$560 double. All rates include daily continental breakfast. Rates for the entire Hacienda or separate villas consisting of 3 suites each are also available. MC, V. Very limited street parking available. **Amenities:** Full menu of en-suite breakfast, lunch, and dinner, or private chef available; restaurant; concierge; complimentary Internet access; 2 outdoor pools. *In room:* A/C, TV/DVD, CD player, hair dryer.

Hotel Playa Los Arcos ★★ This is one of Vallarta's perennially popular hotels, with a stellar location in the heart of Los Muertos Beach, central to the Olas Altas sidewalk-cafe action. The lovely four-story structure is U-shaped and faces the ocean. Guest rooms are small but beautifully decorated, with carved wooden furniture painted pale pink. They have balconies that overlook the charming courtyard pool that almost extends into the lobby. The hotel grounds include a *palapa* beachside bar with occasional live entertainment, a gourmet coffee shop, and the popular Kaiser Maximilian's gourmet restaurant (see "Where to Dine," below). It's 7 blocks south of the river in the old section of downtown.

Olas Altas 380, 48380 Puerto Vallarta, Jal. ℂ **800/648-2403** in the U.S., or 322/226-7100. Fax 322/226-7101. www.playalosarcos.com. 171 units. High season $150–$170 double; $180–$220 suite; low season $100–$150 double, $150–$175 suite. AE, MC, V. Limited street parking. **Amenities:** Restaurant; lobby bar; outdoor pool. *In room:* A/C, TV.

SOUTH TO MISMALOYA

Casa Tres Vidas ★★ Value Set on a stunning private cove, Tres Vidas gives you the experience of your own private villa, complete with service staff. It offers outstanding value for the location—close to town, with panoramic views from every room. Each villa has at least two levels and over 460 sq. m (4,951 sq. ft.) of mostly open living areas, plus a private swimming pool, heated whirlpool, and air-conditioned bedrooms. The Vida Alta penthouse villa has three bedrooms, plus a rooftop deck with pool and bar. Vida Sol villa's three bedrooms sleep 10 (two rooms have two king-size beds each). Directly on the ocean, Vida Mar is a four-bedroom villa, accommodating eight. The staff prepares gourmet meals in your villa twice a day—you choose the menu and pay only for the food. Service is consistently excellent.

Sagitario 132, Playa Conchas Chinas, 48300 Puerto Vallarta, Jal. ℂ 888/640-8100 or 801/531-8100 in the U.S., or 322/221-5317. Fax 322/221-53-27. www.casatres vidas.com. 3 villas. High season $750–$800 villa; low season $550–$600 villa. Rates include services such as housekeeping and meal preparation. Special summer 1- or 2-bedroom rates available; minimum 3 nights. AE, MC, V. Very limited street parking. **Amenities:** 2 prepared daily meals; concierge; private outdoor pool. *In room:* A/C (in bedrooms).

Dreams Puerto Vallarta Resort & Spa The all-inclusive Dreams Resort sits on a beautiful beach with soft white sand in a private cove. Set apart from other properties, with a lush mountain backdrop, it's still only a 5- to 10-minute ride to town. The hotel consists of two buildings: the 250-room main hotel, which curves gently with the shape of the Playa Las Estacas, and the newer 11-story Club Tower, also facing the beach and ocean. Standard rooms in the aging main building are large; some have sliding doors opening onto the beach, and others have balconies. Club Tower rooms (from the sixth floor up) have expanded marble bathrooms and balconies with whirlpool tubs. All rooms feature ocean views, vibrant colors, marble floors, and artwork by local artist Manuel Lepe. The grounds include two swimming pools (including an adults-only tranquillity pool) and health club and spa. Food served in the resort is so-so.

Carretera Barra de Navidad Km 3.5, Playa Las Estacas, 48300 Puerto Vallarta, Jal. ℂ 866/237-3267 in the U.S. and Canada, or 322/226-5000. Fax 322/221-6000. www.dreamsresorts.com. 337 units. All-inclusive rates are per person and include all meals, premium drinks, activities, airport transfers, tips, and taxes. $440 double; $570 junior suite; $860 suite. AE, DC, MC, V. Free secured parking. **Amenities:** 5 restaurants; lobby bar; pool bar; kids' club; fully equipped health club with yoga; 3 outdoor pools w/daytime activities; room service; shows at night in high season; spa; 2 lighted grass tennis courts; nonmotorized watersports;. *In room:* A/C, TV, MP3 players, hair dryer, minibar, Wi-Fi.

Quinta María Cortez ★★ (Finds) An eclectic, imaginative B&B on the beach, this is Puerto Vallarta's most original place to stay—and one of Mexico's most memorable inns. Most of the seven large suites, uniquely decorated with antiques, whimsical curios, and original art, have a kitchenette and balcony. Sunny terraces, a small pool, and a central gathering area with fireplace and *palapa*-topped dining area (where an excellent full breakfast is served) occupy different levels of the seven-story house. A rooftop terrace offers another sunbathing alternative—and is among the best sunset-watching spots in town. The quinta sits on a beautiful cove on Conchas Chinas beach. A terrace fronting the beach accommodates chairs for taking in the sunset. Air-conditioned areas are limited, due to the open nature of the suites and common areas. Those who love it return year after year, charmed by this remarkable place and by the consistently gracious service.

Sagitario 132, Playa Conchas Chinas, 48300 Puerto Vallarta, Jal. ℂ **888/640-8100** or 801/536-5850 in the U.S., or 322/221-5317. Fax 322/221-53-27. www.quinta-maria.com. 7 units. High season $140–$260 double; low season $120–$195 double. Rates include breakfast. AE, MC, V. Very limited street parking. Children younger than 18 not accepted. **Amenities:** Concierge; small outdoor pool. *In room:* Fridge, hair dryer.

YELAPA

Verana ★★★ (Moments) The magical Verana is among my favorite places to stay in Mexico. It has an unparalleled ability to inspire immediate relaxation and a deep connection with the natural beauty of the spectacular coast. Although Yelapa is 30 minutes by water taxi from town, even those unfamiliar with the village should consider it. Verana has eight rustic yet sophisticated suites and bungalows, set into a hillside with sweeping views of the mountains and ocean. Each is a work of art, hand-crafted with care and creativity by owners Heinz Leger, a former film production designer, and prop stylist Veronique Lieve. Each suite has a king bed and private deck—but you won't find TVs, telephones, or other distractions. My favorite suite is the Studio; it's the most contemporary, with a wall of floor-to-ceiling windows that perfectly frame the spectacular view. The European-trained chef prepares scrumptious creations—global cuisine with a touch of Mexico. Verana also has a magically crafted spa and a yoga hut where daily classes take place.

Calle Zaragoza 404, 48304 Yelapa, Jal. ℂ **866/687-9358** or 310/455-2425 in the U.S., or 322/222-0878. www.verana.com. 8 villas. Winter/high season $360–$480 villa per night with 5-night minimum; $750 3-bedroom Casa Grande per night; extra person $70 per night. Mandatory daily breakfast and dinner charge $80 per person; lunch and beverages extra. Shorter stays based on availability. Closed during summer months. AE, MC, V. Management helps arrange transportation from Puerto Vallarta to Boca, where a private boat runs to Yelapa; from there, Verana is a gentle hike or mule ride. **Amenities:** Restaurant/bar; 2 prepared daily meals; library; outdoor pool; spa w/massage services; morning yoga classes. *In room:* No phone.

3 WHERE TO DINE

Puerto Vallarta has the most exceptional dining scene of any resort town in Mexico. Over 250 restaurants serve cuisines from around the world, in addition to fresh seafood and regional dishes. Chefs from

France, Switzerland, Germany, Italy, and Argentina have come for visits and stayed to open restaurants. In celebration of this diversity, Vallarta's culinary community hosts a 2-week-long gourmet dining festival each November.

Dining is not limited to high-end options—there are plenty of small, family-owned restaurants, local Mexican kitchens, and vegetarian cafes. Vallarta also has branches of the Hard Rock Cafe, Outback Steakhouse, and even Hooters. I won't bother to review these restaurants, where the quality and decor are so familiar.

Of the inexpensive local spots, one favorite is **El Planeta Vegetariano,** Iturbide 270, just down from the main church (© **322/222-3073**), serving an inexpensive, bountiful, and delicious vegetarian buffet, which changes for breakfast and lunch/dinner. It's open daily. Breakfast ($5) is served from 8am till noon; the lunch and dinner buffets ($7.50) are served from noon to 10pm; no credit cards are accepted.

TIPS ON DINING
Mealtimes

MORNING   The morning meal, known as *el desayuno,* can be something light, such as coffee and sweetbread, or something more substantial: eggs, beans, tortillas, bread, fruit, and juice. It can be eaten early or late and is always a sure bet in Mexico. The variety and sweetness of the fruits is remarkable, and you can't go wrong with Mexican egg dishes.

MIDAFTERNOON   The main meal of the day, known as *la comida* (or *el almuerzo*), is eaten between 2 and 4pm. Stores and businesses often close, and many people go home to eat and perhaps take a short afternoon siesta before going about their business. The first course is the *sopa,* which can be either *caldo* (soup) or *sopa de arroz* (rice) or both; then comes the main course, which ideally is a meat or fish dish prepared in some kind of sauce and served with beans, followed by dessert.

EVENING   Between 8 and 10pm, most Mexicans have a light meal called *la cena.* If eaten at home, it is something like a sandwich, bread and jam, or perhaps tacos made from some of the day's leftovers. At restaurants, the most common thing to eat is *antojitos* (literally, "little cravings"), a general label for light fare. Antojitos include tostadas, tamales, tacos, and simple enchiladas, and are big hits with travelers. Large restaurants offer complete meals as well.

Dining Out

Avoid eating at those inviting sidewalk restaurants that you see beneath the stone archways that border the main plazas. These places usually cater to tourists and don't need to count on getting any return business. But they are great for getting a coffee or beer.

For the main meal of the day many restaurants offer a multicourse blue-plate special called *comida corrida* or *menú del día.* This is the least expensive way to get a full dinner.

In Mexico, you need to ask for your check; it is generally considered inhospitable to present a check to someone who hasn't requested it. If you're in a hurry to get somewhere, ask for the check when your food arrives.

Tips are about the same as in the United States. You'll sometimes find a 15% **value-added tax** on restaurant meals, which shows up on the bill as "IVA." This is a boon to arithmetically challenged tippers, saving them from undue exertion.

To summon the waiter, wave or raise your hand, but don't motion with your index finger, which is a demeaning gesture that may even cause the waiter to ignore you. Or if it's the check you want, you can motion to the waiter from across the room using the universal pretend-you're-writing gesture.

Most restaurants do not have **nonsmoking sections;** when they do, I mention it in the reviews. But Mexico's wonderful climate allows for many open-air restaurants, usually set inside a courtyard of a colonial house, or in rooms with tall ceilings and open windows.

MARINA VALLARTA

Most of the best restaurants in the Marina are in hotels, but a number of quality options line the boardwalk bordering the marina yacht harbor as well.

Benitto's CAFE   Wow, what a sandwich! This tiny cafe inside the Plaza Neptuno serves simple, delicious food and has excellent service. It's popular with locals for light breakfasts, casual lunches, and fondue and wine in the evenings. Benitto's is the best place in the area to find pastrami, corned beef, or vegetarian sandwiches, all served on your choice of gourmet bread. Draft beer and wine are available, and the cafe also serves specialty infused waters and a variety of fresh juices.

Inside Plaza Neptuno. ✆ **322/209-0287.** Breakfast $3–$6; main courses $5–$8. No credit cards. Mon–Sat 8:30am–9:30pm.

Porto Bello ★★ ITALIAN   One of the first restaurants in the marina, Porto Bello serves flavorful Italian dishes. For starters, the fried calamari is delicately seasoned, and the grilled vegetable antipasto could easily serve as a full meal. Signature dishes include fusilli prepared with artichokes, black olives, lemon juice, basil, olive oil, and Parmesan cheese; and sautéed fish filet with shrimp and clams in saffron tomato sauce. I love the lightly broiled butterfly shrimp served with spaghetti or, for a splurge, the pecan-crusted rack of French lamb. The elegant indoor dining room is air-conditioned, and there's

also marina front seating. The restaurant occasionally schedules live
music on weekend evenings.

Marina Sol, Loc. 7 (Marina Vallarta *malecón*). ☎ **322/221-0003.** Reservations recommended for dinner. Main courses $15–$44. AE, MC, V. Daily noon–11pm.

DOWNTOWN
Expensive
Café des Artistes/Thierry Blouet Cocina del Autor ★★★

FRENCH/INTERNATIONAL The award-winning chef and owner, Thierry Blouet, is both a member of the French Academie Culinaire and a Maitre Cuisinier de France. The dining experience of the Café has evolved over the years into a trio of special places, including the upscale Bar Constantini lounge and the Thierry Blouet Cocina del Autor dining area. Together, they're located in a restored house that resembles a castle. The interior of the original Café des Artistes showcases murals, lush fabrics, and an array of original works of art, and those who prefer to dine outside can opt instead for the picturesque garden terrace. The Café's menu is a changing delight of French gourmet bistro fare, drawing on Chef Blouet's French training and incorporating regional specialty ingredients. Noteworthy entrees include sea bass filet served with a lentil, bacon, and coriander stew; and the renowned roasted duck glazed with honey, soy, ginger, and lime sauce, and served with a pumpkin risotto. At the Cocina de Autor, the atmosphere is sleek and stylish, and the fixed-priced tasting menu (prices depend on the number of plates you select, from three to five) offers a choice of the chef's most sumptuous creations. Choose any combination of starters, entrees, and desserts. Portions are generally small. After dining, you're invited to the cognac and cigar room, an exquisite blend of old adobe walls, flickering candles, and elegant leather chairs. Or, order your nightcap in the adjacent Bar Constantini, which offers live piano music in a regal setting.

Chef Thierry also oversees the kitchen at **Thierry's Prime Steak-house** in the Plaza Peninsula mall (Blvd. Francisco Medina Ascencio 2485, Loc. Ancla Sub. A; ☎ **322/331-1212;** www.thierrysprime. com). It features aged prime steaks, plus a limited selection of fish and chicken dishes. The steakhouse is open for lunch and dinner daily.

Guadalupe Sánchez 740, corner with Vicario. ☎ **322/222-3228,** -3229, or -3230. www.cafedesartistes.com. Reservations recommended. Main courses $19–$33. Cocina de Autor tasting menu $59–$75 without wine, $96–$137 with wine. AE, DC, MC, V. Daily 6–11:30pm (lounge until 2am).

Moderate
Daiquiri Dick's ★★★ PACIFIC RIM/MEDITERRANEAN A Vallarta dining institution, Daiquiri Dick's has been around for 3

decades, evolving its winning combination of decor, service, and scrumptious cuisine. The name belies the casual beachfront elegance of this popular restaurant, and the genuinely warm staff and open-air location fronting Los Muertos Beach add to the experience. As lovely as the restaurant is, though, the food is the main attraction, incorporating Mediterranean and pan-Asian influences. Start with lemon grass–scented gazpacho or an order of lobster tacos. For main courses, my favorites are giant grilled prawns in a chimichurri marinade, rib-eye steak served medium, and whole grilled snapper. For something lighter, the salmon salade niçoise hits the mark. Chocolate banana-bread pudding makes a perfect finish. It may come as no surprise that the flavored daiquiris are dangerous and delicious. Daiquiri Dick's is a great place for groups as well as for a romantic night out. It's one of the few places that is equally enjoyable for breakfast, lunch, and dinner.

Olas Altas 314. ✆ **322/222-0566.** www.ddpv.com. Main courses $17–$26. AE, MC, V. Daily 9am–10:30pm. Closed Sept.

de Santos ★★ MEDITERRANEAN   De Santos is the place to see and be seen, a trendy restaurant co-owned by one of the members of the wildly popular Latin group Maná. The menu is Mediterranean inspired; best bets include lightly breaded calamari, paella Valenciana, and thin-crust pizza. The cool, refined interior feels more urban than resort oriented, and the sound system is the best in town (a DJ spins to match the mood of the crowd). Guests can also dine on the open-air terrace in the back. Prices seem quite reasonable, given the restaurant's quality and popularity. The adjacent club remains among the hottest nightspots in town (see "Puerto Vallarta After Dark," in chapter 3). De Santos has a sister restaurant in Manhattan as well.

Morelos 771, Centro. ✆ **322/223-3052.** www.desantos.com.mx. Reservations recommended during high season. Main courses $13–$29. AE, MC, V. Daily 5pm–1am; bar closes at 4am on weekends.

Hacienda San Angel ★ MEXICAN   Meals at Hacienda San Angel became so popular with its guests that the owner decided to share the experience with other visitors to Puerto Vallarta. In addition to the exquisite beauty of the Hacienda itself, diners are treated to one of the most stunning views of town, overlooking the city lights and the bay beyond. The menu changes periodically and features classic Mexican fare along with international favorites. Starters include crispy fried calamari with a selection of sauces, grilled seasonal vegetables in a tomato, olive oil, and basil balsamic vinaigrette, and a shrimp and coconut cream soup accented with brandy. The house specialty is the grilled *Cabreria,* a tender bone-in steak, served with garlic mashed potatoes, a portobello mushroom ragout, and a three-chili sauce. Other standouts include chicken *mole* and the herb-crusted rack of lamb in a green-pepper sauce. Start the evening by arriving between 6 and 8pm for a sunset cocktail hour featuring live mariachi music—you may also enjoy strolling the grounds.

Miramar 336, Centro. ☏ **322/222-2692.** www.haciendasanangel.com. Reservations required. Main courses $22–$39, with 20% gratuity added to all checks. MC, V. Daily 6–10pm.

Las Palomas ★ MEXICAN One of Puerto Vallarta's first restaurants, this is the power-breakfast place of choice—and a popular hangout for everyone else throughout the day. Authentic in atmosphere and menu, it's one of Puerto Vallarta's few genuine Mexican restaurants. Breakfast is the best value. The staff pours mugs of steaming coffee spiced with cinnamon as soon as you're seated. Try classic *huevos rancheros* or *chilaquiles* (tortilla strips, fried and topped with red or green spicy sauce, cream, cheese, and fried eggs or shredded chicken). Lunch and dinner offer traditional Mexican specialties, plus a selection of stuffed crepes. The best places for checking out the *malecón* and watching the sunset while sipping an icy margarita are the spacious bar and the upstairs terrace.

Paseo Díaz Ordaz 610. ☏ **322/222-3675.** www.laspalomaspvr.com. Breakfast $3.50–$10; lunch $8.50–$20; main courses $8.50–$22. AE, MC, V. Daily 8am–11pm.

Trio ★★★ (Finds) INTERNATIONAL Trio is the darling of Vallarta restaurants, with diners beating a path to the modest but stylish cafe where chef-owners Bernhard Güth and Ulf Henricksson's undeniable passion for food imbues each dish. Trio is noted for its perfected melding of Mexican and Mediterranean flavors and exquisite presentation. Consider starting with the cilantro-ginger-marinated calamari with avocado and a jalapeño salsa. For a main course, I recommend the herb risotto with toasted sunflower seeds and quail; or the pan-roasted sea bass with glazed grapes, mashed potatoes, and sauerkraut in a white-pepper sauce. These dishes may not be on the menu when you arrive, though—it's a constantly changing work of art. The atmosphere is always comfortable and welcoming. In high season, the rooftop bar area allows for a more comfortable wait for a table or for after-dinner coffee. Most locals will tell you this is their favorite restaurant in town. The same owners run Vitea, below.

Guerrero 264. ☏ **322/222-2196.** www.triopv.com. Reservations recommended. Main courses $18–$28. AE, MC, V. Daily 6–11:30pm.

Xitomates ★ MEXICAN In the heart of downtown, this creative Mexican restaurant changed locations in 2007, adding raves for the creative, intimate atmosphere. The warm dining room is accented with tin star lamps and flickering candles. The menu mixes Mexican

Tapas, Anyone?

Certainly much of modern Mexico's culture draws on the important influence of Spain, so it only makes sense that Spanish culinary traditions would be evident as well. Within the last several years, dining on tapas has soared in popularity here. Of the many options, these are my favorite places: the long-standing **Barcelona Tapas,** Matamoros and 31 de Octubre streets (© **322/222-0510**), a large and lovely restaurant on a terrace built high on a hillside, with sweeping views of the bay. They serve tapas and a selection of Spanish entrees, including paella, from 5pm to midnight. **La Esquina de los Caprichos,** Miramar 402, corner of Iturbide (© **322/222-0911**), is a tiny place, known as having the most reasonably priced ($3.50–$8) tapas in town, and perhaps the tastiest. Hours are Monday to Saturday from 11am to 10pm. It closes from July to the end of August.

with Caribbean, Asian, and Mediterranean influences, and the presentation is as creative as the preparation. Starters include the signature coconut shrimp in a tangy tamarind sauce, thinly sliced scallops with cucumber and jicama julienne, or mushrooms stuffed with shrimp or *huitlacoche* (a mushroom that grows on corn stalks). There's a new menu of creative seviche—seafood prepared in lime juice and served cold—as well as a number of vegetarian selections. Main courses range from grilled salmon filet in a poblano chile sauce, to a tender rib-eye steak with mushrooms, delicately flavored with the Mexican herb epazote. The house specialty dessert is a Toluca ice-cream cake. An excellent wine list and full bar complement the exquisite dining.

Morelos 601, corner with Aldama. © **322/222-9434.** www.losxitomates.com. Main courses $8–$30. AE, MC, V. Daily 6pm–midnight.

Inexpensive

Agave Grill ★ MEXICAN   Agave Grill has gradually taken over the space at the Casa de Tequila in central downtown. The location is lovely, in a beautiful garden setting within a classic hacienda-style building. They'll start you out with fresh salsa made at your table (spiced to your preference); I'd suggest you follow this with an order of the *pulpa* (octopus) sautéed to tenderness in a delectable chile and garlic sauce. My favorite main courses include seafood enchiladas, and beef tenderloin prepared with *mole*. For a sweet finish, you'll love the

chocolate "tamale" served with homemade vanilla ice cream. All tortillas and savory salsas are handmade. An elegant bar at the entry
serves Vallarta's most original selection of fine tequilas, many from
small distilleries. A three-course chef's tasting menu is also available.

Morelos 589. ℂ **322/222-2000.** Main courses $15–$30, chef's tasting menu $27.
MC, V. Mon–Sat noon–11pm, Sun 4–11pm.

El Arrayán ★★★ (Finds) MEXICAN   The spirited Arrayán is the
pot of gold at the end of the rainbow for anyone in search of authentic Mexican cuisine. The casual open-air dining area surrounds a cozy
courtyard, while its exposed brick walls and funky-chic decor showcase a modern view of Mexican classics—tin tubs serve as sinks in the
bathrooms, while colorful plastic tablecloths and Huicholean art
enliven the dining room. Start with an order of delicious seviche,
sumptuous plantain empanadas filled with black beans, or a traditional salad of diced *nopal* cactus paddles with fresh cheese. Favorite
main courses include chiles rellenos packed with shrimp, and Mexican duck *carnitas* served in an *arrayán*-orange sauce. (*Arrayán*, the
namesake of the place, is a small bittersweet fruit native to the region.)
The homemade ice creams and sorbets make for a tasty and refreshing
finish to your meal. The full bar offers an extensive selection of tequilas, regional liquors, Mexican wines, and nonalcoholic *aguas frescas*, a
blended drink of fresh fruit and water. Sample their signature *raicilla*
martini—made with the potent local spirit *raicilla* and infused with
herbs for a unique flavor. Excellent service rounds out this requisite
dining experience.

Allende 344, just past Matamoros, on the corner with Miramar. ℂ **322/222-7195.**
www.elarrayan.com.mx. Reservations recommended. Main courses $15–$24. AE,
MC, V. Wed–Mon 6–11pm. Closed Tues.

Vitea ★★★ (Finds) INTERNATIONAL   This beachfront bistro
opened in late 2004 by the chef/owners of Trio, and their recipe for
success took hold from day one—the bustling restaurant has become
a favorite among locals. Due to strategically placed mirrors on the
back wall, every seat has a view of the ocean, while the interior is
cheerful and inviting. Seating is at small bistro-style tables with intricately designed wrought-iron chairs, along a banquette that runs the
length of the back wall or at umbrella-topped tables on the wide
promenade fronting the restaurant. Starters include succulent shrimp
tempura with pumpkin seeds, spicy garlic, and chili; and a fresh
Greek salad that just explodes with flavor. Main courses change regularly and may include barbecue red snapper with wilted spinach,
chickpea ravioli with portobello mushrooms, or traditional steak
frites. Dinner selections offer a choice of smaller or larger portions.
Lunch offers lighter fare, and breakfast is now served as well.

Malecón no. 2, at Libertad. © **322/222-8703.** www.viteapv.com. Reservations recommended during peak dining hours. Main courses $8.50–$32. MC, V. Daily 8am–11pm.

SOUTH OF THE RIO CUALE TO OLAS ALTAS

South of the river is the densest restaurant area, where you'll find Basilio Badillo, the street nicknamed "Restaurant Row." A second main dining drag has emerged along Calle Olas Altas, with a variety of cuisines and price categories. Cafes and espresso bars, generally open from 7am to midnight, line its wide sidewalks.

Expensive

Archie's Wok ★★★ (Finds) ASIAN/SEAFOOD Since 1986, Archie's has been legendary in Puerto Vallarta for serving original cuisine influenced by the intriguing flavors of Thailand, China, and the Philippines. Archie was Hollywood director John Huston's private chef during the years he spent in the area. Today his wife Cindy upholds his legacy at this tranquil Asian-inspired retreat, where fountains trickle and table candles flicker by night. The Thai Mai Tai and other tropical drinks, made from only fresh fruit and juices, are a good way to kick off a meal, as are the consistently crispy and delicious Filipino spring rolls. The popular Singapore fish filet features lightly battered filet strips in sweet-and-sour sauce; Thai garlic shrimp are prepared with fresh garlic, ginger, cilantro, and black pepper. Vegetarians have plenty of options, including broccoli, tofu, mushroom, and cashew stir-fry in black-bean-and-sherry sauce. Thursday through Saturday from 7:30 to 10:30pm, there's live classical harp and flute in Archie's Oriental garden.

Francisca Rodríguez 130 (a half-block from the Los Muertos pier). © **322/222-0411.** Main courses $7–$21. MC, V. Mon–Sat 2–11pm. Closed Sept.

Café Kaiser Maximilian ★★ INTERNATIONAL Designed to resemble a 19th-century Viennese cafe, Kaiser Maximilian presents a casually elegant atmosphere with a genuine European feel. It's the prime place to go if you want to combine exceptional food with great people-watching. Austrian-born owner Andreas Rupprechter is almost always on hand to ensure that the service is impeccable and the food delicious. Indoor, air-conditioned dining takes place at cozy tables; sidewalk tables are larger and great for groups of friends. The cuisine merges old-world European preparations with regional fresh ingredients. My favorite is filet of trout with spinach and a celery purée; equally notable is the mustard chicken with mashed potatoes, and the rack of lamb with polenta, mustard crust, and green beans. Desserts are especially tempting, as are the gourmet coffees—Maximilian has an Austrian cafe and pastry shop next door.

Olas Altas 380-B (at Basilio Badillo, in front of the Hotel Playa Los Arcos), Zona Romántica. ✆ 322/223-0760. www.kaisermaximilian.com. Reservations recommended in high season. Main courses $18–$30. AE, MC, V. Mon–Sat 6–11pm.

Espresso ★★ ITALIAN   This popular eatery is Vallarta's best late-night dining option. The two-level restaurant is on one of the town's busiest streets—across from El Torito's sports bar, and cater-cornered from the lively Señor Frog's—meaning that traffic noise is a factor, though not a deterrent. The cuisine is superb, the service attentive, and the prices more than reasonable. Owned by a partnership of lively Italians, it serves food that is authentic in preparation and flavor, from thin-crust, brick-oven pizza to savory homemade pastas and oven-baked breads. My favorite pizza is the Quattro Stagioni, topped with artichokes, black olives, ham, and mushrooms. Excellent calzones and panini (sandwiches) are also options. I prefer the rooftop garden area for dining, but many patrons gravitate to the pool table in the air-conditioned downstairs, which features major sports and entertainment events on satellite TV. Espresso also has full bar service and draft beer.

Ignacio L. Vallarta 279. ✆ 322/222-3272. Entrees $7–$19. AE, MC, V. Daily noon–1am.

Fajita Republic ★ MEXICAN/SEAFOOD/STEAKS   Fajita Republic has hit on a winning recipe: delicious food, ample portions, welcoming atmosphere, and low prices. The specialty is, of course, fajitas, grilled to perfection in every variety: steak, chicken, vegetarian, shrimp, combo, and occasionally lobster. All come with a generous tray of salsas and toppings. This "tropical grill" also serves sumptuous barbecued ribs, Mexican *molcajetes* with incredibly tender strips of marinated beef filet, and grilled shrimp. Starters include fresh guacamole served in a giant spoon and the ever-popular Maya cheese sticks (breaded and deep-fried). Try an oversize mug or pitcher of Fajita Rita Mango Margaritas. A second location in Nuevo Vallarta, across from the Grand Velas Resort, draws equal raves with the same menu and prices.

Basilio Badillo 188, 1 block north of Olas Altas. ✆ 322/222-3131. Main courses $9–$18. MC, V. Daily 5pm–midnight.

La Palapa ★★★ SEAFOOD/MEXICAN   This open-air, *palapa*-roofed restaurant on the beach is a decades-old local favorite, and with each visit I have found the quality of the food and the service keeps improving. For lunch and dinner, seafood is the specialty; featured dishes include miso Chilean sea bass, pepper-crusted yellowfin tuna, and grilled shrimp in tequila. The Palapa's location, in the heart of Los Muertos Beach, makes it an excellent place to start or end the day, and equally enticing for breakfast or, even better, a late-night sweet temptation and specialty coffee while watching the moon over the bay. The bar area features acoustic guitars and vocals nightly from 8 to 11pm, performed on Monday and Tuesday nights by the owner, Alberto. Other nights, an incredibly talented flutist who looks a bit like Moses joins the duo.

Pulpito 103. ✆ **322/222-5225.** www.lapalapapv.com. Reservations recommended for dinner in high season. Breakfast $6–$12; main courses $20–$39. AE, MC, V. Daily 8am–11:30pm.

Moderate

Le Bistro ★★ MEXICAN/INTERNATIONAL I love this place—with a large garden deck set right over the river between the two sections of downtown. Breakfast here is one of Vallarta's most enchanted experiences, with piano music in the morning and an assortment of traditional Mexican and American dishes, including vegetarian options. One of the best is the vegetarian omelet with squash, sautéed mushrooms, goat cheese, and pesto. Le Bistro's specialty is crepes, which come in a variety of flavors for breakfast, lunch, or dinner. The lunch-and-dinner menu also offers fine cuisine, including duck in a blackberry sauce and rock Cornish hen stuffed with herbed rice, dried tropical fruits, and nuts, finished in mango-cilantro sauce. The vegetarian offerings are more creative than most. An extensive wine list and ample selection of specialty coffees complement the menu, and live jazz music plays Thursday through Saturday nights.

Isla Río Cuale 16-A (just east of northbound bridge). ✆ **322/222-0283.** www. lebistro.com.mx. Reservations recommended for dinner in high season. Breakfast $6–$15; main courses $19–$32. AE, MC, V. Mon–Sat 9am–midnight.

Inexpensive

Café de Olla ★★ (Value) MEXICAN One of my favorite Vallarta restaurants, the Café de Olla serves up the most consistently delicious Mexican food in town. The atmosphere is simple and festive, and the typically packed dining room is served by a staff that's quick and efficient. Mexican standards like enchiladas, quesadillas, chiles rellenos, fajitas, and tacos are prepared in large portions. I recommend an order of fresh, thick guacamole as a starter or to accompany your meal. The margaritas are terrific. Don't come here for romance or refinement, but do come here for great authentic fare, friendly service, and a fun experience. Only cash is accepted.

Francisco I. Madero 218 ✆ **322/223-1626.** Main courses $6–$22. No credit cards. Wed–Mon 9am–11pm. Closed Tues.

Café San Angel (Moments) CAFE   This comfortable, classic sidewalk cafe is a local gathering place from sunrise to sunset. For breakfast, choose a burrito stuffed with eggs and chorizo sausage, a three-egg Western omelet, crepes filled with mushrooms, such Mexican classics as huevos rancheros and *chilaquiles,* or a tropical fruit plate. Deli sandwiches, crepes, pastries, and simple Mexican plates like quesadillas, enchiladas, and tostadas round out the small but ample menu. The cafe also serves exceptional fruit smoothies and perfectly made espresso and other coffee drinks. Although the service is occasionally slow, keep in mind that this place affords the best people-watching in the area. Bar service and Internet access are available.

Olas Altas 449 (at Francisco Rodríguez). ℂ **322/223-1273.** Breakfast $4–$8; main courses $4–$9. No credit cards. Daily 8am–2am.

Red Cabbage Café (El Repollo Rojo) ★★★ (Finds) MEXICAN   The tiny, hard-to-find cafe is worth the effort—a visit here will reward you with exceptional traditional Mexican cuisine and a whimsical crash course in contemporary culture. The small room is covered wall-to-wall with photographs, paintings, movie posters, and news clippings about the cultural icons of Mexico. Frida Kahlo figures prominently in the decor, and a special menu duplicates dishes she and husband Diego Rivera prepared for guests. Specialties from all over Mexico include *chiles en nogada* (poblanos stuffed with ground beef, pine nuts, and raisins, topped with a sweet walnut cream sauce sprinkled with pomegranates and served cold); intricate chicken *mole* from Puebla; and a hearty Mexican plate with steak, a chile relleno, quesadilla, guacamole, rice, and beans. In addition, the vegetarian menu is probably the most diverse and tasty in town. This is not a place for an intimate conversation, however—the poor acoustics cause everyone's conversations to blend together.

Calle Rivera del Río 204A (across from Río Cuale). ℂ **322/223-0411.** www.red cabbagepv.com. Main courses $9–$20. Tasting menu $35. No credit cards. Daily 5–10:30pm.

JUNGLE RESTAURANTS

One of the unique attractions of Puerto Vallarta is its "jungle restaurants," south of town toward Mismaloya. They offer open-air dining in a tropical setting by the sea or beside a mountain river. The many varieties of "jungle" and "tropical" tours include a stop for swimming and lunch. If you travel on your own, a taxi is the best transportation—the restaurants are quite a distance from the main highway. Taxis are usually waiting for return patrons.

The most recommendable of the jungle restaurants is the ecologically sensitive **El Nogalito** ★ (ℂ/fax **322/221-5225**). Located beside a clear jungle stream, the exceptionally clean, beautifully landscaped ranch serves lunch, beverages, and snacks on a shady, relaxing terrace. Several hiking routes depart from the grounds, and the restaurant provides a guide (whom you tip) to point out the native plants, birds, and wildlife. It's much closer to town than the other jungle restaurants: To find it, travel to Punta Negra, about 8km (5 miles) south of downtown Puerto Vallarta. A well-marked sign points up Calzada del Cedro, a dirt road, to the ranch. It's open daily from noon to 5:30pm. No credit cards are accepted.

Just past Boca de Tomatlán, at Hwy. 200 Km 20, is **Chico's Paradise** (© **322/223-6005**). It offers spectacular views of massive rocks—some marked with petroglyphs—and the surrounding jungle and mountains. There are natural pools and waterfalls for swimming, plus a small market selling pricey trinkets. The menu features excellent seafood as well as Mexican dishes. The quality is quite good, and the portions are generous, although prices are higher than in town—remember, you're paying for the setting. It's open daily from 10am to 6pm. No credit cards are accepted.

Exploring Puerto Vallarta & Beyond

by Shane Christensen

Beyond the cobblestone streets, graceful cathedral, and welcoming atmosphere, Puerto Vallarta offers a wealth of natural beauty and man-made pleasures.

Ecotourism activities flourish—from canopy tours to whale-watching, ocean kayaking, and diving with giant mantas in Banderas Bay. Forty-two kilometers (26 miles) of beaches, many in pristine coves accessible only by boat, extend around the bay. High in the Sierra Madre, the mystical Huichol Indians still live in relative isolation in an effort to protect their centuries-old culture from outside influences.

Villages such as **Rincón de Guayabitos, Barra de Navidad,** and **Melaque** are laid-back and almost undiscovered. Starkly different from the spirited resort towns, they offer travelers a glimpse into local culture. Excursions to these smaller villages make easy day trips or extended stays.

1 BEACHES, ACTIVITIES & EXCURSIONS

Travel agencies can provide information on what to see and do in Puerto Vallarta and can arrange tours, fishing trips, and other activities. Most hotels have a tour desk on-site. Of the many travel agencies in town, I highly recommend **Tukari Servicios Turísticos,** Av. España 316 (© **322/224-7177;** fax 322/224-2350; www.tukari.com), which specializes in ecological and cultural tours. Another source is **Xplora Adventours** (© **322/223-0661**), in the Huichol Collection shop on the *malecón.* It has listings of all locally available tours, with photos, explanations, and costs; however, be aware that a timeshare resort owns the company, so part of the information you receive will be an invitation to a presentation, which you may decline. One of the tour companies with the largest—and best-quality—selection of boat cruises and land tours is **Vallarta Adventures ★★★** (© **888/303-2653** in the

U.S., or 322/297-1212; www.vallarta-adventures.com). I can highly recommend any of their offerings. Book with them directly and get a 10% discount when you mention Frommer's.

THE BEACHES

For years, beaches were Puerto Vallarta's main attraction. Although visitors today are exploring more of the surrounding geography, the sands are still a powerful draw. Over 42km (26 miles) of beaches extend around the broad Bay of Banderas, ranging from action-packed party spots to secluded coves accessible only by boat.

IN TOWN The easiest to reach is **Playa Los Muertos** (also known as Playa Olas Altas or Playa del Sol), just off Calle Olas Altas, south of the Río Cuale. The water can be rough, but the wide beach is home to a diverse array of *palapa* restaurants that offer food, beverage, and beach-chair service. The most popular are the adjacent El Dorado and La Palapa, at the end of Pulpito Street. On the southern end of this beach is a section known as "Blue Chairs"—the most popular gay beach. Vendors stroll Los Muertos, and beach volleyball, parasailing, and jet-skiing are all popular pastimes. The **Hotel Zone** is also known for its broad, smooth beaches, accessed through the resorts.

SOUTH OF TOWN **Playa Mismaloya** is in a beautiful sheltered cove about 10km (6¼ miles) south of town along Hwy. 200. The water is clear and beautiful, ideal for snorkeling off the beach. Entrance to the public beach is just to the left of the **Barceló La Jolla de Mismaloya** (© 322/226-0600). This is where the *Night of the Iguana,* the movie that made Puerto Vallarta famous with the international jet set, was filmed.

The beach at **Boca de Tomatlán,** just down the road, houses numerous *palapa* restaurants where you can relax for the day—you buy drinks, snacks, or lunch, and you can use their chairs and *palapa* shade.

The two beaches are accessible by public buses, which depart from the corner of Basilio Badillo and Insurgentes every 15 minutes from 5:30am to 10pm and cost just 50¢.

Las Animas, Quimixto, and **Yelapa** beaches are the most secluded, accessible only by boat (see "Getting Around," in chapter 1, for information about water-taxi service). They are larger than Mismaloya, offer intriguing hikes to jungle waterfalls, and are similarly set up, with restaurants fronting a wide beach. Overnight stays are available at Yelapa (see "Side Trips from Puerto Vallarta," later in this chapter).

NORTH OF TOWN The beaches at **Marina Vallarta** are the least desirable in the area, with darker sand and seasonal inflows of stones.

EXPLORING PUERTO VALLARTA & BEYOND

3

BEACHES, ACTIVITIES & EXCURSIONS

ATTRACTIONS ●
Gringo Gulch
  (neighborhood) **16**
Isla del Río Cuale **20**
Main Square **11**
Municipal Flea Market **17**
Museo del Cuale **21**
Parish of Nuestra Señora
  de Guadalupe **12**

ACCOMMODATIONS ■
Hacienda San Angel **15**
Hotel Playa Los Arcos **27**

*Bahía de
Banderas*

Playa
Los Muertos
Pier
(water taxi)

DINING ◆
Agave Grill **10**
Archie's Wok **29**
Barcelona Tapas **2**
Bar Constantini **4**
Café de Olla **25**
Café des Artistes/
  Thierry Blouet Cocina
  del Autor **4**
Café Kaiser Maximilian **27**

Café San Angel **28**
Carlos O'Brian's **5**
Daiquiri Dick's **26**
de Santos **6**
El Arrayán **3**
El Planeta Vegetariano **13**
Espresso **23**
Fajita Republic **24**
Hacienda San Angel **15**
La Bodeguita del Medio **1**

La Esquina de los Caprichos **14**
La Palapa **30**
Las Palomas **8**
Le Bistro **22**
Red Cabbage Café
  (El Repollo Rojo) **31**
Trio **18**
Vitea **19**
Xitomates **9**
Z'Tai **7**

The entire northern coastline from Bucerías to Punta Mita is a succession of sandy coves alternating with rocky inlets. For years the beaches to the north, with their long, clean breaks, have been the favored locale for surfers. The broad, sandy stretches at **Playa Anclote, Playa Piedras Blancas,** and **Playa Destiladeras,** which all have *palapa* restaurants, have made them favorites with local residents looking for a quick getaway.

You can also hire a *panga* (small motorized boat) at Playa Anclote to take you to the **Marietas Islands ★★★** just offshore. These uninhabited islands are a great place for bird-watching, diving, snorkeling, or just exploring. Blue-footed booby birds (found only here and in the Galapagos) dawdle along the islands' rocky coast, and giant mantas, sea turtles, and colorful tropical fish swim among the coral cliffs. The islands are honeycombed with caves and hidden beaches—including the stunning Playa de Amor (Beach of Love) that appears only at low tide. Humpback whales congregate around these islands during the winter months, and *pangas* can be rented for a do-it-yourself whale-watching excursion. Trips cost about $40 per hour. You can also visit these islands aboard one of the numerous day cruises that depart from the cruise-ship terminal in Puerto Vallarta.

ORGANIZED TOURS

BOAT TOURS Puerto Vallarta offers a number of boat trips, including sunset cruises and snorkeling, swimming, and diving excursions. They generally travel one of two routes: to the **Marietas Islands,** a 30- to 45-minute boat ride off the northern shore of Banderas Bay, or to **Yelapa, Las Animas,** or **Quimixto** along the southern shore. The trips to the southern beaches make a stop at **Los Arcos,** an island rock formation south of Puerto Vallarta, for snorkeling. Prices range from $45 for a sunset cruise or a trip to one of the beaches with open bar, to $85 for an all-day outing with open bar and meals. Travel agencies sell tickets and distribute information on all cruises.

One of the best outings is a day trip to **Las Caletas ★★**, the cove where John Huston made his home for years. **Vallarta Adventures** (© **888/303-2653** in the U.S., or 322/297-1212; www.vallarta-adventures.com) holds the exclusive lease on the private cove and has done an excellent job of restoring Huston's former home, adding exceptional day-spa facilities, and landscaping the beach, which is wonderful for snorkeling. The trip sets out every Monday through Saturday from Nuevo Vallarta at 8:30am or from Vallarta's Maritime Terminal at 9am, and includes a light breakfast, buffet lunch, open bar, snorkeling and kayaking equipment, and guided tours.

Whale-watching tours become more popular each year. Viewing humpback whales is almost a certainty from mid- to late November to March. The majestic whales have migrated to this bay for centuries (in the 17th c. it was called "Humpback Bay") to bear their calves. The noted local authority is **Open Air Expeditions,** Guerrero 339 (*©*/fax **322/222-3310;** www.vallartawhales.com). It offers ecologically oriented, oceanologist-guided 4-hour tours on the soft boat *Prince of Whales,* the only boat in Vallarta specifically designed for whale-watching. Cost is $95 for adults, $82 for children 5 to 10, and travel is in a group of up to 12 (there's a discount for booking online). The tour departs at 9:30am. **Vallarta Adventures** (see above) offers a variety of whale-watching excursions that may combine time for snorkeling, or simply focus on photographing these exquisite mammals. Prices range from $70 to $85, and offer a choice of boats—from small boats (to bring you closest for photos) to graceful sailboats.

LAND TOURS   **Tukari Servicios Turísticos** (see "Beaches, Activities & Excursions," above) can arrange trips to the fertile birding grounds near **San Blas,** 3 to 4 hours north of Puerto Vallarta in the state of Nayarit, and shopping trips to **Tlaquepaque** and **Tonalá** (6 hr. inland, near Guadalajara). A day trip to **Rancho Altamira,** a 20-hectare (49-acre) working ranch, includes a barbecue lunch and horseback riding, and then a stroll through **El Tuito,** a small nearby Colonial-era village. The company can also arrange an unforgettable morning at **Terra Noble Art & Healing Center ★★** (*©* **322/223-3530** or 322/222-5400; www.terranoble.com), a mountaintop day spa and center for the arts where participants can get a massage, *temazcal* (ancient indigenous sweat lodge—available only for groups), or treatment; work in clay and paint; and have lunch in a heavenly setting overlooking the bay. Call ahead for reservations.

Hotel travel desks and travel agencies, including Tukari and American Express, can also book the popular **Tropical Tour** or **Jungle Tour** ($45), a basic orientation to the area. These excursions are expanded city tours that include a drive through the workers' village of Pitillal, the affluent neighborhood of Conchas Chinas, the cathedral, the market, the Taylor–Burton houses, and lunch at a jungle restaurant. The **Sierra Madre Expedition** is another excellent tour offered by **Vallarta Adventures** (see "Boat Tours," above). The daily excursion travels in Mercedes all-terrain vehicles north of Puerto Vallarta through jungle trails, stops at a small town, ventures into a forest for a brief nature walk, and winds up on a pristine secluded beach for lunch and swimming. The $88 outing is worthwhile because it takes tourists on exclusive trails into scenery that would otherwise be off-limits.

STAYING ACTIVE
DIVING & SNORKELING   Underwater enthusiasts, from beginner to expert, can arrange scuba diving or snorkeling through **Vallarta**

Adventures (© 888/303-2653 in the U.S., or 322/297-1212, ext. 3; www.vallarta-adventures.com), a five-star PADI dive center. You may snorkel or dive at Los Arcos, a company-owned site at Caletas Cove (where you'll dive in the company of sea lions), Quimixto Coves, the Marietas Islands, or the offshore La Corbeteña, Morro, and Chimo reefs. The company runs a full range of certification courses (up to Instructor). **Chico's Dive Shop,** Díaz Ordaz 772–5, near Carlos O'Brian's (© **322/222-1895;** www.chicos-diveshop.com), offers similar diving and snorkeling trips and is also a PADI five-star dive center. Chico's is open daily from 8am to 10pm, with branches at the Marriott, Fiesta Americana, and Playa Los Arcos. You can also snorkel off the beaches at Mismaloya and Boca de Tomatlán; elsewhere, there's not much to see besides a sandy bottom.

ECOTOURS & ACTIVITIES   Open Air Expeditions (www.vallarta whales.com) offers nature-oriented trips, including birding and ocean kayaking in Punta Mita. **Ecotours de México,** Ignacio L. Vallarta 243 (©/fax **322/222-6606;** www.ecotoursvallarta.com), runs eco-oriented tours, including seasonal (Aug–Dec) trips to a turtle preservation camp where you can witness hatching baby Olive Ridley turtles.

A popular Vallarta adventure activity is **canopy tours.** You glide from treetop to treetop, getting an up-close-and-personal look at a tropical rainforest canopy and the trails far below. Tours depart from the **Vallarta Adventures** (see "Diving & Snorkeling," above) offices in both Marina Vallarta and Nuevo Vallarta at 8am, returning at 2pm. The price ($79 for adults, $53 for children 8–11) includes the tour, bottled water, and light snacks. A second option is available in the southern jungles of Vallarta, over the Orquidias River, through **Canopy Tours de Los Veranos** (© **322/223-6060;** www.canopytours-vallarta.com). This tour will pick you up at the Canopy office, near the south-side Pemex station, to transport you to their facilities upriver from Mismaloya. Departures are on the hour, from 9am to 2pm. In addition to the 14 cables—the longest being a full 350m (1,148 ft.)—it offers climbing walls and water slides. Price is $79 for adults, or $58 for children ages 6 and older.

FISHING   Arrange fishing trips through travel agencies or through the **Cooperativa de Pescadores (Fishing Cooperative),** on the *malecón* north of the Río Cuale, next door to the Rosita Hotel (© **322/222-1202**). Fishing charters cost $150 per person, for one to eight people; or select from other options where the price varies with the size of the boat; a boat can be rented for 8 hours for $600. It's open Monday through Sunday from 7am to 10pm, but make arrangements a day ahead. You can also arrange fishing trips at the

Marina Vallarta docks, or by calling **Fishing with Carolina** (© 322/ 224-7250, cell 044-322/292-2953; fishingwithcarolina@hotmail. com), which uses a 9m (30-ft.) Uniflite sportfisher, fully equipped with an English-speaking crew. Fishing trips cost $350 for up to four people for 4 hours and include equipment and bait, but drinks, snacks, and lunch are optional, at $15 per person.

GOLF   Puerto Vallarta is an increasingly popular golf destination; six courses have opened in the past 7 years, bringing the total in the region to nine. The Joe Finger–designed private course at the **Marina Vallarta Golf Club** (© 322/221-0073) is an 18-hole, par-74 course that winds through the Marina Vallarta peninsula and affords ocean views. It's for members only, but most luxury hotels in Puerto Vallarta have membership for their guests. Greens fees are $135 year-round, and $100 after 2pm. Fees include golf cart, range balls, and tax. A caddy costs $12. Club rentals, lessons, and special packages are available.

North of town in the state of Nayarit, about 15km (9¼ miles) beyond Puerto Vallarta, is the 18-hole, par-72 **Los Flamingos Club de Golf** (© 329/296-5006; www.flamingosgolf.com.mx). It features beautiful jungle vegetation and is open from 7am to 7pm daily, with a full pro shop and snack bar (no restaurant). The daylight greens fee is $139, which drops to $89 after 2pm. It includes the use of a golf cart; hiring a caddy costs $20 plus tip, and club rental is $35 to $45.

There are now two breathtaking Jack Nicklaus Signature courses at the **Punta Mita Golf Club ★★★** (© 329/291-6000; www.four seasons.com/puntamita), with the newest addition opened in October 2008. The original "Pacifico" course features 8 oceanfront holes and an ocean view from every hole. Its hallmark is the 3rd hole, the "Tail of the Whale," with a long drive to a green on a natural island— the only natural-island green in the Americas. It requires an amphibious cart to take you over when the tide is high, and there's an alternate hole for when the ocean or tides are not accommodating. The second Jack Nicklaus Signature course, "Bahia," intertwines with the original course, and also affords stunning seaside holes; its finishing hole is adjacent to the new St. Regis Resort. The courses are open only to members or guests staying in the Punta Mita resorts, or to other golf club members with a letter of introduction from their pro. Greens fees are $252 for 18 holes and $173 for 9 holes, including cart, with (Calloway) club rentals for $75. Lessons are also available.

Another Jack Nicklaus course is located at the **Vista Vallarta Golf Club** (© 322/290-0030; www.vistavallartagolf.com), along with one designed by Tom Weiskopf. These courses were the site of the 2002 PGA World Cup Golf Championships. The club is the foothills of the Sierra Madre, behind the bullring in Puerto Vallarta. A round costs

$194 per person, including cart, or $135 after 2pm. Club rentals are available for $55.

The Robert von Hagge–designed **El Tigre** course at Paradise Village (© **866/843-5951** in the U.S., or 322/297-0773; www.eltigre golf.com), in Nuevo Vallarta, is a 7,239-yard course on a relatively flat piece of land, but the design incorporates challenging bunkers, undulating fairways, and water features on several holes. Greens fees are $167 a round, or $110 if you play after 2pm. Club rentals are $52.

HORSEBACK-RIDING TOURS   Travel agents and local ranches can arrange guided horseback rides. **Rancho Palma Real,** Carretera Vallarta, Tepic 4766 (© **322/222-0501**), has an office 5 minutes north of the airport; the ranch is in Las Palmas, 40 minutes northeast of Vallarta. It is by far the nicest horseback-riding tour in the area. The price ($70; American Express or cash only) includes continental breakfast, drinks, and lunch.

Another excellent option is **Rancho El Charro,** Av. Francisco Villa 895 (© **322/224-0114,** cell 044-322/294-1689; www.ranchoel charro.com), which has beautiful, well-cared-for horses and a variety of rides for all levels, departing from their ranch at the base of the Sierra Madre Mountains. Rides range in length from 3 to 8 hours, and in price from $62 to $120. Rancho El Charro also has multiple-day rides—check their website for details. **Rancho Ojo de Agua,** Cerrada de Cardenal 227, Fracc. Las Aralias (©/fax **322/224-0607;** www.mexonline.com), also offers high-quality tours, from its ranch located 10 minutes by taxi north of downtown toward the Sierra Madre foothills. The rides last 3 hours (10am and 3pm departures) and take you up into the mountains overlooking the ocean and town. The cost is $62. Both of the ranches listed above have other tours available, as well as their own comfortable base camp for serious riders who want to stay out overnight.

SWIMMING WITH DOLPHINS   Dolphin Adventure ★★★ (© **888/303-2653** in the U.S., or 322/297-1212; www.vallarta-adventures.com) operates an interactive dolphin-research facility—considered the finest in Latin America—that allows limited numbers of people to swim with dolphins Monday through Saturday at scheduled times. Cost for the swim is $142. Reservations are required, and they generally sell out at least a week in advance. **Dolphin Encounter** ($79) allows you to touch and learn about the dolphins in smaller pools, so you're ensured up-close-and-personal time with them. You can even be a **Trainer for a Day,** a special 7-hour program of working alongside the more experienced trainers and the dolphins, for a cost of $265. The **Dolphin Kids** program, for children ages 4 to 8, is a gentle introduction to dolphins, featuring the Dolphin Adventure

> (Moments   **A Spectacular Sight**
>
> Performances of the **Voladores de Papantla (Papantla Fly-ers)** take place weekend evenings on the *malecón,* adjacent to the "Boy on a Seahorse" statue. In this pre-Columbian religious ritual, four men are suspended from the top of a 50-foot pole, circling and descending it as though in flight, while another beats a drum and plays a flute while balancing himself at the top. It signifies the four cardinal points, and the mystic "center" of the self, a sacred direction for ancient Mexican cultures.

baby dolphins and their mothers interacting with the children par-ticipants ($75).

TENNIS   Many hotels in Puerto Vallarta offer excellent tennis facilities; they often have clay courts. The full-service **Canto del Sol Tennis Club** (© **322/226-0123;** www.cantodelsol.com) is at the Canto del Sol hotel in the Hotel Zone. It offers indoor and outdoor courts (including a clay court), a full pro shop, lessons, clinics, and partner matches.

A STROLL THROUGH TOWN
Puerto Vallarta's cobblestone streets are a pleasure to explore; they're full of tiny shops, rows of windows edged with curling wrought iron, and vistas of red-tile roofs and the sea. Start with a walk up and down the *malecón.*

Among the sights you shouldn't miss is the **municipal building** on the main square (next to the tourism office), which has a large Man-uel Lepe mural inside in its stairwell. Nearby, right up Independencia, sits the picturesque **Parish of Nuestra Señora de Guadalupe church,** Hidalgo 370 (© **322/222-1326**), topped with a curious crown held in place by angels—a replica of the one worn by Empress Carlota during her brief time in Mexico as Emperor Maximilian's wife. On its steps, women sell religious mementos; across the narrow street, stalls sell native herbs for curing common ailments. Services in English are held each Saturday at 5pm, and Sunday at 10am. Regular hours are Monday through Saturday from 7:30am to 8:30pm, Sunday from 6:30am to 8:30pm. Note that entrance is restricted to those properly attired—no shorts or sleeveless shirts allowed. Three blocks south of the church, head east on Libertad, lined with small shops and pretty upper windows, to the **municipal flea market** by the river. (It's the Río Cuale Mercado, but I once overheard a tourist ask for the "real quality" market.) After exploring the market, cross the bridge to the island in the river; sometimes a painter is at work on its banks. Walk down the center of the island toward the sea, and you'll come to the tiny **Museo del Cuale** (no phone; Tues–Sat 10am–2pm and 2–4pm; free admission), which has a small but impressive permanent exhibit of pre-Columbian figurines.

Retrace your steps to the market and Libertad, and follow Calle Miramar to the brightly colored steps up to Zaragoza. Up Zaragoza to the right 1 block is the famous **pink arched bridge** that once connected Richard Burton's and Elizabeth Taylor's houses. In this area, known as **"Gringo Gulch,"** many Americans have houses.

2 SHOPPING

For years, shopping in Puerto Vallarta was concentrated in small, eclectic, independent shops rather than impersonal malls. In the past few years, however, this has changed, with the addition of large, modern shopping centers between the Marina and hotel zone areas. Vallarta is known for having the most diverse and impressive selection of **contemporary Mexican fine art** outside Mexico City. It also has an abundance of tacky T-shirts and the ubiquitous **silver jewelry.**

THE SHOPPING SCENE

The key shopping areas are central downtown, the Marina Vallarta *malecón,* the popular *mercados,* and the beach—where the merchandise comes to you. Some of the more attractive shops are 1 to 2 blocks in **back of the *malecón.*** Start at the intersection of Corona and Morelos streets—interesting shops spread out in all directions from here. **Marina Vallarta** has two shopping plazas, Plaza Marina and Neptuno Plaza, on the main highway from the airport into town, which offer a limited selection of shops, with Plaza Neptuno primarily featuring home decor shops.

An addition to Vallarta's shopping and dining scene is the modern **Plaza Peninsula** (located on Av. Francisco Medina Ascencio 2485, just south of the cruise-ship terminal and north of the Ameca River bridge; no phone number or website), in front of a large waterfront condominium development of the same name. It's home to more than 30 businesses, including Vallarta's first **Starbucks,** as well as art galleries, boutiques, and a varied selection of restaurants. The **Centro Comercial Galerias Vallarta** (on Av. Francisco Medina Ascencio 2920, adjacent to Wal-Mart and directly across from the cruise-ship terminal; ℂ **322/209-1520;** www.galeriasvallarta.com.mx) is a large shopping and entertainment mall anchored by the high-end Mexican department store Liverpool. It houses a variety of boutiques, including Lacoste, Levi, Hugo Boss, and United Colors of Benetton. Among the selections for dining are Chili's, Subway, and Sirloin Stokade. For entertainment, there's a 10-screen movie theater. The mall is open daily from 8am to 2am; most stores are open from 11am to 9pm. There is ample underground parking.

Puerto Vallarta's **municipal flea market** is just north of the Río Cuale, where Libertad and A. Rodríguez meet. The *mercado* sells clothes, jewelry, serapes, shawls, leather accessories and suitcases, papier-mâché parrots, stuffed frogs and armadillos, and, of course, T-shirts. Be sure to comparison-shop, and definitely bargain before buying. The market is open daily from 9am to 7pm. Upstairs, a **food market** serves inexpensive Mexican meals—for more adventurous diners, it's probably the best value and most authentic dining experience in Vallarta. An **outdoor market** is along Río Cuale Island, between the two bridges. Stalls sell crafts, gifts, folk art, and clothing. In most of the better shops and galleries, shipping, packing, and delivery to Puerto Vallarta hotels are available. Some will also ship to your home address. Note that while bargaining is expected in the *mercados* and with beach vendors, stores generally charge fixed—and fair—prices for their wares.

THE LOWDOWN ON HUICHOL INDIAN ART

Puerto Vallarta offers the best selection of Huichol art in Mexico. Descendants of the Aztec, the Huichol are one of the last remaining indigenous cultures in the world that has remained true to its ancient traditions, customs, language, and habitat. The Huichol live in adobe structures in the high Sierras (at an elevation of 1,400m/4,592 ft.) north and east of Puerto Vallarta. Due to the decreasing fertility (and therefore productivity) of the land surrounding their villages, they have come to depend more on the sale of their artwork for sustenance.

Huichol art has always been cloaked in a veil of mysticism—probably one of the reasons serious collectors seek out this form of *artesanía*. Colorful, symbolic yarn "paintings," inspired by visions experienced during spiritual ceremonies, characterize Huichol art. In the ceremonies, artists ingest peyote, a hallucinogenic cactus, which induces brightly colored visions; these are considered messages from their ancestors. The visions' symbolic and mythological imagery influences the art, which encompasses not only yarn paintings but also fascinating masks and bowls decorated with tiny colored beads.

The Huichol might be geographically isolated, but they are learning the importance of good business and have adapted their art to

(Fun Facts) A Huichol Art Primer

Puerto Vallarta offers the best selection of Huichol art in Mexico. Descendants of the Aztec, the Huichol are one of the last remaining indigenous cultures in the world that has remained true to its ancient traditions, customs, language, and habitat. Huichol art falls into two main categories: yarn paintings and beaded pieces. All other items you might find in Huichol art galleries are either ceremonial objects or items used in everyday life.

Yarn paintings are made on a wood base covered with wax and meticulously overlaid with colored yarn. Designs represent the magical vision of the underworld, and each symbol gives meaning to the piece. Paintings made with wool yarn are more authentic than those made with acrylic; however, acrylic yarn paintings are usually brighter and more detailed because the threads are thinner. It is normal to find empty spaces where the wax base shows. Usually the artist starts with a central motif and works around it, but it's common to have several independent motifs that, when combined, take on a different meaning. A painting with many small designs tells a more complicated story than one with only one design and fill-work on the background. Look for the story of the piece on the back of the painting. Most Huichol artists write in pencil in Huichol and Spanish.

Beaded pieces are made on carved wooden shapes depicting different animals, wooden eggs, or small bowls made from gourds. The pieces are covered with wax, and tiny *chaquira* beads are applied one by one to form designs. Usually the beaded designs represent animals; plants; the elements of fire, water, or air; and certain symbols that give a special meaning to the whole. Deer, snakes, wolves, and scorpions are traditional elements; other figures, such as iguanas, frogs, and any animals not indigenous to Huichol territory, are incorporated by popular demand. Beadwork with many small designs that do not exactly fit into one another is more time-consuming and has a more complex symbolic meaning. This kind of work has empty spaces where the wax shows.

meet consumer demand. Original Huichol art, therefore, is not necessarily traditional. Iguanas, jaguars, sea turtles, frogs, eclipses, and eggs appear in response to consumer demand. For more traditional works, look for pieces that depict deer, scorpions, wolves, or snakes.

The Huichol have also had to modify their techniques to create more pieces in less time and meet increased demand. Patterned fill-work, which is faster to produce, sometimes replaces the detailed designs that are used to fill the pieces. The same principle applies to yarn paintings. While some are beautiful depictions of landscapes and even abstract pieces, they are not traditional themes.

You may see Huichol Indians on the streets of Vallarta—they are easy to spot, dressed in white clothing embroidered with colorful designs. A number of fine Huichol galleries are in downtown Puerto Vallarta (see individual listings under "Crafts & Gifts" and "Decorative & Folk Art," below).

One place to learn more about the Huichol is **Huichol Collection,** Morelos 490, across from the sea-horse statue on the *malecón* (© 322/223-2141). Not only does this shop offer an extensive selection of Huichol art in all price ranges, but it also has a replica of a Huichol adobe hut, informational displays explaining more about their fascinating way of life and beliefs, and usually a Huichol artist at work. However, note that this is a timeshare sales location, so don't be surprised if you're hit with a pitch for a "free" breakfast and property tour. **Peyote People,** Juárez 222 (© 322/222-2302 or -6268; www.peyotepeople.com), is a more authentic shop specializing in Huichol yarn paintings and bead art from San Andres Cohamiata, one of the main villages of this indigenous group, up in the high Sierra. The shop is open Monday through Friday from 10am until 9pm, and Saturday and Sunday 10am to 6pm.

CLOTHING

Vallarta's locally owned department store, **LANS,** has branches at Juárez 867 (© **322/226-9100;** www.lans.com.mx) and in Plaza Caracol, next door to the supermarket Gigante, in the Hotel Zone (© **322/226-0204**). Both offer a wide selection of name-brand clothing, accessories, footwear, cosmetics, and home furnishings.

CONTEMPORARY ART

Known for sustaining one of the stronger art communities in Latin America, Puerto Vallarta has an impressive selection of fine galleries featuring quality original works. Several dozen galleries get together to offer art walks every Wednesday from 6 to 10pm between November and April. Most of the participating galleries serve complimentary cocktails during the art walks. It's a very popular weekly event among the local expat residents.

Corsica   Among the best of Vallarta's galleries, Corsica features an exquisite collection of sculptures, installations, and paintings, from world-renown contemporary artists from Mexico. They offer professional packing and worldwide shipping with purchases. There are two locations—at Guadalupe Sanchez 735 and Leona Vicario 230. Open Monday through Saturday 11am to 10pm. ☎ **322/223-1821.** www.galeria corsica.com.

Galería des Artistes   This stunning gallery features contemporary painters and sculptors from throughout Mexico, Europe, and Latin America, including the renowned original "magiscopes" of Feliciano Bejar. Paintings by Vallarta favorite Evelyn Boren, as well as a small selection of works by Mexican masters, including Orozco, can be found here, among the exposed brick walls and stylish interior spaces. It's open Monday to Saturday 11am to 10pm. Just across the street, affiliate **Galería Omar Alonso** (☎ **322/222-5587;** www.galeria omaralonso.com) exhibits photography by internationally renowned artists. Open Monday through Saturday 11am to 10pm. Leona Vicario 248. ☎ **322/223-0006.**

Galería Pacífico   Since opening in 1987, Galería Pacífico has been considered one of the finest in Mexico. On display is a wide selection of sculptures and paintings in various media by midrange masters and up-and-comers alike. The gallery is 1½ blocks inland from the fantasy sculptures on the *malecón*. Among the artists whose careers Galería Pacífico has influenced are rising talent Brewster Brockman, internationally renowned sculptor Ramiz Barquet, and other notables, including Marco Alvarez. Open Monday through Saturday from 10am to 8pm, Sunday by appointment. Between June and October, check for reduced hours or vacation closings. Aldama 174, 2nd floor, above La Casa del Habano cigar store. ☎ **322/222-1982.** galeriapacifico@prodigy.net.mx.

Galería Uno   One of Vallarta's first galleries, the Galería Uno features an excellent selection of contemporary paintings by Latin American artists, plus a variety of posters and prints. During the high season, featured exhibitions change every 2 weeks. In a classic adobe building with open courtyard, it's also a casual, salon-style gathering place for friends of owner Jan Lavender. Open Monday through Saturday from 10am to 10pm. Morelos 561 (at Corona). ☎ **322/222-0908.**

Gallería Dante   This gallery-in-a-villa showcases contemporary art as well as sculptures and classical reproductions of Italian, Greek, and Art Deco bronzes—against a backdrop of gardens and fountains.

Works by more than 50 Mexican and international artists are represented, including the acclaimed local talent Rogelio Diaz, Guillermo Gomez, and Israel Zzepada, as well as Alejandro Colunga and Tellosa. Located on the "Calle de los Cafés," the gallery is open during the winter Monday through Friday from 10am to 5pm, and by appointment. Basilio Badillo 269. ✆ 322/222-2477. www.galleriadante.com.

CRAFTS & GIFTS

Alfarería Tlaquepaque   Opened in 1953, this is Vallarta's original source for Mexican ceramics and decorative crafts, all at excellent prices. Talavera pottery and dishware, colored glassware, birdcages, baskets, and wood furniture are just a few of the many items in this warehouse-style store. Open Monday through Saturday 9am to 9pm and Sunday from 9am to 3pm in high season, with reduced hours in low season. Av. México 1100. ✆ 322/223-2121.

La Casa del Feng Shui   I am enchanted by this shop's selection of Australian and local crystals, candles, talismans, fountains, and wind chimes—along with many more items designed to keep the good energy flowing in your home, office, or personal space. Why not take home something to add more harmony to your life? Open Monday through Saturday from 9am to 8pm. Corona 165, around the corner from Morelos. ✆ 322/222-3300.

Safari Accents   Flickering candles glowing in colored-glass holders welcome you to this highly original shop overflowing with creative gifts, one-of-a-kind furnishings, and reproductions of paintings by Frida Kahlo and Botero. Open daily from 10am to 6pm. Olas Altas 224, Loc. 4. ✆ 322/223-2660.

DECORATIVE & FOLK ART

Banderas Bay Trading Company ★   This shop features fine antiques and one-of-a-kind decorative objects for the home, including contemporary furniture, antique wooden doors, religious-themed items, original art, hand-loomed textiles, glassware, and pewter. This unique selection is handpicked by one of the area's most noteworthy interior designers, Peter Bowman. Open Monday to Saturday 10am to 6pm. Lázaro Cárdenas 263 (near Ignacio L. Vallarta). ✆ 322/223-4352. There's also a bodega (warehouse) annex of the shop located at Constitución 319 (at Basilio Badillo). ✆ 322/223-9817.

Lucy's CuCu Cabaña (Finds)   Owners Lucy and Gil Givens have assembled an exceptionally entertaining and eclectic collection of Mexican folk art. Each summer they travel through Mexico and personally select the handmade works created by over 200 indigenous artists and artisans. Items include metal sculptures, Oaxacan wooden animals, *retablos* (altars), and fine Talavera ceramics. Open Monday through Friday from 10am to 8pm, and Saturday from 10am to 3pm. The store is closed from May 15 to October 15. Basilio Badillo 295 (at Constitución). ℂ 322/222-1220.

Olinala This shop contains two floors of fine indigenous Mexican crafts and folk art, including an impressive collection of museum-quality masks and original contemporary art by gallery owner Brewster Brockman. Open Monday through Friday from 10am to 2pm and 5 to 8pm, Saturday from 10am to 2pm. Lázaro Cárdenas 274. ℂ 322/222-4995.

Puerco Azul Set in a space that actually has a former pig-roasting oven, Puerco Azul features a whimsical and eclectic selection of art and home accessories, much of it created by owner and artist Lee Chapman (aka Lencho). You'll find many animal-themed works in bright colors, including his signature *puercos azules* (blue pigs), and a wide selection of children's books and vintage clothing. Open Monday to Saturday from 10am to 6pm, closed on Sunday. Constitución 325, just off Basilio Badillo's "restaurant row." ℂ 322/222-8647.

Querubines (Finds Owner Marcella García travels across the country to select the items, which include exceptional artistic silver jewelry, embroidered and hand-woven clothing, bolts of loomed fabrics, tin mirrors and lamps, glassware, pewter frames and trays, high-quality wool rugs, straw bags, and Panama hats. Open Monday through Saturday from 9am to 9pm. Under the same ownership and open the same hours, **Serafina,** Basilio Badillo 260 (ℂ 322/223-4594), features a more extensive selection of cotton clothing and handmade jewelry. Juárez 501A (at Galeana). ℂ 322/223-1727.

TEQUILA & CIGARS

La Casa del Habano This fine tobacco shop has certified quality cigars from Cuba, along with humidors, cutters, elegant lighters, and other smoking accessories. It's also a local cigar club, with a walk-in humidor for regular clients. In the back, you'll find comfy leather couches, TV sports, and full bar service—in other words, a manly place to take a break from shopping. Open Monday through Saturday from noon to 9pm. Aldama 170. ℂ 322/223-2758.

La Casa del Tequila ★ Here you'll find an extensive selection of premium tequilas, plus information and tastings. Also available are books, tequila glassware, and other tequila-drinking accessories. The shop has been downsized to accommodate the **Agave Grill** (see "Where to Dine," in chapter 2) in the back, but now you can enjoy tasty Mexican fare and margaritas while you shop. Open Monday through Saturday from noon to 11pm, and Sunday from 5pm to midnight. Morelos 589. ℂ 322/222-2000.

3 PUERTO VALLARTA AFTER DARK

Puerto Vallarta's spirited nightlife reflects the town's dual nature—part resort, part colonial town. In the past, Vallarta was known for its live music scene, but in recent years the nocturnal action has shifted to DJ clubs with an array of eclectic, contemporary music. A concentration of nightspots lies along Calle Ignacio L. Vallarta (the extension of the main southbound road) after it crosses the Río Cuale. Along a 3-block stretch, you'll find a live blues club, sports bar, live mariachi music, a gay dance club, and the obligatory **Señor Frog's.** Walk from place to place and take in a bit of it all.

The *malecón,* which used to be lined with restaurants, is now known more for hip dance clubs and a few more relaxed options, all of which look out over the ocean. You can first stroll the broad walkway by the water's edge and check out the action at the back-to-back bars and clubs.

Marina Vallarta's clubs offer a more upscale, indoor, air-conditioned atmosphere. South of the Río Cuale, the **Olas Altas** zone's small cafes and martini bars buzz with action. In this zone, there's also an active gay and lesbian club scene.

PERFORMING ARTS & CULTURAL EVENTS

Truth be told, cultural nightlife beyond the **Mexican Fiesta** is limited. Culture centers on the visual arts; the opening of an exhibition has great social and artistic significance. Puerto Vallarta's gallery community comes together in the central downtown area to present weekly **art walks,** where new exhibits are presented, featured artists attend, and complimentary cocktails are served. Check listings in the daily English-language newspaper *Vallarta Today,* or the events section of **www.virtualvallarta.com**.

FIESTA NIGHTS

Major hotels in Puerto Vallarta feature frequent fiestas for tourists—extravaganzas with open bars, Mexican buffet dinners, and live entertainment. Some are fairly authentic and make a good introduction for first-time travelers to Mexico; others can be a bit cheesy. Shows are usually held outdoors but move indoors when necessary. Reservations are recommended.

Rhythms of the Night (Cruise to Caletas) ★★★ (Moments)

This is an unforgettable evening under the stars at John Huston's former home at the pristine cove called Las Caletas. The smooth, fast Vallarta Adventures catamaran travels here, entertaining guests along the way. Tiki torches and drummers dressed in native costumes greet you at the dock. There's no electricity—you dine by the light of candles, the stars, and the moon. The evening includes dinner, open bar, and entertainment. The buffet dinner is delicious—steak, seafood, and generous vegetarian options. The entertainment showcases indigenous dances in contemporary style. The cruise departs at 6:30pm from the Vallarta Adventure Center in Nuevo Vallarta or at 7pm from the Puerto Vallarta Maritime Terminal and returns by 11pm. ✆ 888/303-2653 in the U.S., or 322/297-1212. www.vallarta-adventures.com. Cost $89 (includes cruise, dinner, open bar, and entertainment).

THE CLUB & MUSIC SCENE
Restaurants & Bars

Bar Constantini ★★ The most sophisticated lounge in Vallarta is set in the elegant eatery Café des Artistes. The plush sofas are enticing, and the list of champagnes by the glass, signature martinis, and specialty drinks is suitably tempting. Live jazz and blues in an intimate atmosphere draws crowds, as do the regular wine tastings. An ample appetizer and dessert menu make it appropriate for late-night dining and drinks. Open daily from 6pm to 1am. Guadalupe Sánchez 740. ✆ 322/222-3229.

Carlos O'Brian's Vallarta's original nightspot was once the only place for an evening of revelry. Although the competition is stiffer nowadays, COB's still packs them in—especially the 20-something set. The late-night scene resembles a college party. Open daily from noon to 2am or later; happy hour is from noon to 8pm. Paseo Díaz Ordaz (malecón) 786, at Pípila. ✆ 322/226-8850. Weekend cover $11 (includes 2 drinks).

La Bodeguita del Medio This authentic Cuban restaurant and bar is known for its casual energy, terrific live Cuban music, and mojitos. It is a branch of the original Bodeguita in Havana (reputedly Hemingway's favorite restaurant there), which opened in 1942. If you can't get to that one, the Vallarta version has successfully imported the essence—and has a small souvenir shop that sells Cuban cigars, rum, and other items. The food is less memorable here than the music and atmosphere, so I recommend coming just for drinks and dancing. A Cuban band plays salsa, cumbia, and other tropical rhythms nightly (except Mon) after 10pm. Open daily from 11:30am to 2am (weekends until 4am). Paseo Díaz Ordaz 858 (malecón), at Allende. ✆ 322/223-1585.

Z'Tai ★ Z'Tai is a stunning array of spaces that span an entire city block. Enter from the *malecón,* and you'll discover ZBar, an upstairs lounge with chill-out music, backlit orange lighting, bay views, and comfortable banquettes to relax on. Venture farther into this club, and you'll find an expansive open air garden area that serves cocktails, as well as an array of Asian-inspired dining and snacking options, accompanied by electronic music at a level still appropriate for conversation. Faux-leather sofas and chairs comprise the seating, overlooking Zen gardens and flowing ponds. There is a 1,000-bottle wine menu, but the favorite drink here is their signature cucumber martini. Open daily for food service from 6pm to 2am, with bar service until 4am and 2-for-1 domestic drinks from 6 to 10pm. They also offer valet service or shuttle service to wherever you parked your car. Morelos 737, Col. Centro. ℂ 322/222-0306.

Rock, Jazz & Blues

El Faro Lighthouse Bar ★   A circular cocktail lounge at the top of the Marina lighthouse, El Faro is one of Vallarta's most romantic nightspots. Live or recorded jazz plays, and conversation is manageable. Drop by at twilight for the magnificent panoramic views, but don't expect anything other than a drink and, if you get lucky, some popcorn. Open daily from 5:30pm to 1:30am. Royal Pacific Yacht Club, Marina Vallarta. ℂ 322/221-0541 or -0542.

Mariachi Loco   This lively mariachi club features singers belting out boleros and ranchero classics. The mariachi show begins at 11:30pm—the mariachis stroll and play as guests join in impromptu singing—and by midnight it gets going. After 2am the mariachis play for pay, which is around $15 for each song played at your table. There's Mexican food from 8 to 10:30pm. Open daily from 8pm to 6am. Cárdenas 254 (at Ignacio Vallarta). ℂ 322/223-2205. Cover is generally $7, but varies depending on guest performances.

Night Clubs & Dancing

A few of Vallarta's clubs charge admission, but generally you pay just for drinks: $6 for a margarita, $4.50 for a beer, more for whiskey and mixed drinks. Keep an eye out for discount passes frequently available in hotels, restaurants, and other tourist spots. Most clubs are open from 10pm to 4am.

Christine   This dazzling club draws a crowd with an opening laserlight show, pumped-in dry ice, flashing lights, and a dozen largescreen video panels. Once a disco—in the true sense of the word—it is now a more modern dance club, with techno, house, and hip-hop the primary tunes played. The sound system is truly amazing, and the mix of music can get almost anyone dancing. Dress code: no tennis shoes or flip-flops, no shorts for men. Open daily from 10pm to 4am; the light show begins at 11pm. In the Krystal Vallarta hotel, north of downtown off Av. Francisco Medina Ascencio. ℂ 322/224-0202. Cover $10 ladies, $20 men.

Collage Club   A multilevel monster of nighttime entertainment, Collage includes a pool salon, video arcade, bowling alley, and the always-packed dance club, with frequent live entertainment. It's just past the entrance to Marina Vallarta, air-conditioned, and very popular with a young, mainly local crowd. Open daily from 10am to 6am. Calle Proa s/n, Marina Vallarta. ② **322/221-0505.** Cover $5.50–$40, which varies by theme party being offered that night.

de Santos ★★★   Vallarta's chic de Santos restaurant is even better known for the hip urban crowd its bar draws, and the adjacent club has become known as the place for the superchic to party. The lower level holds an air-conditioned bar and dance floor (after midnight, when dining tables have been cleared away), where a DJ spins the hottest of house and techno. Upstairs there's an open-air rooftop bar with chill-out music and acid jazz. One partner, a member of the superhot Latin rock group Maná, uses Vallarta as a home base for writing songs. The crowd, which varies in age from 20s on up, shares a common denominator of cool style. The restaurant bar is open daily from 6pm to 2am; the club is open Wednesday through Saturday from 10pm to 4am. Morelos 771. ② **322/223-3052** or -3053.

Hilo   You'll recognize Hilo by the giant sculptures that practically reach out the front entrance and pull you into this high-energy club, which has become a favorite with the 20-something set. Music ranges from house and electronic to rock. It seems the later the hour, the more crowded the place becomes. Open daily from 4pm to 6am. Malecón, btw. Aldama and Abasolo sts. ② **322/223-5361.** Cover $10 weekends and holidays. No cover weekdays.

J & B Salsa Club   This is the locally popular place to go for dancing to Latin music—from salsa to samba, the dancing is hot and the atmosphere electric. On Fridays, Saturdays, and holidays, the air-conditioned club hosts live bands. Open daily from 10pm to 6am. Av. Francisco Medina Ascencio Km 2.5 (Hotel Zone). ② **322/224-4616.** Cover $10.

Mandala   The sister club to Hilo is geared toward a slightly more sophisticated crowd. The two-level bar and dance club has oversized windows overlooking the *malecón* and ongoing music video screens, with giant Buddha sculptures situated throughout the Pan Asian–inspired club. But there's little meditating here amid the din of house and Latin pop. Currently the hottest place in town, it attracts a sleek and suntanned crowd. It's open daily from 11am to 6am. There's basic bar service from opening until 8pm, when a DJ spins into action. Paseo Díaz Ordaz (malecón) 600 at Abasolo. ② **322/223-0966.** Cover (nighttime) $10–$20, depending on the promotion of the evening.

Rio Latino   For those seeking steamy salsa dancing, this new, classy locale has been a welcome addition in town since it opened in 2007.

Although the dance floor is rather small for all that action, the excellent music—ranging from regional Mexican to Cuban salsa—is drawing strong crowds of mostly local residents. It's on the upper level of Plaza Peninsula, open Thursday to Sunday from 10pm to 6am. Francisco M. Ascencio #2485. Local C2 y C3. © 322/209-2042. Cover $15.

Zoo This is your chance to be an animal and get wild in the night. A giant elephant head emerges out of a jungle-themed mural near the entrance, and the Zoo even has cages to dance in if you're feeling unleashed. This packed club boasts a killer sound system and a hot variety of dance music, including techno, reggae, and rap. Every hour's happy hour, with two-for-one drinks. Zoo opens daily at noon and closes in the wee hours. Paseo Díaz Ordaz (malecón) 630. © 322/222-4945. www.zoobardance.com. Cover $15 weekends only (includes 2 drinks).

A Sports Bar

Steve's Sports Bar With a multitude of old-school TVs, Steve's Sports Bar is popular with veterans and American expats. It shows most NBA, NHL, NFL, and MLB broadcast events. Steve's serves simple American fare and plenty of beer. It's open daily from 11am to midnight. Basilio Badillo 286 (at corner of Constitución) in the Zona Romantica. © 322/222-0256.

Gay & Lesbian Clubs

Vallarta has a vibrant gay community with a wide variety of clubs and nightlife options, including special bay cruises and evening excursions to nearby ranches. Most of the gay nightlife happens in so-called Zona Romantica on the south side of the Rio Cuale, where the busiest street lined with restaurants, cafes, and bars is Olas Altas. The free *Gay Guide Vallarta* (www.gayguidevallarta.com) specializes in gay-friendly listings, including weekly specials and happy hours.

Garbo This small, cozy club is gay friendly, but not exclusively gay, and features great recorded music and occasional live music on weekends, including piano and jazz. It's open daily from 6pm to 2am and is air-conditioned. Pulpito 142. © 322/223-5753.

La Noche A casual, intimate "neighborhood bar" catering to a gay clientele, with great prices on drinks, and a menu of tequila cocktails. Beers are always two-for-one. Open daily from 6pm to 2am. Lazaro Cardenas 257 (2 doors from Ignacio Vallarta). © 322/222-3364.

Mañana ★ The town's most popular gay club is located in the Zona Romantica. There are two dance floors, a pool with a waterfall, and candlelit tables. Weekends bring drag shows and strip teases. It's open daily from noon to 6am and is air-conditioned. Venustiano Carranza 290. © 322/222-7772. Cover $12 weekends, $5 weekdays.

4 SIDE TRIPS FROM PUERTO VALLARTA

YELAPA: ROBINSON CRUSOE MEETS JACK KEROUAC ★

It's a cove straight out of a tropical fantasy, and only a 45-minute trip by boat from Puerto Vallarta. Yelapa has no cars and one paved (pedestrian-only) road, and only recently acquired electricity. It's accessible only by boat. Its tranquillity, natural beauty, and seclusion make it a popular home for hipsters, artists, writers, and a few expats (looking to escape the stress of the world, or perhaps the law). A seemingly strange mix, but you're unlikely to ever meet a stranger—Yelapa remains casual and friendly.

To get there, travel by excursion boat or inexpensive water taxi (see "Getting Around," in chapter 1). You can spend an enjoyable day, but I recommend a longer stay—it provides a completely different perspective.

Once you're in Yelapa, you can lie in the sun, swim, snorkel, eat fresh grilled seafood at a beachside restaurant, or sample the local moonshine, *raicilla*. The beach vendors specialize in the most amazing pies you've ever tasted (coconut, lemon, or chocolate). Equally amazing is how the pie ladies balance the pie plates on their heads as they walk the beach; they sell crocheted swimsuits, too. You can tour this tiny town or hike up a river to see one of two waterfalls; the closest to town is about a 5-minute walk straight up from the pier. *Note:* If you use a local guide, agree on a price before you start out. Horseback riding, guided birding, fishing trips, and paragliding are also available.

For overnight accommodations, local residents frequently rent rooms, and there's also the rustic **Hotel Lagunita ★** (© **322/209-5056** or -5055; www.hotel-lagunita.com). Its 29 cabañas have private bathrooms, and the hotel has electricity, a saltwater pool, a primitive spa with massage, an amiable restaurant and bar, as well as the Barracuda Beach lounge and brick-oven pizza cafe, plus a gourmet coffee shop. Though the prices are high for what you get, it is the most accommodating place for most visitors. Double rates run $120 during the season and $90 in the off season. Special rooms are available now for honeymooners, for $150 (MasterCard and Visa are accepted). Lagunita has become a popular spot for yoga retreats, and regularly features yoga classes.

An alternative is the fashionable **Verana ★★★** (© **800/530-7176** or 322/222-2360; www.verana.com). See "Where to Stay," in chapter 2, for details.

If you stay over on a Wednesday or Saturday during the winter, don't miss the regular dinner-dance at the **Yelapa Yacht Club** ★ (no phone). Typically tongue-in-cheek for Yelapa, the "yacht club" consists of a cement dance floor and a disco ball, but the DJ spins a great range of tunes, from Glenn Miller to Kanye West, attracting all ages and types. Dinner ($6–$13) is a bonus—the food may be the best anywhere in the bay. The menu changes depending on what's fresh. Ask for directions; it's in the main village, on the beach.

NUEVO VALLARTA & NORTH OF VALLARTA: ALL-INCLUSIVES

Many people assume Nuevo Vallarta is a suburb of Puerto Vallarta, but it's a stand-alone destination over the state border in Nayarit. It was designed as a megaresort development, complete with marina, golf course, and luxury hotels. Although it got off to a slow start, it has finally come together, with a collection of mostly all-inclusive hotels on one of the widest, most attractive beaches in the bay. The biggest resort, Paradise Village, has a full marina and an 18-hole golf course inland from the beachside strip of hotels, plus a growing selection of condos and homes for sale. The Mayan Palace also has an 18-hole course here. The Paradise Plaza shopping center, next to Paradise Village, amplifies the area's shopping, dining, and services. It's open daily from 10am to 10pm. To get to the beach, you travel down a lengthy entrance road from the highway, passing by a few remaining fields (which used to be great for birding) but mostly real estate under construction.

A 16-mile trip into downtown Puerto Vallarta takes about 30 minutes by taxi, costs about $20 to $25, and is available 24 hours a day. The ride is slightly longer by public bus, which costs $1.50 and operates from 7am to 11pm.

Marival Grand & Club Suites   This all-inclusive hotel sits almost by itself at the northernmost end of Nuevo Vallarta. Designed in Mediterranean style, it offers a complete vacation experience, including extensive land sports, water sports, and daytime activities for kids, teenagers, and adults. Cooking and Spanish lessons, golf clinics, yoga classes, bicycle riding, rock climbing, beach volleyball, tennis, and soccer are among the many options. There are a large variety of room types, ranging from studios to one-, two-, and three-bedroom suites. Rooms and suites have balconies or terraces with garden, pool, or ocean views. The broad white-sand beach is one of the real assets here—it stretches over 450m (1,476 ft.).

Paseo de los Cocoteros and Bulevar Nuevo Vallarta s/n, 63735 Nuevo Vallarta, Nay. ⓒ **450/686-0226** in Canada, and 322/297-0100 or 322/226-8200. Fax 322/297-0262. www.gomarival.com. 495 units. $200 and up double; $300 and up suite.

Rates are all-inclusive. Ask for seasonal specials. AE, MC, V. From the Puerto Vallarta airport, enter Nuevo Vallarta from the 2nd entrance; Club Marival is the 1st resort to your right on Paseo de los Cocoteros. Free parking. **Amenities:** 6 restaurants; 8 bars; 4 outdoor pools and an adults-only whirlpool; spa; 4 lighted tennis courts; extensive watersports, land sports, and daytime activities. *In room:* A/C, TV, hair dryer, Wi-Fi (fee).

Paradise Village ★   The collection of pyramid-shaped buildings, designed in Maya-influenced style, houses well-designed all-suite accommodations in studio and one-, two-, and three-bedroom configurations. All have sitting areas and kitchenettes, making the resort ideal for families or groups of friends. Truly a village, this self-contained resort set on an exquisite stretch of beach offers a full array of services. The Maya theme extends to both oceanfront pools, with mythical creatures forming water slides and waterfalls. The exceptional spa is reason enough to book a vacation here, with treatments, hydrotherapy, massage (including massage on the beach), and fitness and yoga classes. Special spa packages are always available. A compelling attraction is the El Tigre golf course (details earlier in this chapter, under "Golf"); their on-site marina continues to draw a growing number of boats and yachts. Paradise Village has begun to feel a bit dated around the edges.

Paseo de los Cocoteros 001, 63731 Nuevo Vallarta, Nay. (✆ **800/995-5714** in the U.S., or 322/226-6770. Fax 322/226-6713. www.paradisevillage.com. 700 units. $150–$300 junior or 1-bedroom suite; $300–$400 2-bedroom suite; $500–$600 3-bedroom suite. All-inclusive rates available for $89 additional per person. AE, DC, MC, V. Free covered parking. **Amenities:** 3 restaurants; 2 beachside snack bars; basketball court; beach volleyball; complete fitness center; championship golf club w/18-hole course; kids' club; marina; petting zoo; 2 beachside pools; lap pool; European spa; 4 tennis courts; watersports center. *In room:* A/C, TV, hair dryer, minibar.

BUCERIAS: A COASTAL VILLAGE ★

Only 18km (11 miles) north of the Puerto Vallarta airport, Bucerías ("boo-seh-*ree*-ahs," meaning "place of the divers") is a small coastal fishing village of 10,000 people in Nayarit state on Banderas Bay. It has caught on as an alternative to Puerto Vallarta for those who find the pace of life there too invasive. Bucerías offers a seemingly contradictory mix of accommodations—trailer-park spaces and exclusive villa rentals tend to dominate, although there's a small selection of hotels as well.

To reach the town center by car, take the exit road from the highway out of Vallarta and drive down the shaded, divided street that leads to the beach. Turn left when you see a line of minivans and taxis (which serve Bucerías and Vallarta). Go straight ahead 1 block to the main plaza. The beach, with a lineup of restaurants, is a half-block farther. You'll see cobblestone streets leading from the highway to the beach, and hints of villas and town homes behind high walls. If you take the bus to Bucerías, exit when you see the minivans and taxis to and from Bucerías on the street that leads to the beach. To use public transportation from Puerto Vallarta, take a minivan or bus marked BUCERIAS (they run 6am–9pm). The last minivan stop is Bucerías's town square. There's also 24-hour taxi service.

Exploring Bucerías

Come here for a day trip from Puerto Vallarta just to enjoy the long, wide, uncrowded beach, along with the fresh seafood served at the beachside restaurants or at one of the cafes listed below. On Saturdays and Sundays, many of the streets surrounding the plaza are closed to traffic for a *mercado* (street market)—where you can buy anything from tortillas to neon-colored cowboy hats.

The **Coral Reef Surf Shop,** Heroe de Nacozari 114-F (✆ 329/298-0261), sells a great selection of surfboards and gear, and offers surfboard and boogie board rentals, surf lessons, and ATV and other adventure tours to surrounding areas.

Where to Stay

There are few quality hotels in Bucerías, and most people who choose to stay here opt for a private home rental. Check out the available vacation rentals at **Sunworx** (✆ 329/298-0060; www.sunworx.com), which will book accommodations in Bucerías including villas, houses, and condos. Call ahead, or ask for directions to the office when you get to Bucerías.

Where to Dine

Besides those mentioned below, there are many seafood restaurants fronting the beach. The local specialty is *pescado zarandeado,* a whole fish smothered in tasty sauce and slow-grilled.

Karen's Place ★ INTERNATIONAL/MEXICAN This casual oceanside restaurant offers classic cuisine, plus Mexican favorites in a style that appeals to North American appetites. Known for Sunday champagne brunch (9am–3pm), it is a perfect place to enjoy a light beach lunch, or a romantic dinner. The casual, comfortable restaurant features live music on Tuesday and Friday at 7pm. It also has a decked terrace dining area with spectacular views, as well as a sushi menu.

On the beach at the Costa Dorada, Calle Lázaro Cárdenas. ✆ 329/298-3176. www.all.at/karens. Breakfast $5–$7; Sun brunch (9am–3pm) $18; main courses $5.50–$16. MC, V. Mon–Sat 9am–9pm, Sun 9am–3pm.

Le Fort ★★★ (Moments) FRENCH What an unforgettable dining experience. The evening consists of watching as Chef Gilles Le Fort prepares your gourmet meal and teaches you how to re-create it. The

U-shaped bar adjacent to the kitchen accommodates diners, who sip fine wines and nibble on pâté while the master works. Chef Le Fort is the winner of numerous culinary awards, and his warm conviviality is the real secret ingredient of this unusual experience. Once dinner is served, the chef and his wife, Margarita, will join the table, entertaining with stories of their experiences in Mexico. Le Fort probably has the most extensive wine cellar in the bay—some 3,000 bottles. Homemade sausages, pâtés, and more delicacies are available in the adjoining shop.

Calle Lázaro Cárdenas 71, 1 block from the Hotel Royal Decameron. **329/298-1532.** www.lefort.com.mx. Reservations required. Cooking class, 3-course dinner, wines, and recipes $55 per person. No credit cards. Daily 8–10:30pm; cooking classes available 10am–1:30pm.

Mark's ★★ (Finds) ITALIAN/STEAK/SEAFOOD   It's worth a special trip to Bucerías just to eat at this covered-patio restaurant. The most popular American hangout in town, Mark's offers a great assortment of thin-crust pizza and flatbread, baked in its brick oven and seasoned with fresh herbs grown in the garden. Everything has exquisite flavorings—some favorites include shrimp tempura with fruit salad, macadamia-crusted red snapper filet, ahi tuna served rare, and filet mignon with blue-cheese ravioli. Multitalented chef Jan Marie (Mark's charming wife and partner) runs an adjacent boutique, featuring elegant home accessories and unique gift items. The bar televises all major sporting events.

Calle Lázaro Cárdenas 56 (½-block from the beach). **329/298-0303.** Pasta $17–$25; main courses $20–$37. MC, V. Daily 5–10:30pm. From the hwy., turn left just after bridge, where there's a small sign for Mark's; double back left at next st. (immediately after you turn left) and turn right at next corner; Mark's is on the right.

Mezzogiorno ★★ ITALIAN   The owners of this lovely oceanfront *trattoria* built a reputation with their Mezzaluna restaurant in Vallarta, then moved the business to their former home in Bucerías when the traffic became too much to deal with the commute. And diners on the north shore are so very grateful. It's the most attractive dining option north of Vallarta, in a sleekly restored home overlooking the bay. But as stunning as the setting is, it takes second place to the savory dishes served. Large, flavorful salads overflow with fresh ingredients. My favorite combines grilled chicken with mixed greens, sun-dried tomatoes, goat cheese, and a currant-balsamic vinaigrette. For main dishes, pasta is the specialty, with best-sellers that include fettuccini Alfredo, lasagna, and spaghetti with grilled vegetables. Also delightful are the shrimp, scallops, and fish served over black fettuccine, with black olives, capers, and a spicy tomato sauce.

Av. del Pacífico 33. **329/298-0350.** www.mezzogiorno.com.mx. Main courses $7.50–$19. MC, V. Daily 6–11pm.

PUNTA MITA: EXCLUSIVE SECLUSION ★★★

At the northern tip of the bay is an arrowhead-shaped, 600-hectare (1,482-acre) peninsula bordered on three sides by the ocean, called Punta Mita. Considered a sacred place by the Indians, this is the point where Banderas Bay, the Pacific Ocean, and the Sea of Cortez come together. It's magnificent, with white-sand beaches and coral reefs just offshore. Stately rocks jut out along the shoreline, and the water is a dreamy translucent blue. Punta Mita is evolving into one of Mexico's most exclusive developments. The master plan calls for resorts, several high-end residential communities, and up to three championship golf courses. Today what you'll find is the elegant Four Seasons Resort, its Jack Nicklaus Signature golf course, and a selection of luxury rental villas and condos. In 2008, a 120-room St. Regis Resort opened (see below), along with Punta Mita's second Jack Nicklaus Signature golf course.

Casa de Mita ★★ (Finds)   Previously known as Casa Las Brisas, this hotel isn't technically in Punta Mita, but it's near enough to convey a sense of the area's relaxed seclusion. It's located on the back road that runs from Punta Mita to Sayulita, on the small, pristine Careyeros Bay. The six rooms and two suites are set in a villa overlooking the exquisite beach. The villa itself is a work of white stucco walls, tile floors and patios, thatched and tiled roofs, and guayaba-wood balcony detailing. Patios and intimate indoor-outdoor seating areas on varying levels are ideal for an afternoon read or an evening cocktail. Interiors of the guest rooms are simple and elegant, with touches such as carved armoires, headboards, and doors from Michoacán. Private balconies with ocean views surround the pool, which features submerged sunning chairs and a small fountain. A big plus here is the delicious dining, included in the price of your stay.

Playa Careyeros, 63734 Punta de Mita, Nay. (℗) 866/740-7999 in the U.S., 329/298-4114. Fax 329/298-4112. www.casademita.com. 8 rooms and suites. High season $525–$655 suite; low season $445–$575 suite. Rates include all meals and drinks. Minimum 3-night stay required. AE, DC, MC, V. Limited street parking. **Amenities:** Restaurant; entertainment room w/TV, DVD, and VCR; universal gym station; small outdoor pool; spa; tour services, including horseback riding and surfing lessons. *In room:* A/C, minibar, no phone.

Four Seasons Resort Punta Mita ★★★   The Four Seasons Resort set the standard for luxury along Mexico's Pacific Coast, and few places in the world can match it. The gorgeous resort offers seclusion, pampering service, and comfort. Accommodations are in three-story *casitas* surrounding the main building, which houses the beautiful open-air lobby, cultural center, restaurants, shopping arcade, and oceanfront infinity pool. Every guest room offers breathtaking views of the ocean from a large terrace or balcony. Most suites have a private plunge pool, sitting room with a sofa bed, separate bedroom, bar, and a powder room. Rooms are plush and spacious, with a king or two double beds, a seating area, and an oversize bathroom with a deep soaking tub, separate glass-enclosed shower, and dual-vanity sink. The Four Seasons also has an adults-only tranquillity pool, with a champagne and caviar bar surrounded by cabañas available for daily rent, as well as an incredible kids' pool in the form of a lazy river. The resort also rents out magnificent four- and five-bedroom villas with private butlers. Service is unerringly warm and unobtrusive throughout this little paradise. At least 45 minutes from Puerto Vallarta's activities, it's an ideal getaway, with a full-service spa, tennis center, and two championship golf courses.

63734 Bahía de Banderas, Nay. (© **800/332-3442** in the U.S., or 329/291-6000. Fax 329/291-6060. www.fourseasons.com. 173 units. High season $545–$1,175 double, $1,685–$16,000 suite; low season $375–$925 double, $1,025–$8,750 suite. AE, DC, MC, V. Free valet parking. **Amenities:** 3 restaurants; lobby bar; beachfront bar; children's programs; concierge; cultural center w/lectures, cooking classes, Spanish classes, dance classes, and other daily activities; full-service fitness center; horseback riding; Jacuzzi; oceanfront pool; adults-only pool surrounded by private cabañas; lazy river kids' pool; room service; European-style spa; tennis center w/10 courts of various surfaces; watersports equipment; yoga. *In room:* A/C, flatscreen TV/DVD, iHome audio system and alarm clock, hair dryer, high-speed Internet, minibar.

St. Regis ★★   Opened in late 2008, this ultra-exclusive St. Regis is the first in Latin America, set on a stunning expanse of beach in Punta Mita. Guest rooms and suites are almost hidden amid the 33 two-story casitas spread throughout the property, where palm-filled gardens and three infinity pools compete with the endless ocean for guests' attention. Beautifully appointed rooms incorporate handmade tiles, custom Mexican furnishings, and large marble bathrooms with indoor and outdoor showers. Other features include flatscreen TVs, Remède bath amenities, and the St. Regis signature butler service. Throughout the resort, touches of Provence combine with chic Mexican designs that draw on river stone, marble, onyx, wood, and clay. The resort's spa merits special mention for its pampering service, which will adopt treatments and massages to guest preferences. Although there's a kids' program, the resort targets adults looking for privacy and usually feels very quiet. The three gourmet restaurants give you variety, so you never need leave the property.

Lote H-4 Carretera Federal 200, Km 19.5, Punta de Mita, 63734, Nayarit. (© **800/ 598-1863** in the U.S., or 329/291-5800. Fax 329/291-5801. www.stregis.com/punta mita. 120 units. $595 and up double; $2,000 and up suite. AE, DC, MC, V. Free valet parking. **Amenities:** 3 restaurants; 3 bars, babysitting; kids' club; concierge; full-service fitness center & spa; Jacuzzi; 3 pools; room service; 8 tennis courts; water-sports equipment. *In room:* A/C, flatscreen TV, hair dryer, high-speed Internet, minibar.

SAYULITA: MEXICO'S CURRENT HOT SPOT

Sayulita is only 40km (25 miles) northwest of Puerto Vallarta, on Hwy. 200 to Tepic, yet it feels like a world apart. It captures the simplicity and tranquillity of beach life that has long since left Vallarta—but hurry, because it's exploding in popularity. For years, Sayulita has been principally a surfers' destination—the main beach in town is known for its consistent break and long, rideable waves. Visitors and locals who find Vallarta to be too cosmopolitan have started to flock here. The major travel press noticed this trend and popularized the place to a near tipping point. You'll now find more real estate offices than surf shops, and more fine jewelry stores than juice bars, but Sayulita is still gently holding on to her charms.

An easygoing attitude still prevails in this beach town, despite the niceties popping up amid the basic accommodations, inexpensive Mexican food stands, and handmade, hippie-style-bauble vendors. It's quickly becoming gentrified with new cafes, sleek shops, aromatherapy-infused spas, and elegant villas for rent. Boutique art and clothes shops surround the festive central plaza.

Sayulita is most popular for surfing. Any day, you'll witness an army of surfers seeking perfect swells offshore from the main beach. You may just as easily encounter a Huichol Indian family that has come down from the Sierra to sell their wares.

To get to Sayulita, you can rent a car or take a taxi from the airport or downtown Vallarta. The rate is about $70 to get to the town plaza. The taxi stand is on the main square, or you can call for pickup at your hotel. The trip to the airport from Sayulita costs about $60. Guides also lead tours to Puerto Vallarta, Punta Mita, and other surrounding areas, including a Huichol Indian community.

Where to Stay

Sayulita has several private homes for rent. One local expert on Sayulita rentals is **Upi Viteri** (upiviteri@prodigy.net.mx), who has access to some of the nicest properties.

Villa Amor Villa Amor is a collection of charming guest rooms—think of it as your private villa by the sea. Owner Rod Ingram and his design team have carefully crafted each space and individual suite. The exterior walls curve invitingly and open to breathtaking views all around. The one- and two-bedroom "villa" suites have fully equipped kitchenettes, plus open-air seating or dining areas (or both); some have plunge pools. Note there are many stairs and steep walkways throughout the property. Weddings are often hosted here.

Camino Playa Los Muertos s/n, 63732 Sayulita, Nay. ☏ **619/819-5407** from the U.S.; 329/291-3010. Fax 329/291-3018. www.villaamor.com. 33 units. $110–$260 1-bedroom villa; $380–$550 2-bedroom villa; $750 3-bedroom villa; rates include continental breakfast. MC, V. **Amenities:** Restaurant; bar; concierge; room service; tennis court; watersports equipment/rentals, including boogie boards, kayaks, and surfboards. *In room:* A/C, fan.

Where to Dine

If you are in Sayulita, chances are, you heard about it because of **Don Pedro's,** the most popular restaurant in town, in the heart of the main beach. More popular than fine dining in Sayulita, however, are the pervasive stands hawking cheap fish tacos and other street fare— which are the best way to dine.

Don Pedro's INTERNATIONAL   Many say it's Don Pedro's that has brought so much attention to Sayulita in recent years. Vallarta area visitors came for the food, then booked their next vacation in this funky town. Choose between a two-level indoor dining area or shaded tables on the beach for breakfast, lunch, or dinner. Starters include grilled artichoke, tuna and crab seviche, and fresh salads. Main courses feature thin-crust pizza, fresh fish artfully prepared, and a changing selection of savory pasta and meat dishes, such as the organic pork chop served with sweet potato purée. Grilled ahi tuna with mashed potatoes is also a favorite. Delicious homemade flatbread accompanies your meal. At night, torches and clay pot fireplaces warm the beachfront tables. In the bar area, TVs broadcast sporting events of any relevance, from college football to Mexican *futból* (soccer).

Marlin 2, on the beachfront. ☏ **329/291-3090.** Main courses $15–$30. MC, V. Daily 8am–11pm.

Rollie's ★★ ⒻⒾⓃⒹⓈ BREAKFAST   Breakfast heaven. This family restaurant emanates a happy aura that puts its patrons in a good mood. The menu reflects the tone of the place, welcoming "travelers, strangers, or lonely locals" with a sense of "love and nurturing" for all diners. Recommended plates include Adriana's Rainbow (an omelet with cheese, tomatoes, green peppers, and onions) and my personal favorite, Indian Pipe Pancakes. All dishes come with Rollie's famous lightly seasoned, pan-fried new potatoes. Rollie's has expanded its service to dinner as well, served from 5:30 to 9pm. Specialties include paella. There's also an upstairs espresso bar.

Breakfast $5–$8; dinner $6–$15. No credit cards. Daily Nov–Apr 7:30am–noon and
5:30–9pm. Closed May–Oct.

Surfing

There are two main surf spots in Sayulita—the most popular is the
break fronting the main beach in the village, which is a right long-
board break. A faster, left break is found just north of the river mouth,
in front of the campground. Surf instruction and board rentals are
available at **Lunazul Surf School** (ⓒ **329/291-2009**), located at
Marlin #4, where this street ends at the beachfront. The 90-minute
surf lessons cost $40 for individual instruction, or $30 for group
instruction. They also offer 2-day weekend clinics for $80 or week-
long clinics for $200. Included in all lessons is the use of a surfboard
and rashguard. Board rentals through Lunazul are $20 for the day, or
$140 for the week. Lunazul also has a surf shop, where you can pur-
chase surf gear ranging from wax to boards.

Among the growing number of surfer-chic shops, the standout is
Pachamama (ⓒ **329/291-3468;** Defin #4B, www.lesgazelles.com),
which sells Tahitian black pearl jewelry, generally strung on leather
cords in exquisite yet casual designs, as well as a tightly edited selection of clothing and home design items. The boutique—owned and
operated by a group of free-spirited, lovely French girls with a passion
for surfing and sunshine—is an enchanting visit, whether you end up
with a purchase or not.

Nightlife

Nightlife in Sayulita is as laid-back by night as by day, but options are
plentiful—ranging from rowdier bars to live music venues. The locals
seem to gravitate to a different locale each night, so when you arrive,
ask around to see where the evening's hot spot will be. One depend-
able option is the **Buddha Mar** (ⓒ **329/291-3869**), located at Calle
Marlin #8, on the second floor just next to Don Pedros (you can't
miss the neon pink sign). Having recently changed its name from
Buddha Bar to Buddha Mar, this cool ambient bar serves sushi and
sashimi as well as luscious libations amid Buddha statues, pillowed
banquettes, and lounge music. On weekends, there is often live music
from 9pm until 1am, which tends to draw a dancing crowd. It's open
each evening from 6:30pm until about 2am, or when the crowd
abates. Housed upstairs under a big *palapa* next to the main plaza,
Calypso (ⓒ **329/291-3704**), at Av. Revolución 44, is a popular bar/
restaurant serving simple Mexican dishes alongside a full collection of
tequilas and other favorite liquors. Traditional Mexican music plays in
the background. It's open daily from 5 to 11pm.

SAN SEBASTIAN: MOUNTAIN HIDEAWAY ★★★

If you haven't heard about San Sebastián yet, it probably won't be long—its remote location and historic appeal have made it the Mexican media's new darling destination. Originally discovered in the late 1500s and settled in 1603, the town peaked as a center of mining operations, swelling to a population of over 30,000 by the mid-1800s. Today, with roughly 600 year-round residents, San Sebastián retains all the charm of a village locked in time, with an old church, a coffee plantation, an underground tunnel system—and wholly without a T-shirt shop.

Getting There

By car, it's a $2^1/_2$-hour drive up the Sierra Madre from Puerto Vallarta on an improved road, but it can be difficult during the summer rainy season, when the road washes out frequently. **Vallarta Adventures** (© **888/303-2653** in the U.S., or 322/297-1212; www.vallarta-adventures.com) runs 7-hour long day trips (by land; no longer by air) from Puerto Vallarta. The cost is $80 including round-trip transportation, lunch, guided tour, and bottled water. The small private airport can also arrange flights. **Aerotron** (© **322/221-1921;** www.aerotron.com.mx) charges about $140 round-trip, **Aéro Taxis de la Bahía** (© **322/221-1990** and 322/222-2049) about $100 round-trip, depending on the type of plane and number of passengers.

Where to Stay

There are two places to stay in San Sebastián. The first is the very basic **El Pabellón de San Sebastián,** which faces the town square. Its nine simply furnished rooms surround a central patio. Don't expect extras here; rates run $50 per double. The town's central phone lines handle reservations—you call (© **322/297-0200**) and leave a message or send a fax, and hopefully the hotel will receive it. Except on holidays, there is generally room at this inn. No credit cards.

A more enjoyable option, the stately **Hacienda Jalisco ★★** (© **322/222-9638;** www.haciendajalisco.com), built in 1850, was once the center of mining operations in town. The beautifully landscaped, rambling old hacienda is near the airstrip, a 15-minute walk from town. The five extra-clean rooms have wood floors, rustic furnishings and antiques, and working fireplaces; some are decorated with pre-Columbian reproductions. The ample bathrooms are beautifully tiled and have skylights. Hammocks grace the upstairs terrace, while a sort-of museum on the lower level attests to the celebrity guests and importance the hacienda has enjoyed over the years.

Because of its remote location, all meals are included. Rates are $80 per person per night and include full breakfast and dinner; alcoholic beverages are extra. Reserve through e-mail (pmt15@hotmail.com or info@haciendajalisco.com), through the town telephone (© **322/297-0200**), or on their website. Group rates and discounts for longer stays are available. No credit cards are accepted. Guided horseback, walking, or mine tours can be arranged through the Hacienda.

Costa Alegre: Puerto Vallarta to Barra de Navidad

by Shane Christensen

In my view, Costa Alegre is Mexico's most spectacular coastal area, a 232km (144-mile) stretch that connects tropical forests with a series of dramatic cliff-lined coves and a few of the most exclusive accommodations in the world. Tiny outpost towns line the coast, while dirt roads trail down to a succession of magical coves with pristine beaches, most of them steeped in privileged exclusivity. The sunset vistas and nighttime stargazing here are incredible—without any light pollution, it feels like you can reach up and grab the stars. Considered one of Mexico's greatest undiscovered treasures, this coast is becoming a favored hideaway for publicity-fatigued celebrities and those in search of natural seclusion.

The area is referred to as **Costa Alegre (Happy Coast)**—the marketer's term—and **Costa Careyes (Turtle Coast),** after the many sea turtles that nest here. It is home to an eclectic array of the most captivating and exclusive places to stay in Mexico, with a selective roster of activities that includes championship golf and polo. Along the line, however, you will encounter the funky beach towns that were the original lure for travelers who discovered the area.

Stops along Hwy. 200, as it meanders between Puerto Vallarta to the north and Manzanillo to the south, can be an enjoyable day trip, but travelers usually make the drive en route to a destination along the coast.

EXPLORING COSTA ALEGRE   Costa Alegre is more an ultimate destination than a place to rent a car and take a drive. Most of the beaches are tucked into coves accessible by dirt roads that can extend for kilometers inland. If you do drive along this coast, Hwy. 200 is safe, but it's not lit and it curves through the mountains, so travel only during the day. A few buses travel this route, but they stop only at the towns that line the highway; many of them are several kilometers inland from the resorts along the coast. For more information about

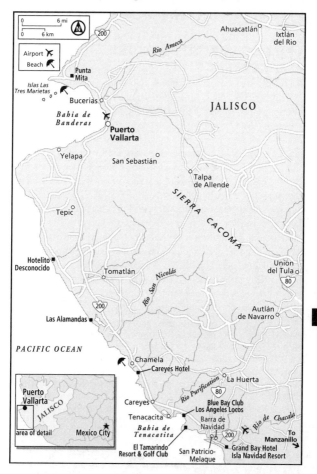

traveling to this area, visit **www.costalegre.ca**. It's now possible to visit Hotelito Desconocido, Las Alamandas, and El Tamarindo (see below) for 6 or 9 nights as part of an exclusive package arranged by the hotels; visit **www.mexicoboutiquehotels.com** for rates and details.

1 ALONG COSTA ALEGRE (NORTH TO SOUTH)

CRUZ DE LORETO'S LUXURY ECO-RETREAT

Hotelito Desconocido ★★★ Ⓜ**Moments** The fact that the Hotelito Desconocido ("little unknown hotel") is ecologically minded is a bonus, but it's not the principal appeal. A cross between *Out of Africa* and *Blue Lagoon,* Hotelito Desconocido is among my favorite places in Mexico. Think camping with luxury linens, romantic candles everywhere, and a symphony performed by cicadas, birds, and frogs. The rustic, open-air rooms, called *palafitos,* are in cottages perched on stilts over a lagoon. A grouping of suites is on the sand bar that separates the tranquil estuary from the Pacific Ocean. Ceiling fans cool the air, and water is solar heated. It's easy to disconnect here. In fact, it's mandatory: There's no electricity; no phones; no neighboring restaurants, nightclubs, or shopping—just delicious tranquillity. At night, there are only candles, lanterns, and flashlights to guide you. Rates do not include meals or drinks; a meal plan is mandatory, because there are no other options nearby (making the entire package somewhat pricey)—but it's a unique experience. The secluded beach offers a variety of nonmotorized watersports.

Playón de Mismaloya s/n, Cruz de Loreto, 48360 Tomatlán, Jal. Ⓒ **800/851-1143** in the U.S. and Canada (reservations Ⓒ **01-800/013-1313** in Mexico, or 322/281-4010 or 322/222-2546). Fax 322/281-4178. www.hotelito.com. 24 units. High season $800–$1,490 double; low season $510–$900 double. Mandatory daily meal plan $120 per person. Children are discouraged. AE, MC, V. Take Hwy. 200 south for 1 hr., turn off at exit for Cruz de Loreto, and continue on clearly marked route on unpaved road for about 25 min. All activities are subject to an extra charge. Free parking. **Amenities:** 2 restaurant/bars; beach volleyball; mountain bikes; billiards; birding tours; hiking trails; horseback riding; kayaks; sailboards; sauna; primitive-luxury spa; whirlpool. *In room:* No phone.

LAS ALAMANDAS: AN EXCLUSIVE LUXURY RESORT

Las Alamandas ★★★ Almost equidistant between Manzanillo (2 hr.) and Puerto Vallarta (2 hr.) lies Mexico's original ultraexclusive resort. A dirt road winds for about a mile through a tiny village to the guardhouse of Las Alamandas, set on 28 hectares (69 acres) of beachfront and low hills that are part of a 600-hectare (1,500-acre) estate. The resort consists of colorful villas and *palapas* spread among four stunning private beaches, gardens, lakes, lagoons, and a bird sanctuary. It's designed for serenity—guests rarely catch a glimpse of one another. The resort has air-conditioning, telephones, and a beachside massage *palapa*, yet manages to keep the experience natural. Las Alamandas accommodates a maximum of 30 guests, with over 100 staff members serving them.

The six spacious villas house a total of 14 suites splashed in pinks, yellows, and blues. These suites can easily be joined to form larger accommodations, and all have tiled verandas with magnificent ocean or garden views. Some villas are on the beach, others across a cobblestone plaza. The food here is excellent, with most of the organic products grown right on the enormous property. When you reserve your room, you can arrange for van transportation to and from Manzanillo ($250 one-way) and Puerto Vallarta ($250 one-way), as well as air transport from Puerto Vallarta. This is one of my favorite resorts in Mexico.

Hwy. 200, Km 83 48850 Manzanillo–Puerto Vallarta, Jal. Mailing address: Domicilio Conocido Costa Alegre QUEMARO Jalisco, Apdo. Postal 201, 48980 San Patricio Melaque, Jal. © **888/882-9616** in the U.S. and Canada, or 322/285-5500. Fax 322/285-5027. www.alamandas.com. 14 units. High season $488–$2,070; low season $371–$1,499. Meal plans $120. AE, MC, V. Free parking. **Amenities:** Restaurant; bar; art gallery; mountain bikes; birding tours; boat tours; boogie boards; concierge; hiking trails; horseback riding; landing strip (make advance arrangements); 18m (59-ft.) outdoor pool; room service; lighted tennis court; video library; weight room. *In room:* A/C, TV w/DVD/VCR available upon request, minibar.

CAREYES

The Careyes Hotel ★★   The Careyes is a gem of a resort on a small, pristine cove between dramatic cliffs adorned by the exclusive villas of Careyes. (This area has practically defined the architectural style that defines Mexico beach chic—with bold washes of vibrant colors, open spaces, and tropical gardens.) Stylishly simple, if dated, accommodations all face the ocean. Guests come primarily to get away from it all, although the resort is as popular with families as with couples and you can enjoy many services, including a full European spa and even polo. It's rustic and sophisticated; room facades are awash in scrubbed pastels and form a U around the center lawn and freeform pool. Some rooms have balconies. Twenty rooms have private pools, and villas are available for rent. Roughly 150km (93 miles) south of Puerto Vallarta, the Careyes is about a 2-hour drive north of Manzanillo on Hwy. 200, and about a 1-hour drive from the Manzanillo airport. Taxis from the Manzanillo airport charge around $110 one-way. Manzanillo and Puerto Vallarta airports have car-rental counters. A car would be useful only for exploring the coast—Barra de Navidad and other resorts, for example—and the hotel can make touring arrangements.

Hwy. 200 Km 53.5, 48970 Careyes, Jal. CP. Mailing address: Apdo. Postal 24, 48970 Cihuatlán, Jal. ☎ 888/433-3989 in the U.S. and Canada, 315/351-0000. Fax 315/ 351-0100. www.elcareyesresort.com. 51 units. High season $385–$425 double, $455–$1,269 suite; low season $299–$315 double, $345–$995 suite. AE, MC, V. Free parking. **Amenities:** Restaurant; bar; deli; beach volleyball; bikes; book and DVD library; children's programs (during Christmas and Easter vacations only); horseback riding; kayaks; large beachside pool; hot and cold plunge pools; privileges at exclusive El Tamarindo resort (40km/25 miles south), w/18-hole mountaintop golf course; room service; sauna; state-of-the-art spa; steam room; 2 tennis courts; weight equipment. *In room:* A/C, TV/DVD, CD player, minifridge, hair dryer, minibar.

TENACATITA BAY

Located an hour (53km/33 miles) north of the Manzanillo airport, this jewel of a bay is accessible by an 8km (5-mile) dirt road that passes through a small village set among banana plants and coconut palms. Sandy, serene beaches dot coves around the bay (frolicking dolphins are a common sight), and exotic birds fill a coastal lagoon. Swimming and snorkeling are good, and the bay is a popular stop for luxury yachts. Just south of the entrance to Tenacatita is a sign for the all-inclusive **Sun Resorts Los Angeles Locos,** as well as the exclusive **El Tamarindo** resort and golf club. There is no commercial or shopping area, and dining options outside hotels are limited to a restaurant or two that may emerge during the winter months (high season). Relax—that's what you're here for.

Blue Bay Club Los Angeles Locos Ⓥalue On a 5km (3-mile) stretch of sandy beach, the all-inclusive Los Angeles Locos offers an abundance of activities programs, entertainment, and dining options. It's especially popular with families and groups of friends. Most rooms and all suites have ocean views, with either balconies or terraces. The four-story hotel is basic in decor and amenities, but colorful and comfortable. The attraction here is the wide array of on-site activities, plus a "Mangrove" cruise excursion (included in the room rate). **La Lagarta Disco** is a little on the dark and smoky side but can really rock, depending on the crowd—it's basically the only option on the bay. This is a beautiful location, but a long way from any serious town.

Carretera Federal 200 Km 20, Tenacatita 48989, Municipio de la Huerta, Jal. ☎ 800/483-7986 in the U.S., 800/713-3020 or 315/351-5411 in Mexico. Fax 315/ 351-5412. www.losangeleslocos.com. 204 units. High season $280 double; low season $180 double. Children 5–12 $40 year-round. Rates are all-inclusive. Ask about family specials. AE, MC, V. Free parking. **Amenities:** 2 restaurants and snack bar (w/buffets and a la carte dining); 3 bars; babysitting; basketball court; kids' club; dance club; exercise room; Hobie Cats; horseback riding; kayaks; massage; adult outdoor pool; kids' outdoor pool adjacent to the beach; pool tables; sailboards; 3 tennis courts. *In room:* A/C, TV.

El Tamarindo Beach & Golf Resort ★★★ (Finds)   The most
beautiful resort I know in Mexico, El Tamarindo is a romantic haven
amid lush jungle surroundings, with exquisite facilities, gracious service, and absolute tranquillity. Each thatched-roof casita features a
wrap-around splash pool (many have a whirlpool, too), hammock,
and open-air sitting and dining area that overlooks a private lawn.
The bedrooms—with dark hardwood floors and intricately designed
furnishings—can be closed off for air-conditioned comfort, but the
remaining areas are open to the sea breezes and heady tropical air.
Beachfront bungalows rest on a protected Pacific cove; the nonbeach-
side bungalows arguably have more privacy. There are also three luxurious four-bedroom beachfront residences that can accommodate up
to eight adults. El Tamarindo boasts a championship 18-hole golf
course designed by David Fleming, with 7 oceanside holes and dramatic views. The spa services are exceptional, with most massages and
treatments provided in beachfront *cabañas* or in the resort's Spa Hut.
El Tamarindo's restaurant is the only dining option, but the menu
changes daily and won't disappoint. The flora and fauna here are the
full-time residents of El Tamarindo, and listening to the life around
you is simply exhilarating—there are over 250 species of birds alone.
At night, subtle lighting through the jungle and around the casitas
transforms El Tamarindo into a truly enchanted retreat. On 800
hectares (1,976 acres) of tropical rainforest bordering the Pacific
Ocean, you'll feel as if you've found your own personal bit of heaven
here.

Carretera Barra de Navidad–Puerto Vallarta Km 7.5, 48970 Cihuatlán, Jal. ℂ **866/
717-4316** in the U.S.; 315/351-5031. Fax 315/351-5070. www.eltamarindoresort.
com. 29 bungalows. High season $625–$1,650 villas; low season $500–$1,100 villas. Beachfront residences $2,700–$5,500. AE, MC, V. From Puerto Vallarta (3 hr.) or
the Manzanillo airport (45 min.), take Hwy. 200, then turn west at the clearly
marked exit for El Tamarindo; follow signs for about 25 min. Free valet parking.
Amenities: Restaurant; bar; mountain bikes; estuary bird-watching tours; high-
tech fitness center; hiking trails; kayaks; kids' club; sailboards; Aquafin sailboats;
large beachside pool w/whirlpool; room service; spa services; *temazcal* (pre-Hispanic sweat lodge); 2 clay tennis courts and 1 grass court; yoga classes; waterski-
ing. *In room:* A/C, TV, CD player, hair dryer, Wi-Fi.

---

2 BARRA DE NAVIDAD & MELAQUE

This pair of rustic beach villages (only 5km/3 miles apart) has been
attracting travelers for decades. Only 30 minutes north of Manzanillo's airport and about 100km (62 miles) north of downtown Manzanillo, Barra has a few brick or cobblestone streets, good budget hotels

and restaurants, and funky beach charm. All of this lies incongruously next to the super-luxurious Grand Bay Hotel, which sits on a bluff across the inlet from Barra.

In the 17th century, Barra de Navidad was a harbor for the Spanish fleet; from here, galleons first set off in 1564 to find China. Located on a crescent-shaped bay with curious rock outcroppings, Barra de Navidad and neighboring Melaque are connected by a continuous beach on the same wide bay. It's safe to say that the only time Barra and Melaque hotels are full is during Easter and Christmas weeks. **Barra de Navidad** has more charm, more tree-shaded streets, better restaurants, more stores, and more conviviality between locals and tourists. Barra is very laid-back; faithful returnees adore its lack of flash. Other than the Grand Bay Hotel, on the cliff across the waterway in what is called Isla Navidad (although it's not on an island), nothing is new or modern. But there's a bright edge to Barra, with more good restaurants and limited—but existent—nightlife.

Melaque, on the other hand, is larger, sun baked, treeless, and lacking in attractions. It does, however, have plenty of cheap hotels available for longer stays, and a few restaurants. Although the beach between the two is continuous, Melaque's beach, with deep sand, is more beautiful than Barra's. Both villages appeal to those looking for a quaint, quiet, inexpensive retreat rather than a modern, sophisticated destination.

Isla Navidad Resort has a manicured 27-hole golf course and the superluxurious Grand Bay Hotel, but the area's pace hasn't quickened as fast as expected. The golf is challenging and delightfully uncrowded, with another exceptional course at nearby El Tamarindo. It's a serious golfer's dream.

ESSENTIALS

GETTING THERE & DEPARTING   Regional buses from Manzanillo frequently run up the coast along Hwy. 200 on their way to Puerto Vallarta and Guadalajara. Most stop in the central villages of Barra de Navidad and Melaque. First-class **ETN** buses (www.etn.com. mx) make the 4-hour ride to and from Guadalajara for $35 each way. From the Manzanillo airport, it's only around 30 minutes to Barra, and **taxis** are available. The fare from Manzanillo to Barra is around $45; from Barra to Manzanillo, $35. From Manzanillo, the highway twists through some of the Pacific Coast's most beautiful mountains. Puerto Vallarta is 3 hours by **car** and 5 hours by bus, north on Hwy. 200 from Barra. To arrange a car rental, **Crazy Cactus** (© **315/355-6091**), located at 21 de Noviembre #60, offers car rentals from November through April.

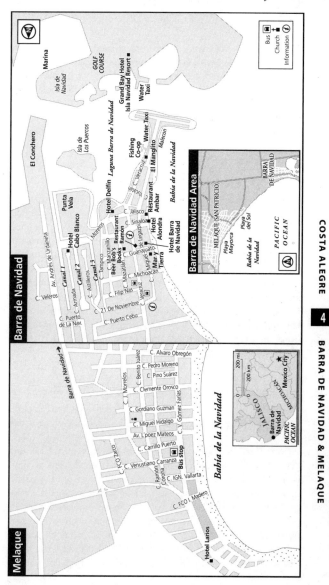

VISITOR INFORMATION   The **tourism office** for both villages is at Jalisco 67 (btw. Veracruz and Mazatlán), Barra (℃/fax **315/355-5100;** www.barradenavidad.com); it's open Monday through Friday from 9am to 5pm.

ORIENTATION   In Barra, hotels and restaurants line the main beachside street, **Legazpi.** From the bus station, beachside hotels are 2 blocks straight ahead, across the central plaza. Two blocks behind the bus station and to the right is the lagoon side. More hotels and restaurants are on its main street, **Morelos/Veracruz.** Few streets are marked, but 10 minutes of wandering will acquaint you with the village's entire layout. There's a taxi stand at the intersection of Legazpi and Sinaloa streets. Legazpi, Jalisco, Sinaloa, and Veracruz streets border Barra's **central plaza.**

ACTIVITIES ON & OFF THE BEACH

Swimming and enjoying the attractive beach and views of the bay take up most tourists' time. You can hire a small boat for a coastal ride or fishing in two ways. Go toward the *malecón* on Calle Veracruz until you reach the tiny boatmen's cooperative, with fixed prices posted on the wall, or walk two buildings farther to the water taxi ramp. The water taxi is the best option for going to Colimilla (5 min.; $2.50) or across the inlet (3 min.; $1) to the Grand Bay Hotel. Water taxis make the rounds regularly, so if you're at Colimilla, wait, and one will be along shortly. At the cooperative, a 30-minute **lagoon tour** costs $20, and a **sea tour** costs $25. **Sportfishing** is $80 for up to four people for a half-day in a small *panga* (open fiberglass boat, like the ones used for water taxis).

   Isla Navidad Country Club (℃ 314/337-9024; www.islanavidad. com) has a beautiful and challenging 27-hole, 7,053-yard, par-72 **golf course** that is open to the public. Greens fees are $200 for 18 holes, $220 for 27 holes (discounts are available for hotel guests). Prices include a motorized cart. Caddies are available, as are rental clubs.

   Beer Bob's Books, Avenida Tampico #8, between Sinaloa and Guanajuato, is a book-lover's institution in Barra and a sort of community service that the rather grouchy Bob does for fun. His policy of "leave a book if you take one" allows vacationers to select from hundreds of neatly shelved paperbacks, as long as they leave a book in exchange. It's open Monday through Friday from noon to 3pm and occasionally in the evenings. "Beer Bob" got his name because in earlier days, when beer was cheap, he kept a cooler stocked, and book browsers could sip and read. (When beer prices went up, Bob put the cooler away.)

Low season in Barra is any time except Christmas and Easter weeks. Except for those 2 weeks, it doesn't hurt to ask for a discount at the inexpensive hotels.

Very Expensive

Grand Bay Hotel Isla Navidad Resort ★★ Across the yacht channel from Barra de Navidad, this grand hotel sits on its own island and is spread out over 480 hectares (1,186 acres) next to a 27-hole golf course. Now operated by Wyndham Resorts, the Grand Bay overlooks the village, bay, and Navidad lagoon. The hotel's swimming pools are spectacular, and there's a narrow beach facing the lagoon. Spacious guest rooms are sumptuously outfitted with marble floors and columns, beautiful bathrooms, hand-carved wood furnishings, and soft colors. Prices vary according to view and size of room, but even the standard rooms are elegantly decorated. Each comes with a king-size or two double beds, ceiling fans plus air-conditioning, and a balcony. Outdoor activities abound, and the luxurious spa offers extensive facial and body treatments for those who prefer to relax indoors. The hotel is a short water-taxi ride across the inlet from Barra de Navidad; it's also on a paved road from Hwy. 200. It's worth a visit even if you're not staying here, although the hotel is not open to nonguests at night unless they're coming for dinner.

Circuito de los Marinos s/n, 28830 Isla Navidad, Col. ✆ **877/999-3223** in the U.S.; 01-800/849-2373 in Mexico, or 314/331-0500. Fax 314/331-0570. www.wyndham. com. 199 units. $200 and up double; $300 and up suite. AE, DC, DISC, MC, V. Free parking. **Amenities:** 3 restaurants; 2 bars; golf club w/food and bar service; babysitting; concierge; fishing, boat tours, and other excursions can be arranged; 27-hole, par-72 golf course; golf club w/pro shop and driving range; 2 Jacuzzis; kids' club; marina w/private yacht club; 3 outdoor pools, including 1 w/waterslides and swim-up bar; room service; full spa; 3 lighted grass tennis courts; small workout room. *In room:* A/C, TV, hair dryer, minibar.

Moderate

Hotel Cabo Blanco ★★ Located on the point where you cross over to Isla Navidad, the Cabo Blanco is an outstanding option for family vacations or longer-term stays. Rooms are pleasantly rustic, with tile floors, large tile tubs, separate dressing areas, and stucco walls. The hotel overlooks the bay, but it's a 5-minute walk to the beach. The beamed-ceiling lobby is in its own building; rooms are in hacienda-style buildings surrounded by gardens. The atmosphere is generally tranquil, except during weekends and Mexican holidays, when this hotel tends to fill up. Because the Cabo Blanco doesn't front the beach, it has an affiliated beach club and restaurant, Mar y Tierra (see "Where to Dine," below).

Armada y Bahía de la Navidad s/n, 48987 Barra de Navidad, Jal. ℭ **800/710-5690** in Mexico; 315/355-6495, -6496. Fax 315/355-6494. www.hotelcaboblanco.com. 101 units. $100 double; $256 suite with kitchenette. All-inclusive plans also available. AE, MC, V. Limited street parking. **Amenities:** Restaurant; concierge; 2 outdoor pools (1 adults only); 2 tennis courts. *In room:* A/C, TV.

Inexpensive

Hotel Alondra ★   One of the town's newest and best hotels, this moderately priced option sits in the heart of the action. It's located next to the church on the main strip of restaurants, shops, and bars, and there's a little beach just in front. Guest rooms are spread out in two buildings, one oceanfront and the other just across the street. Splashed in hues of blue, yellow, and white, the light-filled rooms feature marble floors and small bathrooms with showers only; junior suites have kitchenettes. This friendly hotel, which is especially popular with Canadians, has a small infinity pool in front of the beach, as well as an open-air bar on the 15th floor with a lovely view of the village and sea.

Sinaloa 16, 48987 Barra de Navidad, Jal. ℭ **315/355-8373.** www.alondrahotel. com. 73 units. $119–$128 double; $144 oceanview double. AE, MC, V. **Amenities:** Restaurant; bar; outdoor pool. *In room:* A/C, TV, kitchenette (in some rooms).

Hotel Barra de Navidad ★   At the northern end of Legazpi, this popular, comfortable beachside hotel is among the nicest in the town. It has friendly management and some rooms with balconies overlooking the beach and bay. Other, less-expensive rooms afford only a street view. Only the oceanview rooms have air-conditioning. A nice swimming pool is on the street level to the right of the lobby, and there's a small restaurant called the Banana Cafe.

Legazpi 250, 48987 Barra de Navidad, Jal. ℭ **315/355-5122.** Fax 315/355-5303. www.hotelbarradenavidad.com. 60 units. $86–$108 double. MC, V. Free parking. **Amenities:** Outdoor pool. *In room:* A/C (in some rooms).

Hotel Delfín   The simple four-story (no elevator) Delfín sits on the landward side of the lagoon. It offers basic, well-lit rooms that have tile floors and a queen or two double beds, but no air-conditioning. Two apartments with kitchens have been added. The tiny courtyard, with a small pool and lounge chairs, sits in the shade of an enormous rubber tree. From the third and fourth floor, there's a view of the lagoon. A breakfast buffet goes from 8:30 to 10:30am (see "Where to Dine," below).

Morelos 23, 48987 Barra de Navidad, Jal. ℭ **315/355-5068.** Fax 315/355-6020. www.hoteldelfinmx.com. 26 units. $49 double; ask about low-season discounts. MC, V. Free parking. **Amenities:** Restaurant; gym; heated outdoor pool; Wi-Fi.

El Manglito ★ SEAFOOD/MEXICAN On the placid lagoon, with a view of the palatial Grand Bay Hotel, El Manglito serves home-style Mexican food to a growing number of repeat diners. The whole fried fish accompanied by drawn garlic butter, boiled vegetables, rice, and french fries, is a crowd pleaser. Other enticements include boiled shrimp, chicken in orange sauce, and shrimp salad.

Veracruz 17, near the boatmen's cooperative. No phone. Main courses $7–$18. No credit cards. Daily 10am–11pm.

Hotel Delfín BREAKFAST The second-story terrace of this small hotel is a pleasant place to begin the day. The self-serve buffet offers an assortment of fresh fruit, juice, granola, yogurt, milk, pastries, and unlimited coffee. The price includes made-to-order eggs and delicious banana pancakes—for which the restaurant is known.

Morelos 23. ✆ **315/355-5068.** www.hoteldelfinmx.com. Breakfast buffet $4. No credit cards. Daily 8:30am–noon.

Mar y Tierra INTERNATIONAL Hotel Cabo Blanco's beach club is also a popular restaurant and bar, and a great place to spend a day at the beach. There are shade *palapas* and beach chairs, and a game of volleyball seems constantly in progress. Open during the daytime only, the colorful restaurant is decorated with murals of mermaids. Perfectly seasoned shrimp fajitas come in plentiful portions.

Legazpi s/n (at Jalisco). ✆ **315/355-5028.** Main courses $12–$20. MC, V. Daily 8am–6pm.

Restaurant Ambar ★ CREPES/ITALIAN/FRENCH This cozy beachside restaurant is open to the breezes, and the food is as wonderful as the ambience. The crepes are named after towns in France; the delicious *crêpe Paris,* for example, is filled with chicken, potatoes, spinach, and green sauce. Rich selections of salads and carpaccios are available as starters. Main dishes include grilled fish prepared any way you like, jumbo prawns, beef medallions in a pepper sauce, and lobster tail kabob in a white wine sauce. Pastas and pizzas are also served.

López de Legazpi 150 (corner of Jalisco), across from the church. ✆ **315/355-8169.** Crepes $11–$21; main courses $9–$34. No credit cards. Daily 5pm–midnight.

Restaurant Ramón ⒱alue SEAFOOD/MEXICAN It seems that everybody eats at Ramón's, where the chips and fresh salsa arrive unbidden, and service is prompt and friendly. The food is especially tasty, although many options are fried. Try fresh fried shrimp with french fries or any daily special that features vegetable soup or chicken-fried steak. Box lunches are offered for $7.

Legazpi 260. (© **315/355-6435.** Main courses $6.50–$13. No credit cards. Daily 7am–11pm.

BARRA DE NAVIDAD AFTER DARK

When dusk arrives, visitors and locals alike find a cool spot to sit outside, sip cocktails, and chat. Many outdoor restaurants and stores in Barra accommodate this relaxing way to end the day, adding extra tables and chairs for drop-ins. Most of the nighttime action is centered around the walking area near the church.

During high season, the **Hotel Sands** poolside and lagoon-side bar has happy hour from 2 to 6pm. The colorful **Capri Sunset Bar and Restaurant,** facing the bay at the corner of Legazpi and Jalisco, is a favorite for sunset-watching and a game of oceanside pool or dancing to live or taped music. It's most popular with travelers ages 20 to 30. In the same vein, **Simona & Niños,** at the beachfront adjacent to Hotel Casa Chips at the corner of Yucatán and Legazpi, offers an excellent sunset vista. **Piper Lover Bar & Grill,** Legazpi 154 A (© **315/355-6747;** www.piperlover.com), is done in the style of the Carlos Anderson's chain—but it's not one of them. Still, it is lively, with pool tables and occasional live music.

A VISIT TO MELAQUE (SAN PATRICIO)

For a change of scenery, you may want to wander over to Melaque (aka San Patricio), 5km (3 miles) from Barra on the same bay. You can walk on the beach from Barra or take one of the frequent local buses from the bus station near the main square in Barra. The bus is marked MELAQUE. To return to Barra, take the bus marked CIHUATLAN.

Melaque's pace is even more laid-back than Barra's, and though it's a larger village, it seems smaller. It has fewer restaurants and less to do. Although there are more hotels, or "bungalows," as they are usually called, few manage the charm of those in Barra; if Barra hotels are full on a holiday weekend, Melaque would be a second choice. The paved road ends where the town begins. A few yachts bob in the harbor, and the palm-lined beach is gorgeous.

If you come by bus from Barra, you can exit anywhere in town or stay on until the last stop, which is the bus station in the middle of town a block from the beach. Restaurants and hotels line the beach. Coming into town from the main road, you'll be on the town's main street, **Avenida López Mateos.** You'll pass the main square on the way to the waterfront, where there's a trailer park. The street going left (southeast) along the bay is **Avenida Gómez Farías;** the one going right (northwest) is **Avenida Miguel Ochoa López.**

Where to Stay & Dine

The best hotel in town is **Larios,** at Calle Av. Primavera 60 (© **315/ 355-8058**), just a block from the beach. Opened in 2007, it has 10 rooms that cost $110 per night, cash only. Other motels in town are half that price but far less nice. As for dining, there are a number of rustic *palapa* **restaurants** on the beach and farther along the bay at the end of the beach.

Manzanillo

by Shane Christensen

Manzanillo has long been known as a resort town with wide, curving beaches, legendary sportfishing, and a highly praised diversity of dive sites. Golf is also an attraction here, with two popular courses in the area.

One reason for its popularity could be Manzanillo's enticing tropical geography—vast groves of tall palms, abundant mango trees, and successive coves graced with smooth sand beaches. To the north, mountains blanketed with palms rise alongside the shoreline. And over it all lies the veneer of perfect weather, with balmy temperatures and year-round sea breezes. Even the approach by plane into Manzanillo showcases the promise—you fly in over the beach and golf course. Once on the ground, you exit the airport through a palm grove.

Manzanillo is a dichotomous place—it is both Mexico's busiest commercial seaport and a tranquil, traditional town of multicolor houses cascading down the hillsides to meet the central commercial area of simple seafood restaurants, shell shops, and a few salsa clubs. The activity in Manzanillo divides neatly into two zones: the downtown commercial port and the luxury Santiago Peninsula resort zone to the north. The busy harbor and rail connections to Mexico's interior dominate the downtown zone. A visit to the town's waterfront *zócalo* provides a glimpse into local life. The exclusive Santiago Peninsula, home to the resorts and golf course, separates Manzanillo's two golden sand bays.

---

1 ESSENTIALS

256km (159 miles) SE of Puerto Vallarta; 267km (166 miles) SW of Guadalajara; 64km (40 miles) SE of Barra de Navidad

GETTING THERE & DEPARTING

BY PLANE **Alaska Airlines** (© 800/252-7522 in the U.S., or 314/334-2211) offers service from Los Angeles; **Mexicana** (© 800/531-7921 in the U.S.) connects to U.S. destinations via Mexico City; **US Airways** (© 800/428-4322 in the U.S.) flies from Phoenix. Ask

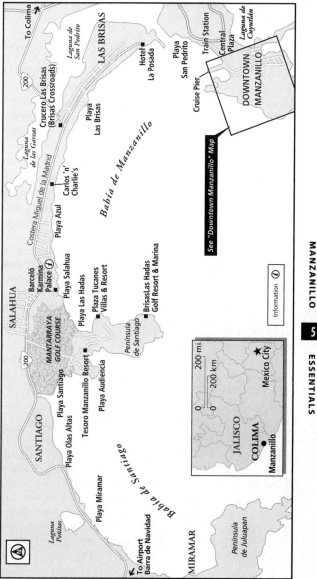

To Colima

Laguna de San Pedro

LAS BRISAS

Laguna de Cuyutlán

Train Station

Central Plaza

Hotel La Posada

Playa San Pedrito

DOWNTOWN MANZANILLO

Cruise Pier

200

Crucero Las Brisas (Brisas Crossroads)

Playa Las Brisas

Laguna de las Garzas

Carlos 'n' Charlie's

Costera Miguel de la Madrid

Bahía de Manzanillo

See "Downtown Manzanillo" Map

Playa Azul

Barceló Karmina Palace (i)

Playa Salahua

SALAHUA

Playa Las Hadas

Plaza Tucanes Villas & Resort

Peninsula de Santiago

BrisasLas Hadas Golf Resort & Marina

Information (i)

200

MANTARRAYA GOLF COURSE

Tesoro Manzanillo Resort

Playa Santiago

Playa Audiencia

SANTIAGO

Playa Olas Altas

Bahía de Santiago

Playa Miramar

Laguna Peñitas

MIRAMAR

To Airport Barra de Navidad

Peninsula de Juluapan

0   200 mi
0   200 km

JALISCO

COLIMA

Manzanillo

★

Mexico City

a travel agent about the numerous **charters** from the States in the winter.

The **Playa de Oro International Airport** (ZLO) is 40km (25 miles) northwest of town. *Colectivo* (minivan) airport service is available from the airport; hotels arrange returns. Make reservations for return trips 1 day in advance. The *colectivo* fare is based on zones and runs $15 to $20 for most hotels. Private taxi service between the airport and downtown area is around $35. **Budget** (② **800/472-3325** in the U.S., or 314/333-1445), **Hertz** (② **314/333-3191**), and **Alamo** (② **314/334-0124**) have counters in the airport open during flight arrivals; they will also deliver a car to your hotel. Daily rates run $60 to $80. You need a car only if you plan to explore surrounding cities and the Costa Alegre beaches.

BY CAR   **Coastal Hwy. 200** leads from Acapulco (south) and Puerto Vallarta (north). From Guadalajara, take **Hwy. 54** through Colima into Manzanillo. Outside Colima you can switch to a toll road, which is faster but less scenic.

BY BUS   Buses run to Barra de Navidad ($1^{1}/_{2}$ hr. north), Puerto Vallarta (5 hr. north), Colima ($1^{1}/_{2}$ hr. east), and Guadalajara ($4^{1}/_{2}$ hr. north), with deluxe service and numerous daily departures. **ETN** (www.etn.com.mx) is the main bus company. Manzanillo's **Central Camionera** (bus station; ② **314/336-4785**) sits about 12 long blocks east of town. If you follow Hidalgo east, the station will be on your right.

VISITOR INFORMATION

The **tourism office** (② **314/333-2277;** www.gomanzanillo.com) is on the Costera Miguel de la Madrid 875-A, Km 8.5. It's open Monday through Friday from 9am to 7pm, and Saturday from 9am to 2pm.

CITY LAYOUT

The town lies at one end of an 11km-long ($6^{3}/_{4}$-mile) beach facing Manzanillo Bay and its commercial harbor. The beach has four sections—**Playa Las Brisas, Playa Azul, Playa Salahua,** and **Playa Las Hadas.** At the other end of the beaches is the high, rocky **Santiago Peninsula.** Santiago lies 11km ($6^{3}/_{4}$ miles) from downtown; it's the site of many beautiful homes and the best hotel in the area, Las Hadas, as well as the hotel's Mantarraya Golf Course. The peninsula juts into the bay, separating Manzanillo Bay from Santiago Bay. Playa Las Hadas sits on the south side of the peninsula, facing Manzanillo Bay, and **Playa Audiencia** is on the north side, facing Santiago

Las Hadas.

Activity in downtown Manzanillo centers on the *zócalo,* officially known as the Jardín Alvaro Obregón. A railroad, shipyards, and a basketball court with constant pickup games separate it from the waterfront. The plaza has flowering trees, a fountain, twin kiosks, and a view of the bay. It's a staple of local life, where people congregate on park benches to swap gossip and throw handfuls of rice to the ever-present *palomas* (doves—really just pigeons). Large ships dock at the pier nearby. **Avenida México,** the street leading out from the plaza's central gazebo, is the town's principal commercial thoroughfare.

Once you leave downtown, the **Costera Miguel de la Madrid** highway (or just Costera Madrid) runs through the neighborhoods of Las Brisas, Salahua, and Santiago to the **hotel zones** on the Santiago Peninsula and at Miramar. Shell shops, mini-malls, and several restaurants dot the way.

There are two main lagoons. **Laguna de Cuyutlán,** almost behind the city, stretches south for miles, paralleling the coast. **Laguna de San Pedrito,** north of the city, parallels the Costera Miguel de la Madrid; it's behind Playa Las Brisas. Both are good birding sites. There are also two bays. **Manzanillo Bay** encompasses the harbor, town, and beaches. The Santiago Peninsula separates it from the second bay, **Santiago.** Between downtown and the Santiago Peninsula lies **Las Brisas,** a flat peninsula with a long stretch of sandy golden beach, a lineup of inexpensive but run-down hotels, and a few good restaurants.

GETTING AROUND

BY TAXI   Taxis in Manzanillo are plentiful. Fares are fixed by zones; rates for trips in town and to more distant points should be posted at your hotel. Daily rates can be negotiated for longer drives outside the Manzanillo area.

BY BUS   The *camionetas* (local buses) make a circuit from downtown in front of the train station, along the Bay of Manzanillo, to the Santiago Peninsula and the Bay of Santiago to the north; the fare is 50¢. The ones marked LAS BRISAS go to the Las Brisas crossroads, to the Las Brisas Peninsula, and back to town; MIRAMAR, SANTIAGO, and SALAHUA buses go to outlying settlements along the bays and to most restaurants mentioned below. Buses marked LAS HADAS go to the Santiago Peninsula and pass the Las Hadas resort and the Tesoro Manzanillo and Plaza Las Glorias hotels. This is an inexpensive way to see the coast as far as Santiago and to tour the Santiago Peninsula.

MANZANILLO

5

ESSENTIALS

(*Fast Facts*)   Manzanillo

American Express American Express has no local office in Manzanillo, but I highly recommend **Bahías Gemelas Travel Agency,** Blvd. Costero Miguel de la Madrid 1556, Las Gaviotas (✆ **314/333-1000;** fax 314/333-0649). It's open Monday through Friday from 9am to 2pm and 4 to 7pm, Saturday from 9am to 2pm.

Area Code The telephone area code is **314.**

***Bank* Banamex,** just off the plaza on Avenida Juárez, downtown (✆ **314/332-0115**), is open Monday through Friday from 9am to 4pm, Saturday 10am to 2pm.

Hospital Contact the **Cruz Roja (Red Cross;** ✆ **314/336-5770**) or the **General Hospital** (✆ **314/332-1903,** -0089).

Police Both the general police and Tourism Police are available by calling ✆ **314/332-1004,** -1002.

Post Office The *correo,* Dr. Miguel Galindo 30, opposite Farmacia de Guadalajara, downtown (✆ **314/332-0022**), is open Monday through Friday from 8:30am to 4pm, Saturday from 9am to 1pm.

2 ACTIVITIES ON & OFF THE BEACH

Activities in Manzanillo revolve around its golden-sand beaches, which sometimes accumulate a film of black mineral residue from nearby rivers. Most of the resort hotels are completely self-contained. Manzanillo's public beaches provide an opportunity to see more local color and scenery. They are the daytime playground for those staying at places off the beach or without pools.

BEACHES

Playa Audiencia, on the Santiago Peninsula, offers the best swimming as well as snorkeling, but **Playa San Pedrito,** shallow for a long way out, is the most popular beach for its proximity to downtown. **Playa Las Brisas,** located south of Santiago Peninsula as you're heading to downtown Manzanillo, offers an optimal combination of location and good swimming. **Playa Miramar,** on the Bahía de Santiago past the Santiago Peninsula, is popular with bodysurfers, windsurfers, and boogie boarders. It's accessible by local bus from town. The major

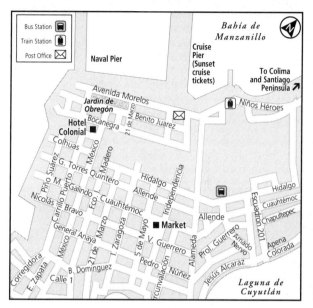

Bus Station

Train Station

Post Office

Naval Pier

Bahía de Manzanillo

Cruise Pier (Sunset cruise tickets)

To Colima and Santiago Peninsula

Niños Héroes

Avenida Morelos

Jardin de Obregón

Bocanegra

21 de Marzo

Benito Juarez

Hotel Colonial

Colhuas

México

Madero

G. Torres Quintero

Prto Suárez

Fco. Cuauhtémoc

M. Galindo

Carrillo Puerto

Nicolás Bravo

Hidalgo

Allende

Independencia

Hidalgo

Cuauhtémoc

Escuadron 201

Chapultepec

Allende

General Anaya

México

21 de Marzo

I. Zaragoza

5 de Mayo

V. Guerrero

Alameda

Prol. Guerrero

Amado Nervo

Apena Colorada

Corregidora

E. Zapata

B. Dominguez

Calle 1

rcurvalación

Pedro Núñez

Jesús Alcaraz

Market

Laguna de Cuyutlán

MANZANILLO

5

ACTIVITIES ON & OFF THE BEACH

part of **Playa Azul,** also south of the Santiago Peninsula, drops off sharply but is noted for its wide stretch of golden sand beach.

BIRDING

Birding is good in several lagoons along the coast. As you go from Manzanillo past Las Brisas to Santiago, you'll pass **Laguna de Las Garzas (Lagoon of the Herons),** also known as Laguna de San Pedrito, where many white pelicans and huge herons fish in the water. They nest here in December and January. Directly behind downtown is the **Laguna de Cuyutlán** (follow the signs to Cuyutlán), where you'll usually find birds in abundance; species vary between summer and winter.

DIVING

Underworld Scuba–Scuba Shack ★★ (© **314/333-3678;** www.divemanzanillo.com), located at Blvd. M. de la Madrid Km 15, is owned by longtime resident and local diving expert Susan Dearing and conducts professional diving expeditions and classes. Susan's warm enthusiasm and intimate knowledge of the area make this one of my top recommendations for dive outfitters in Mexico. Many locations are so close to shore that there's no need for a boat. Close-in dives include the jetty, with coral growing on the rocks at 14m (46 ft.), and a nearby sunken frigate downed in 1959 at 8m (26 ft.). Divers can see abundant sea life, including coral reefs, sea horses, giant puffer fish, and moray eels. A dive requiring a boat costs $60 per person for one tank (with a three-person minimum) or $85 for two tanks ($10 discount if you have your own equipment). You can also rent weights and a tank for beach dives for $10. A three-stop snorkel trip costs $45. All guides are certified divemasters, and the shop offers PADI certification classes in intensive courses of various durations. The owner offers a 10% discount on your certification when you mention Frommer's. MasterCard and Visa are accepted.

ESCORTED TOURS

Because Manzanillo is so spread out, you might consider a city tour. Reputable local tour companies include **HECtours** (© 314/333-1707; www.hectours.com) and **Bahías Gemelas Travel Agency** (© 314/333-1000). Schedules are flexible; a half-day city tour costs around $25. Other tours include the daylong Colima Colonial Tour ($69), which stops at Colima's Archaeological Museum and principal colonial buildings, and passes the active volcano. Offerings change regularly, so ask about new tours.

FISHING

Manzanillo is famous for its fishing, particularly sailfish. Marlin and sailfish are abundant year-round. Winter is best for dolphin fish and dorado (mahimahi); in summer, wahoo and rooster fish are in greater supply. The international sailfish competition is held around the November 20 Revolution Day holiday, and the national sailfish competition is in February. You can arrange fishing through travel agencies or directly at the fishermen's cooperative (© 314/332-1031), located downtown where the fishing boats moor. Call from 6am to 2pm or 5 to 8pm. A fishing boat is approximately $45 for eight people to $55 for 12 people per hour, with most trips lasting about 5 hours.

GOLF

The 18-hole **La Mantarraya Golf Course** (© 314/331-0101) is open to nonguests as well as guests of Las Hadas. At one time, La Mantarraya was among the top 100 courses in the world, but newer entries have surpassed it. Still, the compact, challenging 18-hole course designed by Roy and Pete Dye is a beauty, with banana trees, blooming bougainvillea, and coconut palms at every turn. A lush and verdant place (12 of the 18 holes are played over water), it remains a favorite.

When the course was under construction, workers dug up pre-Hispanic ceramic figurines, idols, and beads where the 14th hole now lies. It is believed to have been an important ancient burial site. The course culminates with its signature 18th hole, with a drive to the island green off El Tesoro (the treasure) beach, directly in front of the Karminda Palace Resort. Local lore says this beach still may hold buried treasure from Spanish galleons, whose crews were the first to recognize the perfection of this natural harbor, and who used it during the 16th century as their starting point for voyages to the Pacific Rim. Greens fees are $150 for 18 holes, $90 for 9 holes; cart rental costs $50 for 18 holes and $35 for 9 holes.

The fabulous Isla Navidad Country Club 27-hole golf course associated with the **Grand Bay Hotel** (© 314/337-9024) in Barra de Navidad, an easy distance from Manzanillo, is also open to the public. The Robert von Hagge design is long and lovely, with each hole amid rolling, tropical landscapes. It is wide open, with big fairways and big greens, and features plenty of water (2 lagoon holes, 13 lakeside holes, and 8 holes along the Pacific). The greens fees, including a motorized cart, are $180 for 18 holes, $200 for 27 holes. Barra is about a 1- to 1 1/2-hour drive north of Manzanillo on Hwy. 200.

A MUSEUM

The **Museum of Archaeology and History** (© 314/332-2256) is a small but impressive structure that houses exhibits depicting the region's history, plus rotating displays of contemporary Mexican art. It's on Avenida Niños Héroes at Avenida Teniente Azueta, on the road leading between the downtown and Las Brisas areas. Every Friday evening, the museum hosts free cultural events, which might be a trio playing romantic ballads or a chamber music ensemble. Performances begin at 8pm. Hours are Tuesday through Saturday from 10am to 2pm and 5 to 8pm, Sunday from 10am to 1pm. *Note:* This museum was being renovated at press time.

SHOPPING

Manzanillo has numerous shops that carry Mexican crafts and clothing, mainly from Guadalajara. Almost all fall on downtown streets near the central plaza. Shopping downtown is an experience—for example, you'll find a shop bordering the plaza that sells a combination of shells, religious items (including shell-framed Virgin of Guadalupe nightlights), and orthopedic supplies. The Plaza Manzanillo is an American-style mall on the road to Santiago, and a traditional *tianguis* (outdoor) market in front of the entrance to Club Maeva sells touristy items from around Mexico. Most resort hotels also have boutiques or shopping arcades.

SUNSET CRUISES

To participate in this popular activity, buy tickets from a travel agent or your hotel tour desk. Most cost around $35. The trips vary in their combinations of drinks, music, and entertainment, and last 1¹/₂ to 2 hours. Departing from Las Hadas are **El Explorer** and **Antares.**

---

3 WHERE TO STAY

Manzanillo's strip of coastline consists of three areas: **downtown,** with its shops, markets, and commercial activity; **Las Brisas,** the hotel-lined beach area immediately north of the city; and **Santiago,** the town and peninsula, now virtually a suburb, to the north at the end of Playa Azul. Transportation by bus or taxi makes all three areas fairly convenient to each other. Reservations are recommended during the Easter, Christmas, and New Year's holidays.

DOWNTOWN

Hotel Colonial ★ An old favorite, this three-story colonial-style hotel sits in the central downtown district. Popular for its consistent quality, ambience, and service, it features beautiful blue-and-yellow tile and colonial-style carved doors and windows in the lobby and restaurant. Rooms provide basic comforts, with minimal furniture and red-tile floors. The hotel lies 1 block inland from the main plaza at Juárez and Galindo.

Av. México 100 and González Bocanegra, 28200 Manzanillo, Col. ✆ **314/332-1080,** -0668, or -1230. 42 units. $50 double. MC, V. Limited street parking. **Amenities:** Restaurant; bar. *In room:* A/C, cable TV, free Wi-Fi.

LAS BRISAS

Some parts of the Las Brisas area look run-down; however, it still lays claim to one of the best beaches in the area and is known for its constant gentle sea breezes—a pleasure in the summer.

Hotel La Posada ★ This charming inn has a bright-pink stucco facade with a large arch that leads to a broad tiled patio and swimming pool right next to the beach. Guest rooms incorporate exposed brick walls, tile floors, and simple furnishings with Mexican decorative accents. It remains popular with longtime travelers to Manzanillo. The atmosphere is casual and informal—help yourself to beer and soft drinks; at the end of your stay, owners Juan and Lisa Martinez will count the bottle caps you deposited in a bowl labeled with your room number. The restaurant, which also welcomes non–hotel guests, is open daily from 8am to 3pm. A meal costs around $6. Stop by for a drink at sunset; the bar's open until 10pm all year. The hotel lies at the end of Las Brisas Peninsula, closest to downtown, and is on the local Las Brisas bus route.

Av. Lázaro Cárdenas 201, Las Brisas (Apdo. Postal 135), 28200 Manzanillo, Col. ©/fax **314/333-1899.** www.hotel-la-posada.info. 23 units. High season $91 double; low season $68 double. Rates include full breakfast. MC, V. Free parking. **Amenities:** Restaurant; bar; Internet kiosk; outdoor pool. *In room:* A/C (in some), ceiling fan.

SANTIAGO

Five kilometers (3 miles) north of Las Brisas lies the wide Santiago Peninsula. The settlement of Salahua is on the highway where you enter the peninsula to reach the hotels Las Hadas, Plaza Las Glorias, and Tesoro Manzanillo, as well as the Mantarraya Golf Course. Buses from town marked LAS HADAS pass by these hotels every 20 minutes. Past the Salahua turnoff, at the end of the settlement of Santiago, an obscure road on the left is marked ZONA DE PLAYAS and leads to the hotels on the other side of the peninsula and Playa de Santiago.

Barceló Karmina Palace ★★ (Kids) The quality of rooms and services at this all-inclusive resort makes the newest of Manzanillo's hotels one of the area's best. The buildings resemble Maya pyramids, and guest rooms are all large suites, with rich wood accents, comfortable recessed seating areas with pull-out couches, and two 27-inch TVs in each room. The extra-large bathrooms have marble floors, twin black marble sinks, separate tubs, and glassed-in showers. Most rooms offer terraces or balconies with views of the ocean, overlooking the tropical gardens and swimming pools. Master suites feature spacious sun terraces with private splash pools, plus a full wet bar, refrigerator, and a large living room area with 42-inch TV. Two full-size bedrooms close off from the living/dining area. The kids' club provides a host of activities—all included in the price. The gym and European-style spa are exceptionally well equipped. If you're looking for a luxurious family vacation in Manzanillo, stay here.

Av. Vista Hermosa 13, Fracc. Península de Santiago, 28200 Manzanillo, Col. **888/234-6222** in the U.S. and Canada, or 01-800/507-4930, 314/334-1300, or 331-1313 in Mexico. Fax 314/334-1108. www.barcelo.com. 324 units. $240 and up double; $450 and up 2-bedroom suites for 4. Rates are all-inclusive. Special packages and Web specials available; ask about seasonal specials. 2 children 7 and younger stay free in parent's room. AE, MC, V. Free parking. **Amenities:** 3 restaurants; snack bar; 5 bars; nightclub; beach volleyball; children's program; concierge; health club; kayaks; 8 pools; room service; sailboards; men's and women's sauna & steam rooms; full spa facilities; tennis courts. *In room:* A/C, TV, hair dryer, minibar.

Brisas Las Hadas Golf Resort & Marina ★★ For me, Las Hadas is synonymous with a visit to Manzanillo. This iconic beachside resort designed in an all-white Moorish style lights up a side of the rocky Santiago peninsula. Rooms are spread over landscaped grounds and overlook the bay; cobbled lanes lined with colorful flowers and palms connect them. The resort is large but maintains an air of seclusion. (Motorized carts are on call for transportation within the property.) Views, room size and quality, and amenities differentiate the six types of accommodations. If you're not satisfied with your room, ask to be moved—some of the accommodations are in need of renovation. Understated and spacious, the better rooms feature white-marble floors, sitting areas, and large, comfortably furnished balconies. Nine suites have private pools. The lobby is a popular place for curling up in one of the overstuffed seating areas or, at night, for enjoying a drink and live music. A stunning free-form pool stretches out beside the small beach in front. Pete and Roy Dye designed La Mantarraya, the hotel's 18-hole, par-71 golf course.

Av. de los Riscos s/n, Santiago Peninsula, 28200 Manzanillo, Col. ⓒ **888/559-4329** in the U.S. and Canada, or 314/331-0101. www.brisas.com.mx. 234 units. High season $206–$327 double; $386–$626 Fantasy Suite; low season $175–$379 double, $386–$626 Fantasy Suite. AE, DC, MC, V. Free guarded parking. **Amenities:** 3 restaurants, including the elegant Legazpi (see "Where to Dine," below); 3 lounges and bars; babysitting; concierge; marina; 2 outdoor pools; room service; sailing cruises; scuba diving; snorkeling; water-skiing; small workout room. *In room:* A/C, TV, hair dryer, minibar.

Plaza Tucanes Villas & Resort ★ The sunset-colored walls of this pueblolike hotel ramble over a hillside on the Santiago Peninsula. The restaurant on top and most rooms afford a broad vista of other red-tiled rooftops and either the palm-filled golf course or the bay. It's one of Manzanillo's undiscovered resorts, known more to wealthy Mexicans than to Americans. Originally conceived as private condominiums, the accommodations were designed for living; each spacious unit is stylishly furnished, and very comfortable. Each has a huge living room; a small kitchen/bar; one, two, or three large bedrooms with tile or brick floors; large bathrooms with Mexican tiles; huge closets; and large furnished private patios with views. Some units contain whirlpool tubs, and a few rooms can be partitioned off and rented by the bedroom only. Rooms can be a long walk from the main entrance, through a succession of stairways and paths. If stair climbing bothers you, try to get a room by the restaurant and pool—you'll have a great view, and a hillside rail elevator goes straight from top to bottom.

Av. de Tesoro s/n, Santiago Peninsula, 28200 Manzanillo, Col. ⓒ **314/334-1625.** Fax 314/334-0090. www.plazatucanes.com.mx. 112 units. $146 double; $250 double all inclusive. Packages available. AE, MC, V. Free parking. **Amenities:** 2

restaurants, including Argentine steakhouse; babysitting (w/advance notice); beach club on Las Brisas beach, w/pool and small restaurant; kids' club; game area; mini golf; recreational park; outdoor pool; room service; transportation to and from beach club (once daily in each direction). *In room:* A/C, TV.

Tesoro Manzanillo Resort ★ (Kids) This 21-floor hotel, overlooking La Audiencia beach, offers all-inclusive package options and a full program of activities, dining, and entertainment. Its excellent kids' program makes it a top choice for families. Onsite is the Corsarlos Water Park, complete with water slides, pools, and activities. Architecturally, it mimics the white Moorish style of Las Hadas that has become so popular in Manzanillo. Inside, it's palatial in scale and awash in pale-gray marble. Room decor picks up the pale-gray theme with armoires that conceal the TV and minibar. Most standard rooms have two double beds or a king-size bed, plus a small table, chairs, and desk. Several rooms at the end of most floors are small, with one double bed, small porthole-size windows, no balcony, and no view. Most rooms, however, have balconies and ocean or hillside views. The 10 honeymoon suites have king-size beds and chaises. Junior suites have sitting areas with couches and large bathrooms. Scuba-diving lessons are held in the pool, and scuba-diving sites are within swimming distance of the shore.

Av. La Audiencia 1, Los Riscos, 28200 Manzanillo, Col. ℂ **866/998-3637** in the U.S., or 314/333-2000. Fax 314/333-2611 www.tesororesorts.com. 332 units. High season $230–$340 double; $240–$370 suite; low season $150 double, $200 suite. Rates are all-inclusive. AE, MC, V. Free parking. **Amenities:** 3 restaurants; 4 bars; grand pool on the beach; children's pool; currency exchange; health club w/exercise equipment, aerobics, and hot tub; men's and women's sauna and steam rooms; spa; room service; 4 lighted tennis courts. *In room:* A/C, TV, hair dryer, minibar.

---

4 WHERE TO DINE

LAS BRISAS

The Hotel La Posada (see "Where to Stay," above) offers breakfast to nonguests at its beachside restaurant; it's also a great place to mingle with other tourists and enjoy the sunset and cocktails.

La Toscana ★★★ (Finds) SEAFOOD/INTERNATIONAL You're in for a treat at La Toscana, one of Manzanillo's most popular and consistently reliable restaurants, located on the beach in Las Brisas. It's homey, casual, and small, so reservations are highly recommended. The exquisite cuisine belies the atmosphere, with starters that include escargot and salmon carpaccio. Among the grilled specialties are shrimp imperial wrapped in bacon, red snapper tarragon, dorado basil, sea bass with mango and ginger, and tender fresh lobsters (four to a serving). Live music frequently sets the scene.

Bulevar Miguel de la Madrid 3177. ℂ **314/333-2515.** Reservations highly recommended. Main courses $10–$30. MC, V. Daily 6:30–11pm. 100m (328 ft.) from Hotel Fiesta Mexicana.

Roca del Mar SEAFOOD   Previously located in the town center, the Roca del Mar has a new beachfront location and menu focused on seafood and, above all else, shrimp. Start with the tasty shrimp cocktail, shrimp prepared in lemon, or even shrimp dressed up in a coconut. The best main courses include snapper grilled with a hot spice, shrimp fettuccini, and a seafood chile relleno. There's even a shrimp hamburger, unusual as this may be. This casual open-air *palapa* restaurant is open for breakfast, too.

Blvd. Miguel de la Madrid 2333. ℂ **314/336-9097.** Main courses $8–$15. MC, V. Mon 9am–6:30pm; Tues–Sun 9am–8pm.

SANTIAGO ROAD

The restaurants below are on the Costera Madrid between downtown and the Santiago Peninsula, including the Salahua area.

Benedetti's Pizza PIZZA   There are several branches in town, so you'll probably find a Benedetti's not far from where you are staying. The variety is extensive; add some *chimichurri* sauce to your sesame-crust pizza to enhance the flavor. Benedetti's specializes in seafood pizza, such as smoked oyster and anchovy. You can also select from pasta, sandwiches, burgers, fajitas, salads, Mexican soups, cheesecake, and pie.

Bulevar Miguel de la Madrid, near the Las Brisas Glorietta on the ocean side (west). ℂ **314/333-1592** or 314/334-0141. Pizza $9–$12; main courses $3–$7. AE, MC, V. Daily 10am–10pm.

Bigotes II SEAFOOD   Locals flock to this large, breezy restaurant (the name translates as "Mustaches") by the water for the good food and festive atmosphere. Strolling singers serenade diners as they dig into large portions of grilled seafood, or their signature "Mustache Shrimp."

Puesta del Sol 3 (2nd location at Blvd. Costa M. de la Madrid 3157). ℂ **314/333-1236.** Main courses $10–$24. AE, MC, V. Daily noon–10pm. From downtown, follow the Costera Madrid past the Las Brisas turnoff; the restaurant is behind the Penas Coloradas Social Club, across from the beach.

El Fogón (Finds) MEXICAN   Locals consider this to be the best Mexican restaurant in town, almost hidden in a small garden setting. The menu features a selection of unique and traditional Mexican dishes. *Molcajetes* (meat, seafood, and vegetables grilled in a stone

dish) are the house specialty; varieties include shrimp, beef, and quail.
A variety of delicious tacos and fajitas are also served.

Bulevar Miguel de la Madrid across from Pacifico Azul. (C) **314/333-3094.** Main courses $9–$14. MC, V. Daily 1pm–midnight. From downtown, follow the Costera Madrid; the restaurant is located just before the Soriana grocery store.

Juanito's MEXICAN/BREAKFAST Manzanillo has few good options for breakfast, but this is one. The cheerful American-run eatery attracts Mexicans and tourists in equal numbers. Pancakes, waffles, and French toast are morning favorites, and customers love the fresh-fruit *licuados,* Mexico's version of smoothies. For lunch and dinner, simple American fare includes burgers, hot dogs, club sandwiches, fried chicken, and barbecue ribs. Diners are served at casual wood tables with green tablecloths. Be prepared for a short wait on weekend mornings.

Bulevar Miguel de la Madrid Km 14. (C) **314/333-7405.** www.juanitos.com. Breakfast $3–$5; main courses $3–$9. AE, MC, V. Daily 8am–11pm.

SANTIAGO PENINSULA

Legazpi ★★ INTERNATIONAL This is a top choice in Manzanillo for sheer elegance, gracious service, and outstanding food. The candlelit tables are set with silver and flowers. Enormous bell-shaped windows on two sides show off the sparkling bay below. The sophisticated menu includes prosciutto with melon marinated in port wine, crayfish bisque, broiled salmon, roast duck, lobster, veal, and flaming desserts.

In the Brisas Las Hadas hotel, Santiago Peninsula. (C) **314/331-0101.** Main courses $8.50–$16. AE, MC, V. High season Thurs–Sat 6:30–11:30pm; closed low season.

---

5 MANZANILLO AFTER DARK

Nightlife in Manzanillo is much more exuberant than you might expect, but then, Manzanillo is not only a resort town—it's a thriving commercial center. Clubs and bars change from year to year, so check with your concierge for current hot spots. Some area clubs have a dress code prohibiting shorts or sandals, principally applying to men.

El Bar de Félix, between Salahua and Las Brisas by the Avis rental-car office ((C) **314/333-1875**), is open Tuesday through Sunday from 2pm to midnight and has an $8 minimum consumption charge. Music ranges from salsa and ranchero to rock and house—it's the most consistently lively place in town, with pool tables and TVs broadcasting sports events. Also very popular—with a built-in crowd—is the nightclub at the **Club Maeva Hotel & Resort** (© **01-800/849-1987** in Mexico), on the inland side of the main highway, north of the Santiago Peninsula. It's open Tuesday, Thursday, and Saturday from 11pm to 2am. Couples are given preferential entrance. Nonguests are welcome but must pay an entrance fee, typically $20 to $30, after which all drinks are included. Note that when Club Maeva is fully booked, entrance to nonguests may be difficult to impossible—ask your hotel front desk if they can secure a pass for you. The fee varies depending on the night of the week and the time of year.

Settling into Guadalajara

by David Baird

As the homeland of mariachi music, the jarabe tapatío (the Mexican hat dance), and tequila, Guadalajara is widely considered the most Mexican of cities. Despite the fact that it's the nation's second-largest metropolis (with 3.5 million inhabitants, it's a very distant second to Mexico City), it isn't hard to navigate, and residents are friendly and helpful. Visitors can enjoy big-city pleasures without the big-city hassles that would beset them in the capital.

While in Guadalajara, you will undoubtedly come across the word *tapatío* (or *tapatía*). In the early days, people from the area were known to trade in threes, called *tapatíos*. The locals came to be called Tapatíos as well, and now the word *tapatío* has come to mean any person, thing, or even style that comes from Guadalajara.

---

1 ORIENTATION

GETTING THERE & DEPARTING

BY PLANE   Guadalajara's **Don Miguel Hidalgo y Costilla International Airport** (GDL) is a half-hour ride from the city. Taxi tickets, priced by zone, are for sale in front of the airport (210 pesos to downtown).

Major Airlines   See "Airline, Hotel & Car Rental Websites," p. 165, for a list of websites for international airlines serving Mexico. Numbers in Guadalajara are: **AeroMar** (✆ 33/3615-8509), **AeroMéxico** (✆ 01-800/021-4010), **American** (✆ 01-800/904-6000), **Click** (✆ 01-800/1225425), **Continental** (✆ 01-800/900-5000), **Delta** (✆ 33/3630-3530), **Mexicana** (✆ 01-800/502-2000), and **United** (✆ 33/3616-9489).

Of the smaller airlines, **Aviacsa** (✆ 33/3123-1751) connects to Los Angeles, Las Vegas, Houston, and Chicago. **Azteca** (✆ 33/3630-4615) offers service to and from Mexico City, and from there to several other cities in Mexico. **Allegro** (✆ 33/3647-7799) operates flights to and from Oakland and Las Vegas via Tijuana. **Alaska Airlines** (© 01-800/426-0333) flies to Los Angeles and Reno.

BY CAR   Guadalajara is at the hub of several four-lane toll roads (called *cuotas* or *autopistas*), which cut travel time considerably but are expensive. From Nogales on the **U.S. border,** follow Hwy. 15 south (21 hr.). From **Tepic,** a quicker route is toll road 15D (5 hr.; 320 pesos). From **Puerto Vallarta,** go north on Hwy. 200 to Compostela; toll road 68D heads east to join the Tepic toll road. Total time is $5^1/_2$ hours, and the tolls add up to 300 pesos. From **Barra de Navidad,** on the coast southeast of Puerto Vallarta, take Hwy. 80 northeast ($4^1/_2$ hr.). From **Manzanillo,** you might also take this road, but toll road 54D through Colima to Guadalajara ($3^1/_2$ hr.; 260 pesos) is faster. From **Mexico City,** take toll road 15D (7 hr.; 550 pesos).

BY BUS   Two bus stations serve Guadalajara. The old one, south of downtown, is for buses to Tequila and other nearby towns; the new one, 10km ($6^1/_4$ miles) southeast of downtown, is for longer trips.

The Old Bus Station   For destinations within 100km (62 miles) of town, including the Lake Chapala area, go to the old bus terminal, on Niños Héroes off Calzada Independencia Sur. For Lake Chapala, take **Transportes Guadalajara-Chapala,** which runs frequent buses and *combis* (minivans).

The New Bus Station   The **Central Camionera** is 15 to 30 minutes from downtown. The station has seven terminals connected by a covered walkway. Each terminal houses bus lines, offering first- and second-class service for different destinations. Buy bus tickets ahead of time from a travel agency in Guadalajara. Ask at your hotel for the closest to you. There are several major bus lines. The best service (big seats and lots of room) is provided by **ETN.**

VISITOR INFORMATION

The **State of Jalisco Tourist Information Office** is at Calle Morelos 102 (© **33/3668-1600,** -1601; http://visita.jalisco.gob.mx) in the Plaza Tapatía, at Paseo Degollado and Paraje del Rincón del Diablo. It's open Monday through Friday from 9am to 8pm, and Saturday, Sunday, and festival days 10am to 2pm. You can get maps, a monthly calendar of cultural events, and good information. Of the **city tourist information booths,** one is in Plaza Liberación (directly behind the cathedral), another in Plaza Guadalajara (directly in front of the cathedral). These are open daily from 9am to 1pm and 3 to 7pm. Ask at either of these about free weekend walking tours.

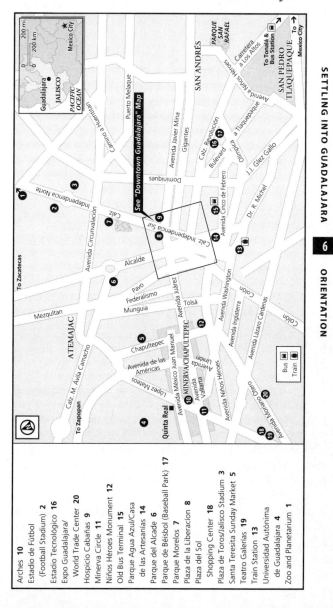

Arches **10**
Estadio de Fútbol
(Football Stadium) **2**
Estadio Tecnologico **16**
Expo Guadalajara/
   World Trade Center **20**
Hospicio Cabañas **9**
Minerva Circle **11**
Niños Héroes Monument **12**
Old Bus Terminal **15**
Parque Agua Azul/Casa
   de las Artesanías **14**
Parque del Alcade **6**
Parque de Béisbol (Baseball Park) **17**
Parque Morelos **7**
Plaza de la Liberacion **8**
Plaza del Sol
Shopping Center **18**
Plaza de Toros/Jalisco Stadium **3**
Santa Teresita Sunday Market **5**
Teatro Galerías **19**
Train Station **13**
Universidad Autónima
   de Guadalajara **4**
Zoo and Planetarium **1**

The **Centro Histórico (city center),** with all its plazas, churches, and museums, will obviously be of interest to the visitor. The **west side** is Guadalajara's modern, cosmopolitan district. In the northwest corner is **Zapopan,** home of Guadalajara's patron saint. On the opposite side of the city from Zapopan, in the southeast corner, are the craft centers of **Tlaquepaque** and **Tonalá.**

The main artery for traffic from downtown to the west side is **Avenida Vallarta.** It starts downtown as **Juárez.** The main arteries for returning to downtown are **México** and **Hidalgo,** both north of Vallarta. Vallarta heads due west, where it intersects another major artery, **Avenida Adolfo López Mateos,** at **Fuente Minerva** (or simply La Minerva, or Minerva Circle). Minerva Circle, a 15-minute drive from downtown, is the central point of reference for the west side. To go to Zapopan from downtown, take **Avenida Avila Camacho,** which you can pick up on Alcalde; it takes 20 minutes by car. To Tlaquepaque and Tonalá, take **Calzada Revolución.** Tlaquepaque is 8km (5 miles) from downtown and takes 15 to 20 minutes by car; Tonalá is 5 minutes farther. Another major viaduct, **Calzada Lázaro Cárdenas,** connects the west side to Tlaquepaque and Tonalá, bypassing downtown.

THE NEIGHBORHOODS IN BRIEF

Centro Histórico   The heart of the city encompasses many plazas, the cathedral, and several historic buildings and museums. Here, too, are the striking murals of José Clemente Orozco, one of the great Mexican muralists. Theaters, restaurants, shops, and clubs dot the area, and an enormous market rounds out the attractions. All of this is in a space roughly 12 blocks by 12 blocks—an easy area to explore on foot, with several plazas and pedestrians-only areas. To the south is a large green space called Parque Agua Azul.

West Side   This is the swanky part of town, with the fine restaurants, luxury hotels, boutiques, and galleries, as well as the American, British, and Canadian consulates. It's a large area best navigated by taxi.

Zapopan   Founded in 1542, Zapopan is a suburb of Guadalajara. In its center is the 18th-century basilica, the home of Guadalajara's patron saint, the Virgin of Zapopan. The most interesting part of Zapopan is clustered around the temple and can be explored on foot. It has a growing arts and nightlife scene.

Tlaquepaque This was a village of artisans (especially potters) that grew into a market center. In the last 30 years, it has attracted designers from all over Mexico. Every major form of art and craft is for sale here: furniture, pottery, glass, jewelry, woodcarvings, leather goods, sculptures, and paintings. The shops are sophisticated, yet Tlaquepaque's center retains a small-town feel that makes door-to-door browsing enjoyable and relaxing.

Tonalá This has remained a town of artisans. Plenty of stores sell mostly local products from the town's more than 400 workshops. You'll see wrought iron, ceramics, blown glass, and papier-mâché. A busy street market operates each Thursday and Sunday.

2 GETTING AROUND

BY TAXI Taxis are the easiest way to get around town. Most have meters, and though some drivers are reluctant to use them, you can insist that they do. There are three rates: for day, night, and suburbia. On my last visit, typical fares were: downtown to the west side, 70 to 90 pesos; downtown or west side to Tlaquepaque, 70 to 100 pesos; to the new bus station, 90 pesos; to the airport, 180 to 220 pesos.

BY CAR Familiarize yourself with the main traffic arteries (see "City Layout," above) before you get behind the wheel. Several important freeway-style thoroughfares crisscross the city. **Dr. R. Michel** leads south from the town center toward Tlaquepaque. Use **González Gallo** for the return direction. **Avenida Vallarta** starts out downtown as **Juárez,** heads west past La Minerva, and eventually feeds onto **Hwy. 15,** bound for Tequila and Puerto Vallarta.

BY BUS For the visitor, the handiest route is the **TUR 706,** which runs from the Centro Histórico southeast to Tlaquepaque (10 pesos), the Central Camionera (the new bus station), and Tonalá. You can catch this bus on Av. 16 de Septiembre. The same bus runs in the reverse direction back to the downtown area.

The **electric bus** is handy for travel between downtown and the Minerva area (5 pesos). It bears the sign PAR VIAL and runs east along Hidalgo and west along the next street to the north, Calle Independencia (not Calzada Independencia). Hidalgo passes along the north side of the cathedral. The Par Vial goes as far east as Mercado Libertad and as far west as Minerva Circle. The city also has a light rail system, **Tren Ligero,** but it doesn't serve areas that are of interest to visitors.

Fast Facts Guadalajara

American Express The local office is at Av. Vallarta 2440, Plaza los Arcos, Local A-1 (© **33/3818-2323**); it's open Monday through Friday from 9am to 6pm, Saturday from 9am to noon.

Area Code The telephone area code is **33.**

Books, Newspapers & Magazines **Gonvil,** a popular book-store chain, has a branch across from Plaza de los Hombres Ilustres on Avenida Hidalgo, and another a few blocks south at Av. 16 de Septiembre 118 (Alcalde becomes 16 de Septiembre south of the cathedral). It carries few English selections. **Sanborn's,** at the corner of Juárez and 16 de Septiembre, does a good job of keeping English-language periodicals in stock, but most are specialty magazines. Many newsstands sell the two English local papers, the *Guadalajara Reporter* and the *Guadalajara Weekly.* For the widest selection of English-language books, try **Sandi Bookstore,** Av. Tepeyac 718 (© **33/3121-0863**), in the Chapalita neighborhood on the west side.

Business Hours Store hours are Monday through Saturday from 10am to 2pm and 4 to 8pm.

Climate & Dress Guadalajara's weather is mostly mild. From November through March, you'll need a sweater in the evening. The warmest months, April and May, are hot and dry. From June through September, the city gets afternoon and evening showers that keep the temperature a bit cooler, but it seems as though the local climate is getting warmer. Dress in Guadalajara is conservative; attention-getting sportswear (short shorts, halters, and the like) is out of place.

Consulates The **American Consular offices** are at Progreso 175 (© **33/3268-2200,** -2100). Other consulates include the **Canadian Consulate,** Mariano Otero 1249, Col. Rinconada del Bosque (© **33/3671-4740**); the **British Consulate,** Calle Jesús Rojas 20, Col. Los Pinos (© **33/3343-2296**); and the **Australian Consulate,** López Cotilla 2018, Col. Arcos Vallarta (© **33/3615-7418**). These offices all keep roughly the same hours: Monday through Friday from 8am to 1pm.

Currency Exchange Three blocks south of the cathedral, on López Cotilla, between Corona and Degollado, are more than 20 *casas de cambio.* Almost all post their rates, which are usually better than bank rates, minus the long lines.

Elevation Guadalajara sits at 1,700m (5,576 ft.).

Emergencies The emergency phone number is ℭ **060.**

Hospitals For medical emergencies, visit the **Hospital México-Americano,** Cólomos 2110 (ℭ **33/3642-7152** or 33/3641-3141).

Internet Access Most of the big hotels have business centers that you can use. There are many Internet cafes in the Centro Histórico; the easiest way to find one is to ask a young person.

Language Classes Foreigners can study Spanish at the **Foreign Student Study Center,** University of Guadalajara, Calle Tomás V. Gómez 125, 44100 Guadalajara, Jal. (ℭ **33/3616-4399**). **IMAC** is a private Spanish school at Donato Guerra 180, in the Centro Histórico (ℭ **33/3613-1080**).

Police Tourists should first try to contact the Jalisco tourist information office in Plaza Tapatía (ℭ **33/3668-1600**). If you can't reach the office, call the municipal police at ℭ **33/3668-7983.**

Post Office The *correo* is at the corner of Carranza and Calle Independencia, about 4 blocks northeast of the cathedral. Standing in the plaza behind the cathedral, facing the Degollado Theater, walk to the left, and then turn left on Carranza; walk past the Hotel Mendoza, cross Calle Independencia, and look for the post office on the left. It's open Monday through Thursday from 9am to 5pm, Saturday from 10am to 2pm.

Safety Guadalajara doesn't have as much crime as Mexico City. Rarely do you hear of muggings. Crimes against tourists and foreign students are infrequent and most often take the form of purse snatching. Criminals usually work in teams and target travelers in busy places, such as outdoor restaurants. Keep jewelry out of sight. Should anyone spill something on you, be alert to your surroundings and step away—accidental spills are a common method for distracting the victim.

3 WHERE TO STAY

Rates shown are the standard rack rates and include the 17% tax. In 2008 and 2009, promotional rates were fairly easy to find, especially with the larger hotels. In some cases, the published rate had fallen, too. Big hotels also are apt to offer business discounts. In some of the cheaper hotels, air-conditioning is a bit feeble.

Most of the luxury hotels in Guadalajara are on the west side, which has the majority of the shopping malls, boutiques, fashionable restaurants, and clubs. The Centro Histórico is also a good option because there's a lot to do, all in walking distance. And Tlaquepaque is a comfortable place to stay—it's relaxing, in that it doesn't have the feel of a big city and is perfect for shoppers; the only drawback is that almost everything shuts down by 7 or 8pm.

Chain hotels not included below are Hilton, Marriott, Camino Real, Howard Johnson, Crowne Plaza, and Best Western.

VERY EXPENSIVE

Hotel Presidente InterContinental ★★★   This hotel offers the most comprehensive list of services and amenities in Guadalajara. The health club here is a standout among other hotels. The rooms are comfortable and quiet, with modern furnishings. Club rooms have discreet check-in, are on limited-access hallways, and come with extras. The extra privacy and services are good for Mexican soap opera stars or repeat guests who like having their preferences known in advance. If you're neither of these, opt for one of the other rooms. The lobby bar is popular; during the season, bullfighters relax here after *la corrida.* Standard rooms come as "superior" or "deluxe." Differences and price aren't that pronounced. The rooms are about the same size and come with attractive midsize bathrooms. Deluxe rooms have a few more amenities. Suites are large and come with large, attractive bathrooms.

Av. López Mateos Sur and Moctezuma (west side), 45050 Guadalajara, Jal. ℂ **800/327-0200** in the U.S. and Canada, or 33/3678-1234. Fax 33/3678-1222. www.interconti.com. 409 units. $224–$250 double; $265 club; $310 and up for suite. Internet promotional rates available. AE, DC, MC, V. Valet parking 45 pesos. **Amenities:** 2 restaurants; bar; babysitting; concierge; executive-level rooms; golf at nearby clubs; health club w/saunas, steam rooms, and whirlpools; outdoor heated pool; room service; smoke-free rooms. *In room:* A/C, TV w/pay movies, hair dryer, minibar, Wi-Fi.

Quinta Real ★★★   This chain specializes in properties that are suggestive of Mexico's heritage. No glass skyscraper here—two five-story buildings made of stone, wood, plaster, and tile capture the feel of Mexican colonial architecture. Suites vary quite a bit: Eight have brick cupolas, and some have balconies. All are large, with a split-level layout and antique decorative touches. And all come with large, great bathrooms with tub/showers. The "grand-class" suites have even bigger bathrooms, with Jacuzzi tubs. They are also a bit larger and come with a few extras, such as a stereo. You can choose between two doubles or one king-size bed. The hotel is 2 blocks from Minerva Circle in western Guadalajara. Ask for a room that doesn't face López Mateos.

9288 in the U.S. and Canada, or 33/3669-0600. Fax 33/3669-0601. www.quintareal. com. 76 suites. $195–$215 master suite; $210–$250 grand-class suite. AE, DC, MC, V. Free secure parking. **Amenities:** Restaurant; bar; babysitting; concierge; fitness room; golf at local club; outdoor heated pool; room service; smoke-free rooms; discounts at local day spa. *In room:* A/C, TV, hair dryer, high-speed Internet access, minibar.

Villa Ganz ★★★   This small, all-suite hotel is on the near west side of the city, near Avenida Chapultepec. It's one of the most comfortable places to stay in Guadalajara. Rooms are big, well furnished, and decorated with flair. Each holds a basket of fruit and a small bottle of wine on check-in. Bathrooms are large and well lit—some have tubs, others just showers. Bed choices include a king, a queen, or two twins. Beds come with down comforters (hypoallergenic option available). Rooms facing the garden are the quietest, but those facing the street are set back from the traffic and have double-glazed windows. The common rooms and rear garden are agreeable places to relax. Service is personal and helpful. Guests can contract with a guide or driver at the hotel. In-room dining can be arranged with one of three nearby restaurants, or arrangements can be made to bring in a chef.

López Cotilla 1739 (btw. Bolivar and San Martín, west side), 44140 Guadalajara, Jal. ℂ **800/728-9098** in the U.S. and Canada, or 33/3120-1416. www.villaganz.com. 10 suites. $234 junior suite; $292 master suite; $328 grand master suite. Rates include continental breakfast. Internet specials often available. AE, MC, V. Free secure parking. Children 11 and under not accepted. **Amenities:** Concierge; golf and tennis at local club; room service. *In room:* A/C, TV, hair dryer, Wi-Fi.

EXPENSIVE

Holiday Inn Hotel and Suites Centro Histórico ★★   This six-story downtown property has comfortable guest rooms and a handy downtown location—just a few blocks from the main square. All rooms were remodeled in 2007, with updated amenities, plush mattresses, and good light. The size is good, and the furniture is comfortable; bathrooms in standard rooms are midsize and well equipped, with ample counter space. The suites are larger, with a few more amenities. Room rates include transportation to (but not from) the airport.

Av. Juárez 211, Centro Histórico, 44100 Guadalajara. Jal. ℂ **800/465-4329** in the U.S. and Canada, 01-800/009-9900 in Mexico, or 33/3560-1200. www.holiday-inn. com. 90 units. $105–$138 double; $120–$150 suite; $170–$204 suite with Jacuzzi. Ask about promotional rates. AE, MC, V. Free secure parking. **Amenities:** Restaurant; bar; fitness room; room service; smoke-free rooms. *In room:* A/C, TV, hair dryer, minibar, Wi-Fi.

Hotel de Mendoza On a quiet street next to the Degollado Theater and Plaza Tapatía, 2 blocks from the cathedral, the Mendoza has perhaps the best location of any downtown hotel. The decor would best be described as a stab at old Spanish, with wood paneling and old-world accents. Standard rooms are midsize. Bed choices are one queen, two full, or two queens. Bathrooms are midsize, with so-so lighting. Suites have an additional sitting area and larger bathrooms, with the recent addition of Jacuzzi tubs. Rooms face the street, an interior courtyard, or the pool. *Note:* The bath towels are the narrowest I've ever seen—obviously the brainchild of a demented cost-cutting expert. If the hotel hasn't changed these, ask for a couple extra after you check in.

Carranza 16, Centro Histórico, 44100 Guadalajara, Jal. ✆ **33/3942-5151.** Fax 33/3613-7310. www.demendoza.com.mx. 104 units. 1,200 pesos double; 1,350 pesos suite. Discounts sometimes available. AE, MC, V. Secure parking 40 pesos. **Amenities:** Restaurant; bar; fitness room; Jacuzzi; small outdoor pool; room service; smoke-free rooms. *In room:* A/C, TV, hair dryer, Wi-Fi.

MODERATE

Hotel Morales ★★ A historical hotel that's attractive and comfortable, the Morales is a good choice for anyone wishing to stay downtown. The standard rooms are called either *suite sencilla* (one queen bed) or *suite doble* (two double beds). The hotel recently replaced all its mattresses, so the beds aren't as firm as they used to be. The rooms are medium or large and come with Pergo floors. The bathrooms are quite attractive, with ceramic-tile floors and good-looking countertops. The showers are strong. The rooms that face the street have balconies with double-glazed windows that do a good job at screening the noise. The imperial suites offer a lot for the money, with super-large bathrooms equipped with a two-person Jacuzzi tub and a separate shower. All rooms are set around an arcaded lobby holding an attractive bar area. There's live music on Thursday and Friday evenings.

Av. Corona 243 (corner of Prisciliano Sánchez) Centro Histórico, 44100 Guadalajara, Jal. ✆ **33/3658-5232.** Fax 33/3658-5239. www.hotelmorales.com.mx. 64 units. 1,050 pesos double; 1,350 pesos junior suite; 1,650 pesos imperial suite. AE, MC, V. Free sheltered parking. **Amenities:** Restaurant; bar; babysitting; fitness room; room service; smoke-free rooms. *In room:* A/C, TV, hair dryer, high-speed Internet access.

La Villa del Ensueño ★ This B&B in central Tlaquepaque is a lovely alternative to big-city hotels. A modern interpretation of traditional Mexican architecture, it contains small courtyards and well-tended grounds bordered by old stucco walls, with an occasional wrought-iron balcony or stone staircase. The rooms have more character

than most hotel lodgings. Doubles have either two twin or two double
beds. The hotel is about 8 blocks from the main plaza.

Fla. 305, 45500 Tlaquepaque, Jal. © **800/220-8689** in the U.S., or 33/3635-8792.
Fax 818/597-0637. www.villadelensueno.com. 20 units. $111 double; $122 deluxe
double; $146 junior suite. Rates include full breakfast and light laundry service. AE,
MC, V. Free valet parking. **Amenities:** Bar; indoor and outdoor pool. *In room:* A/C,
TV, hair dryer, Wi-Fi.

Old Guadalajara ★★ This downtown bed-and-breakfast recommends itself in many ways. In a colonial house, it's well located,
quiet, and beautiful. The rooms reflect the local scene; they speak of
Mexico without shouting it. They are large and airy, with high ceilings, tile floors, and comfortable bathrooms. The colonial architecture makes it possible to live without air-conditioning in the warm
months, and every room is equipped with a ceiling fan. The central
courtyard is cool and shaded by tall bamboo. The common rooms are
open to the courtyard and are stocked with material for readers curious about the city. Paul Callahan prepares filling breakfasts for his
guests using only natural ingredients.

Belén 236, Centro Histórico, 44100 Guadalajara, Jal. ©/fax **33/3613-9958.** www.
oldguadalajara.com. 5 units. $125 double. Rates include full breakfast. AE, MC, V
for deposit; no credit cards at B&B. No children 17 or younger. **Amenities:** Smoke-
free rooms. *In room:* Hair dryer, no phone.

Quinta Don José ★★ (Value) Good value, great location, friendly
English-speaking owners—there are a lot of reasons to like this small
establishment just 2 blocks from Tlaquepaque's main square. Rooms
run the gauntlet from midsize to extra large. They are comfortable,
attractive, and quiet, with some nice local touches. Most of the standard and deluxe doubles have a king or two double beds and an
attractive, midsize bathroom. A couple of them have small private
outdoor spaces. Some of the suites in back come with a full kitchen
and lots of space—more than twice the size of the usual suite, with
one king and one double bed. The breakfasts are good, and recently
the owners have installed a full restaurant open for dinner. Some lodgings just have a good feel to them, and this is one of them.

Reforma 139, 45500 Tlaquepaque, Jal. © **866/629-3753** in the U.S. and Canada,
or 33/3635-7522. www.quintadonjose.com. 15 units. $88 standard; $100 deluxe;
$129–$175 suite. Rates include full breakfast. AE, MC, V. Free secure parking. **Amenities:** Restaurant; bar; babysitting; heated outdoor pool; smoke-free rooms.
In room: A/C, TV, hair dryer, Wi-Fi.

INEXPENSIVE

Hotel Cervantes ★ (Value) This six-story downtown hotel offers
modern amenities at a good price. The rooms are attractive and midsize. They have wall-to-wall carpeting and tile bathrooms with ample

sink areas and tub/showers. The air-conditioning was weak the last time I stayed here. The lower price is for one double bed; the higher price, for a king or two doubles. This is not a noisy hotel, but if you require absolute quiet, request an interior room. The Cervantes is 6 blocks south and 3 blocks west of the cathedral.

Prisciliano Sánchez 442 (corner of Donato Guerra), Centro Histórico, 44100 Guadalajara, Jal. ✆/fax **33/3613-6686.** www.hotelcervantes.com.mx. 100 units. 750–850 pesos double; 1,100 pesos suite. AE, MC, V. Free secure parking. **Amenities:** Restaurant; lobby bar; babysitting; small outdoor heated pool; room service. *In room:* A/C, TV.

Hotel San Francisco Plaza (Value)

This colonial-style downtown hotel is both pleasant and a bargain. Most rooms are medium to large and comfortable, with attractive furnishings. All have rugs or carpeting, and most have tall ceilings. The hotel is built in colonial style around four courtyards, which contain fountains and potted plants. Rooms along the Sánchez Street side are much quieter now that the management has installed double windows. Some units along the back wall of the rear patio have small bathrooms. The San Francisco Plaza is 6 blocks south and 2 blocks east of the cathedral. The air-conditioning has recently been upgraded.

Degollado 267, Centro Histórico, 44100 Guadalajara, Jal. ✆ **33/3613-8954,** -8971. Fax 33/3613-3257. www.sanfranciscohotel.com.mx. 76 units. 550 pesos double. AE, MC, V. Free sheltered parking. **Amenities:** Restaurant; room service. *In room:* A/C, TV.

Plaza Los Reyes (Value)

Okay, so the rooms in this 10-story downtown hotel aren't anything special, but they do have good, individually controlled air-conditioning and strong showers, a rarity for budget hotels. The location is downtown near the market, which is central but in a somewhat decayed part of town. For entertainment, there's a fancy new multiplex cinema across the street that shows first-run Hollywood movies. Guest rooms are midsize and come with either two doubles or a king-size bed. Those on the mezzanine level are larger and often cost the same. Ask for a room facing away from the busy Calzada Independencia. Midsize bathrooms are clean, with good water pressure and plenty of hot water.

Calzada Independencia Sur 168, 44100 Guadalajara, Jal. ✆ **33/3613-9770,** -9775. 189 units. 520 pesos double. AE, MC, V. Free valet parking. **Amenities:** Restaurant; outdoor heated pool; room service; smoke-free rooms. *In room:* A/C, TV, Wi-Fi.

4 WHERE TO DINE

Guadalajara has many excellent restaurants either for fine dining or for typical local fare. Most of the fine-dining spots are on the west side. Tlaquepaque has some good choices, but most close by 8pm.

Good local fare can be had in the Centro Histórico, but for fine dining, head to western Guadalajara or, if it's early in the day, to Tlaquepaque. For a quick bite, there are several **Sanborn's** in the city. This is a popular national chain of restaurants known for their *enchiladas suizas* (enchiladas in cream sauce). If you're downtown and looking for baked goods and coffee, go to **El Globo** (© 33/3613-9926), an upscale bakery at the corner of Pedro Moreno and Degollado. This is also a chain with a couple more locations around Guadalajara. *Tip:* When taking a taxi, keep the address of the restaurant handy; taxi drivers cannot be relied upon to know where even the most popular restaurants are.

Local dishes include *birria* (goat or lamb covered in maguey leaves and roasted). It comes in a tomato broth or with the broth on the side. Another favorite is the *torta ahogada,* a sandwich with pork bathed in a tomato sauce. I'm not particularly fond of them. The most popular drink here is the *paloma,* which combines tequila, lots of lime juice, and grapefruit soda on ice. I am fond of these.

EXPENSIVE

Adobe Fonda ★★★ NUEVA COCINA   This restaurant shares space with a large store on pedestrians-only Independencia. The dining area is open and airy. Homemade bread and tostadas come to the table with an olive oil–based chili sauce, pico de gallo, and *requezón de epazote* (ricotta-like cheese with a Mexican herb). Among the soups are *crema de cilantro* and an interesting mushroom soup with a dark-beer broth. The main courses present some difficult decisions, with intriguing combinations of Mexican, Italian, and Argentine ingredients. Shrimp quesadillas accompanied by *chimichurri* with *nopal* cactus, filet in creamy *chile ancho* sauce, and the crab salad tower were all excellent. Sample the margaritas, too.

Francisco de Miranda 27 (corner of Independencia, Tlaquepaque). © 33/3657-2792. Reservations recommended on weekends. Main courses 150–230 pesos. AE, MC, V. Daily 12:30–6:30pm.

Chez Nené ★★★ FRENCH   In a small and pleasant open-air dining room, you can enjoy a quiet and leisurely meal of delicious French food. After doing just this, I had to meet the owner to see who was behind such work. He turned out to be a French expatriate (whose Mexican wife, Nené, is the restaurant's namesake) with strong ideas about food and dining. Freshness and quality of ingredients are what matter most, and everything (except stews and such) is cooked to order. The daily menu is on a chalkboard and depends on what the owner finds that morning at the market. There are always at least a dozen main courses. The waiter answered every question I put to him and gave excellent service.

Juan Palomar y Arias 426 (continuación Rafael Sanzio, west side). ☎ **33/3673-4564.** Reservations recommended on weekends. Main courses 120–200 pesos. AE, MC, V. Tues 4–11pm; Wed–Sat 1–5:30pm and 7:30–11:30pm; Sun 1–6pm.

El Sacromonte ★★★ ALTA COCINA   The food is so exquisite that I try to dine here every time I'm in Guadalajara. El Sacromonte emphasizes artful presentation and design: Order "Queen Isabel's Crown," and you'll be served a dish of shrimp woven together in the shape of a crown and covered in divine lobster-and-orange sauce. Or try quesadillas with rose petals in a deep-colored strawberry sauce. For soup, consider *el viejo progreso* for its unlikely combination of flavors (blue cheese and chipotle chili). The menu features amusing descriptions in verse. The main dining area is a shaded, open-air patio. The restaurant isn't far from the downtown area, on the near west side.

In the building next door, the owners have opened an updated version of the classic Mexican bar where one drinks while snacking on complimentary *botanas.* You can also order from a limited menu. The place is called **El Duende.**

Pedro Moreno 1398 (corner of Calle Colonias, west side). ☎ **33/3825-5447** or 33/3827-0663. Reservations recommended. Main courses 130–210 pesos. MC, V. Mon–Sat 1:30pm–midnight; Sun 1:30–6pm.

La Tequila ★★ MEXICAN   At its new location, about a block from where it used to be, this restaurant churns out Mexican standards such as *chalupas poblanas,* as well as versions of trendy contemporary Mexican cooking, including pasta stuffed with shrimp and *huitlacoche,* grilled-vegetable salad, and *molcajetes de arrachera* (fajitas with slices of chiles and onions that are cooked and served in a three-legged stone vessel). The cooking is great, the place is lively (the locals love it), and the decorative touches, such as trimmed agaves, give the dining areas a regional point of reference. Indoor/outdoor dining areas and a popular upstairs bar make up the majority of the restaurant. *Tip:* If this place is too crowded or you're simply looking for quieter dining, go to the original site 1 block away (Av. Mexico 2916), where you'll find a restaurant called **La Divina Tentación** (☎ **33/3642-7242**). The menu is similar, tending slightly more toward the style of cooking in Mexico City.

Av. México 2830 (at Napoleón, west side). ☎ **33/3640-3440** or 33/3640-3110. Reservations recommended. Main courses 100–200 pesos. AE, MC, V. Mon–Sat 1pm–midnight; Sun 1–6pm.

MODERATE

Hostería del Angel ★★ TAPAS/SPANISH DELI/WINE BAR   Sip wine and munch on a few tapas in this comfortable patio restaurant and wine bar just a few blocks from the basilica in Zapopan. The chef-owner cooked for years in Spain, where he became fascinated with the making of cheeses and deli meats such as Spanish *jamón serrano*. He serves a variety of tapas, and his baguette sandwiches are popular with the locals. The menu doesn't do a good job of explaining the dishes, so don't hesitate to ask the waitstaff for explanations. Most of the tapas are under the heading "Por la noche," which also includes sandwiches and the *rotolata*—vegetables and cold cuts surrounded by a thin layer of crispy cheese, which is a house specialty. Acoustic music plays from 9 to 11pm Monday through Saturday. The restaurant is a half-block off the pedestrian-only *calzada,* which leads to the plaza in front of the basilica. For breakfast you can get the traditional *molletes.*

5 de Mayo 260, Zapopan (west side). ©/fax **33/3656-9516.** Reservations recommended. Tapas 40–90 pesos; main courses 100–150 pesos. MC, V. Mon–Sat 9am–midnight; Sun 9am–8pm.

I Latina FUSION Warehouse chic with a porcine motif (the owner tells me that the pig is a symbol of abundance in Thailand) is the look here. The menu is absurdly small but is supplemented with lots of daily specials. On my last visit, I sampled a steak with a coffee crust with shoestring sweet potato fries and tossed greens scattered about the plate (quite good), a chicken in peanut sauce that was okay, and a stuffed filet of snapper that was quite tasty. This is a good place for people-watching—you get to see a portion of Guadalajara's hip, intellectual crowd, who enjoy the antiestablishment surroundings, including the metal and plastic tables and chairs. My main problem is the noise, which at times gets to be too much. If you're looking for quiet dining, go elsewhere. Cabs have a hard time finding this place, despite the fact that it's almost right off of Minerva Circle. It's not that difficult—Inglaterra faces the railroad tracks.

Av. Inglaterra (west side). © **33/3647-7774.** Reservations recommended. Main courses 90–180 pesos. MC, V. Wed–Sat 7:30pm–1am; Sun 2–6pm.

La Fonda de San Miguel (Moments) MEXICAN My favorite way to enjoy a good meal in Mexico is to have it in an elegant colonial courtyard. I love the contrast between the bright, noisy street and the cool, shaded patio. This restaurant is in the former convent of Santa Teresa de Jesús. While you enjoy the stone arches and gurgling fountain, little crisp tacos and homemade bread appear at the table. For main courses, try the shrimp *al tequila,* or perhaps the *chiles en nogada* if it's the season. Traditional *mole poblano* is also on the menu. Thursday to Saturday, musicians perform from 3 to 5pm and 9 to 11pm.

Donato Guerra 25 (and Pedro Moreno, downtown). © **33/3613-0809.** Reservations recommended on weekends. Breakfast 50–80 pesos; main courses 90–160 pesos. AE, MC, V. Mon 8:30am–9pm; Tues–Sat 8:30am–midnight.

La Trattoria Pomodoro Ristorante ★ ITALIAN   Good food, good service, and moderate prices make this restaurant perennially popular. The price of pastas and main courses includes a visit to the well-stocked salad bar. Recommendable menu items include the combination pasta plate (lasagna, fettuccini Alfredo, and spaghetti), shrimp linguine, and chicken parmigiana. The Italian owner likes to stock lots of wines from the motherland. The dining room is attractive and casual, with comfortable furniture and separate seating for smokers and nonsmokers.

Niños Héroes 3051 (west side). ℂ 33/3122-1817. Reservations recommended, but not accepted during holidays. Pasta 80–100 pesos; main courses 80–120 pesos. AE, MC, V. Daily 1pm–midnight.

Mariscos Progreso SEAFOOD   On a large, open patio shaded by trees and tile roofs, waiters navigate among the tables carrying large platters of delicious seafood. Mexicans do a wonderful job with seafood, and this popular restaurant does the tradition proud. Grilling over wood is the specialty here, but the kitchen's repertoire includes all the Mexican standards. For a sampling of grilled favorites, try the *parrillada* for two. Sometimes there's quite a bit of ambience, with mariachis adding to the commotion. At other times, the crowd thins and one can rest peacefully from the exertions of shopping with a cold drink. It's a half-block from the Parián.

Progreso 80, Tlaquepaque. ℂ 33/3657-4995. Reservations not accepted. Main courses 100–150 pesos. AE, MC, V. Daily 11am–7pm.

INEXPENSIVE

Café Madrid MEXICAN   This little coffee shop is like many coffee shops used to be—a social institution where people come in, greet each other and the staff by name, and chat over breakfast or coffee and cigarettes. Change comes slowly here. For example, despite the fact that it's an informal place, the waiters wear white jackets with black bow ties, as they did 20 years ago. The coffee and Mexican breakfasts are good, as is the standard Mexican fare served in the afternoon. The front room opens to the street, with a small lunch counter and another room in the back.

Juárez 264 (btw. Corona and 16 de Septiembre, downtown). ℂ 33/3614-9504. Breakfast 25–40 pesos; main courses 60–90 pesos. No credit cards. Daily 7:30am–10:30pm.

La Chata Restaurant REGIONAL/MEXICAN   If you're staying downtown, don't let this place slip off your radar. It does a good job with all the Mexican classics and some regional specialties as well. Unlike most restaurants, this one has the kitchen in front and the dining area in back. For a reasonable sum, you can get a filling bowl of *pozole*. They also offer flautas, *sopes,* quesadillas, and guacamole. There are also traditional *mole* and a couple of combination plates. The chairs are comfortable, and you hang out with lots of locals.

Corona 126 (btw. Juárez and López Cotilla, downtown). © **33/3613-0588.** Reservations not accepted. Breakfast 40–60 pesos; main courses 60–100 pesos. AE, DC, MC, V. Daily 8am–midnight.

La Fonda de la Noche ★★ (Finds) MEXICAN   For a host of reasons, this is my favorite place in the city for a simple supper. The limited menu is excellent, the surroundings are comfortable and inviting, the lighting is perfect, and there's a touch of nostalgia for the Mexico of the '40s, '50s, and '60s. It's not far from downtown or the west side; take a cab to the intersection of Jesús and Reforma, and, when you get there, look for a door behind a small hedge. There's no sign. It's a house with five fun dining rooms. Only Spanish is spoken, and the menu is simple. To try a little of everything, order the *plato combinado,* a combination plate that comes with an *enchilada de medio mole,* an *empanada* called a *media luna,* a *tostada,* and a *sope.* The owner is Carlos Ibarra, an artist from the state of Durango. He has decorated the place with traditional Mexican pine furniture and cotton tablecloths and his personal collection of paintings, mostly the works of close friends. On weekends, La Fonda offers *chiles en nogada.*

Jesús 251 (corner with Reforma, Col. El Refugio). © **33/3827-0917.** Reservations not accepted. Main courses 60–100 pesos. MC, V. Tues–Sun 7:30pm–midnight.

Los Itacates Restaurant ★ (Value) MEXICAN   The Mexican equivalent of down-home cooking at reasonable prices. Office workers pack the place between 2 and 4pm weekdays, and there's a good crowd on weekend nights, but at other times you'll have no problem finding a table. You can dine outdoors in a shaded sidewalk area or in one of the three dining rooms. The atmosphere is bright and colorful. Specialties include *lomo adobado* and chiles rellenos. *Pollo Itacates* is a quarter of a chicken, two cheese enchiladas, potatoes, and rice. Los Itacates is 5 blocks north of Avenida Vallarta. In the evenings, they serve tacos and other *antojitos.*

Chapultepec Norte 110 (west side). © **33/3825-1106,** -9551. Reservations accepted on weekends and holidays. Breakfast buffet 60 pesos; tacos 12 pesos; main courses 50–80 pesos. MC, V. Mon–Sat 8am–11pm; Sun 8am–7pm.

Exploring Guadalajara & Beyond

by David Baird

1 WHAT TO SEE & DO

SPECIAL EVENTS

There's always something going on from September to December. In September, when Mexicans celebrate independence from Spain, Guadalajara goes all out, with a full month of festivities. The celebrations kick off with the **Encuentro Internacional del Mariachi** (www. mariachi-jalisco.com.mx), in which mariachi bands from around the world play before knowledgeable audiences and hold sessions with other mariachis. Bands come from as far as Japan and Russia, and the event takes on a curious postmodern hue. Concerts are held in several venues. In the Degollado Theater, you can hear orchestral arrangements of classic mariachi songs with solos by famous mariachis. You might be acquainted with many of the classics without even knowing it. The culmination is a parade of thousands of mariachis and *charros* (Mexican cowboys) through downtown. It starts the first week of September.

On **September 15,** a massive crowd assembles in front of the Governor's Palace to await the traditional *grito* (shout for independence) at 11pm. The *grito* commemorates Father Miguel Hidalgo de Costilla's cry for independence in 1810. The celebration features live music on a street stage, spontaneous dancing, fireworks, and shouts of *"¡Viva México!"* and *"¡Viva Hidalgo!"* The next day is the official Independence Day, with a traditional parade; the plazas downtown resemble a country fair and market, with booths, games of chance, stuffed-animal prizes, cotton candy, and candied apples. Live entertainment stretches well into the night.

On **October 12, a procession ★★** honoring Our Lady of Zapopan celebrates the feast day of the Virgin of Zapopan. Around dawn, her small, dark figure begins the 5-hour ride from the Cathedral of Guadalajara to the suburban Basilica of Zapopan (see "Other Attractions," below). The original icon dates from the mid-1500s; the procession began 200 years later. Today crowds spend the night along the route and vie for position as the Virgin approaches. She travels in a gleaming new car (virginal, in that it must never have had the ignition turned on), which her caretakers pull through the streets. During the months leading up to the feast day, the figure visits churches all over the city. You will likely see neighborhoods decorated with paper streamers and banners honoring the Virgin's visit to the local church.

The celebration has grown into a month-long event, **Fiestas de Octubre,** which kicks off with an enormous parade, usually on the first Sunday or Saturday of the month. Festivities include performing arts, *charreadas* (rodeos), bullfights, art exhibits, regional dancing, a food fair, and a Day of Nations incorporating all the consulates in Guadalajara. By the time this is over, you enter the **holiday season of November and December,** with Revolution Day (Nov 20), the Virgin of Guadalupe's feast day (Dec 12), and several other celebrations.

DOWNTOWN GUADALAJARA

The most easily recognized building in the city is the **cathedral ★**, around which four open plazas form the shape of a Latin cross. Later a long swath of land was cleared to extend the open area from Plaza Liberación east to the Instituto Cultural Cabañas, creating **Plaza Tapatía.**

Construction on the cathedral started in 1561 and continued into the 18th century. Over such a long time, it was inevitable that remodeling would take place before the building was ever completed. The result is an unusual facade—an amalgam of several styles, including baroque, neoclassical, and Gothic. An 1818 earthquake destroyed the original large towers; their replacements were built in the 1850s, inspired by designs on the bishop's dinner china. Blue and yellow are Guadalajara's colors. The nave is airy and majestic. Items of interest include a painting in the sacristy ascribed to the 17th-century Spanish artist Bartolomé Estaban Murillo (1617–82).

On the cathedral's south side is the **Plaza de Armas,** the oldest and loveliest of the plazas. A cast-iron Art Nouveau bandstand is its dominant feature. Made in France, it was a gift to the city from the dictator Porfirio Díaz in the 1890s. The female figures on the bandstand exhibited too little clothing for conservative Guadalajarans, who clothed them. The dictator, recognizing when it's best to let the people have their way, said nothing.

Facing the plaza is the **Palacio del Gobierno ★★**, a broad, low structure built in 1774. The facade blends Spanish and Moorish elements and holds several eye-catching details. Inside the central courtyard, above the staircase to the right, is a spectacular mural of Hidalgo by the modern Mexican master José Clemente Orozco. The Father of Independence appears high overhead, bearing directly down on the viewer and looking as implacable as a force of nature. On one of the adjacent walls, Orozco painted *The Carnival of Ideologies,* a dark satire on the prevailing fanaticisms of his day. Another of his murals is inside the second-floor chamber of representatives, depicting Hidalgo again, this time in a more conventional posture, writing the proclamation to end slavery in Mexico. The *palacio* is open daily from 10am to 8pm.

In the plaza on the opposite side of the cathedral from the Plaza de Armas is the **Rotonda de los Hombres Ilustres.** Sixteen white columns, each supporting a bronze statue, stand as monuments to Guadalajara's and Jalisco's distinguished sons. Across the street from the plaza, in front of the Museo Regional, you will see a line of horse-drawn buggies. A carriage ride around the Centro Histórico lasts about an hour and costs 200 pesos for one to four people.

Facing the east side of the rotunda is the **Museo Regional de Guadalajara,** Liceo 60 (✆ **33/3613-2703**). Originally a convent, it was built in 1701 in the baroque style and contains some of the region's important archaeological finds, fossils, historic objects, and art. Among the highlights are a giant reconstructed mammoth's skeleton and a meteorite weighing 772 kilograms (1,702 lb.), discovered in Zacatecas in 1792. On the first floor, there's a fascinating exhibit of pre-Hispanic pottery and some exquisite pottery and clay figures recently unearthed near Tequila during the construction of the toll road. On the second floor is a small ethnography exhibit of the contemporary dress of the state's indigenous peoples, including the Coras, Huicholes, Mexicaneros, Nahuas, and Tepehuanes. It's open Tuesday through Saturday from 9am to 5:30pm and Sunday from 9am to 4:30pm. Admission is 40 pesos.

Behind the Cathedral is the Plaza Liberación, with the **Teatro Degollado** (deh-goh-*yah*-doh) on the opposite side. This neoclassical 19th-century opera house was named for Santos Degollado, a local patriot who fought with Juárez against Maximilian and the French. Apollo and the nine muses decorate the theater's pediment, and the interior is famous for both the acoustics and the rich decoration. It hosts a variety of performances during the year, including the Ballet Folclórico on Sunday at 10am. It's open Monday through Friday from 10am to 2pm and during performances.

To the right of the theater, across the street, is the sweet little **church of Santa María de Gracia,** built in 1573 as part of a convent for Dominican nuns. On the opposite side of the Teatro Degollado is the **church of San Agustín.** The former convent is now the **University of Guadalajara School of Music.**

Cathedral **3**
Church of Santa María de Gracia **7**
Instituto Cultural Cabañas **12**
Mercado Libertad **11**
Museo Regional de Guadalajara **5**
Palacio del Gobierno **2**
Plaza de Armas **1**

Plaza Guadalajara **4**
Quetzalcoatl Fountain **10**
Rotonda de los Hombres Ilustres **4**
Teatro Degollado **8**
Universidad de Guadalajara Facultad de Música
& Iglesia de San Agustín **9**

Behind the Teatro Degollado begins the Plaza Tapatía, which leads to the Instituto Cabañas. It passes between a couple of low, modern office buildings. The **Tourism Information Office** is in a building on the right side.

Beyond these office buildings, the plaza opens into a large expanse, now framed by department stores and offices, and dominated by the abstract modern **Quetzalcoatl Fountain.** This fluid steel structure represents the mythical plumed serpent Quetzalcoatl, who figured so prominently in pre-Hispanic religion and culture, and exerts a presence even today.

At the far end of the plaza is the Hospicio Cabañas, formerly an orphanage and known today as the **Instituto Cultural Cabañas ★★**, Cabañas 8 (© **33/3818-2000,** ext. 31009). Admission is 100 pesos. This vast structure is impressive for both its size (more than 23 courtyards) and its grandiose architecture, especially the cupola. Created by the famous Mexican architect Manuel Tolsá, it housed homeless children from 1829 to 1980. Today it's a thriving cultural center offering art shows and classes. The interior walls and ceiling of the main building

Guadalajara Bus Tours

Two companies are now offering bus tours of the city. One is a local company, **Tranvías Turísticos** (no phone), which offers two tours on small buses that look like trolley cars. Get info and buy tickets from the kiosk in Plaza Guadalajara (in front of the cathedral) from 10am until 7pm. There are two routes. One is a circuit through downtown and surrounding neighborhoods. It lasts 1 hour and 10 minutes. The second is a slightly longer tour, going to Tlaquepaque. It lasts 1 1/2 hours. Both cost 90 pesos. The other company, **Tapatío Tours** (© 33/3613-0887; www.tapatiotour.com), has modern, bright red double-decker buses. Its tour goes from downtown to western Guadalajara to Tlaquepaque. The tour costs 90 pesos on weekdays and 110 pesos on weekends. It goes farther out, into western Guadalajara. There are 10 stops; you can get off at any one and catch the next bus when it passes by, which is every 35 minutes. Catch the bus in the plaza on the north side of the cathedral after 10am.

display murals painted by Orozco in 1937. His *Man of Fire,* in the dome, is said to represent the spirit of humanity projecting itself toward the infinite. Other rooms hold additional Orozco works, as well as excellent contemporary art and temporary exhibits.

Just south of the Hospicio Cabañas (to the left as you exit) is the **Mercado Libertad ★**, Guadalajara's gigantic covered central market, the largest in Latin America. This site has been a market plaza since the 1500s; the present buildings date from the early 1950s (see "Shopping," later in this chapter).

OTHER ATTRACTIONS

At **Parque Agua Azul (Blue Water Park),** plants, trees, shrubbery, statues, and fountains create an idyllic refuge from the bustling city. Many people come here to exercise early in the morning. The park is open daily from 7am to 6pm. Admission is 10 pesos for adults, 5 pesos for children.

Across Independencia from the park, cater-cornered from a small flower market, is the **Museo de Arqueología del Occidente de México,** Calzada Independencia at Avenida del Campesino. It houses a fine collection of pre-Hispanic pottery from Jalisco, Nayarit, and

Colima. The museum is open Tuesday through Sunday from 10am to 2pm and 4 to 7pm. There's a small admission charge.

The state-run **Casa de las Artesanías** (© **33/3619-4664**) is at the Instituto de la Artesanía Jalisciense, just past the park entrance at Calzada Independencia and González Gallo (for details, see "Shopping," below).

Also near the park is Guadalajara's rodeo arena, **Lienzo Charro de Jalisco** (© **33/3619-0315**). Mexican cowboys, known as *charros,* are famous for their riding and lasso work, and the arena in Guadalajara is considered the big-time. There are shows and competitions every Sunday at noon. The arena is at Av. Dr. R. Michel 577, between González Gallo and Las Palomas.

Basílica de la Virgen de Zapopan ★

A wide promenade several blocks long leads to a large, open plaza and the basilica. This is the religious center of Guadalajara. On the Virgin's feast day (see "Special Events," above), the plaza fills with thousands of *tapatíos.* The 18th-century church is a combination of baroque and *plateresque* styles. The cult of the Virgin of Zapopan practically began with the foundation of Guadalajara itself. She is much revered and the object of many pilgrimages. In front of the church are several stands selling religious figures and paraphernalia. On one side of the church is a museum and store dedicated to the betterment of the Huichol Indians. It is worth a visit. Admission to the Huichol museum is 5 pesos.

Main Plaza, Zapopan (10km/6¼ miles northwest of downtown). No phone. Free admission. Daily 7am–7pm. Museum Mon–Sat 9:30am–6pm; Sun 10am–2pm.

Museo de la Ciudad

This museum opened in 1992 in a former convent. It chronicles Guadalajara's past. The eight rooms, beginning on the right and proceeding in chronological order, cover the period from just before the city's founding to the present. Unusual artifacts, including rare Spanish armaments and equestrian paraphernalia, give a sense of what day-to-day life was like through the centuries. Descriptive text is in Spanish only.

Independencia 684 (at M. Bárcenas). © **33/3658-2531.** 5 pesos. Tues–Sun 10am–5pm.

Museo de las Artes de la Universidad de Guadalajara

Inside the main lecture hall of this building are some more murals by Orozco. On the wall behind the stage is a bitter denunciation of corruption called *The People and Their False Leaders.* In the cupola is a more optimistic work—*The Five-fold Man,* who works to create a better society and better self. There is also a small permanent collection of modern art, which will look all too familiar because the works seem so derivative of many of the modern masters.

Juárez 975 (enter on López Cotilla). © **33/3134-2222.** www.museodelasartes. udg.mx. 5 pesos. Tues–Sun 10am–8pm.

Museo Pantaleón Panduro ★★★ This museum houses a magnificent collection of ceramic works. Collectors and connoisseurs of pottery will love it, but so will casual students of Mexican popular culture and the arts. This could be one of the great museums of Mexico, but I would change a few things to make it perfect. Every year a national competition is held in Tlaquepaque among ceramists from across Mexico. Prizes are awarded in seven categories and a best of show among these. (*Tip:* The competition is held every June, which is a good time for visiting Tlaquepaque.) The president of Mexico even comes to town to present the awards. After the competition, many of the winning pieces become part the museum's collection. The virtuosity manifested in some of them will take your breath away. It would be wonderful if they were organized by category, with better explanatory text. But for now, the best thing you can do is cajole someone into showing you around and explaining the pieces on display. The staff is actually quite knowledgeable, and at least one member speaks English. The museum occupies a third of a large complex that in colonial times housed a large religious community. It's now called **Centro Cultural El Refugio,** and it's worth ambling through after you've seen the museum's collection.

P. Sánchez 191 (at Calle Florida, Tlaquepaque). © **33/3639-5656.** Free admission. Tues–Sun 10am–6pm.

2 SHOPPING

Many visitors to Guadalajara come specifically for the shopping in Tlaquepaque and Tonalá (see below). If you have little free time, try the government-run **Instituto de la Artesanía Jalisciense** ★, González Gallo 20 at Calzada Independencia (© **33/3619-4664**), in Parque Agua Azul, just south of downtown. This place is perfect for one-stop shopping, with two floors of pottery, silver jewelry, dance masks, glassware, leather goods, and regional clothing from around the state and the country. As you enter, on the right are museum displays showing crafts and regional costumes from the state of Jalisco. The craft store is open Monday through Friday from 10am to 6pm, Saturday from 10am to 5pm, Sunday from 10am to 3pm.

Guadalajara is known for its shoe industry; if you're in the market for a pair, try the **Galería del Calzado,** a shopping center made up exclusively of shoe stores. It's on the west side, about 6 blocks from Minerva Circle, at avenidas México and Yaquis.

Mariachis and *charros* come to Guadalajara from all over Mexico to buy highly worked belts and boots, wide-brimmed sombreros, and embroidered shirts. Several tailor shops and stores specialize in these outfits. One is **El Charro,** which has a store in the Plaza del Sol shopping center, across the street from the Hotel Presidente InterContinental, and one downtown on Juárez.

To view a good slice of what constitutes the material world for most Mexicans, try the mammoth **Mercado Libertad** ★ downtown. Besides food and produce, you'll see crafts, household goods, clothing, magic potions, and more. Although it opens at 7am, the market isn't in full swing until around 10am. Come prepared to haggle.

SHOPPING IN TLAQUEPAQUE & TONALA

Almost everyone who comes to Guadalajara for the shopping has Tlaquepaque (tlah-keh-*pah*-keh) and Tonalá in mind. These two suburbs are traditional handicraft centers that produce and sell a wide variety of *artesanía* (crafts).

Tlaquepaque

Located about 20 minutes from downtown, **Tlaquepaque** ★★★ has the best shopping for handicrafts and decorative arts in all of Mexico. Over the years, it has become a fashionable place, attracting talented designers in a variety of fields. Even though it's a suburb of a large city, it has a cozy, small-town feel; it's a pleasure simply to stroll through the central streets from shop to shop. No one hassles you; no one does the hard sell. There are some excellent places to eat (see "Where to Dine," in chapter 6), or you can grab some simple fare at **El Parián,** a building in the middle of town that houses a number of small eateries.

A taxi from downtown Guadalajara costs 70 pesos, or you can take one of the TUR 706 buses that make a fairly quick run from downtown to Tlaquepaque and Tonalá (see "Getting Around," in chapter 6).

> ## (Tips) Packing It In
>
> If you need your purchases packed safely so that you can check them as extra baggage, or if you want them shipped, talk to **Margaret del Río.** She is an American who runs a large packing and shipping company at Juárez 347, Tlaquepaque (𝄪 **33/3657-5652**). Paying the excess baggage fee usually is cheaper than shipping, but it's less convenient.

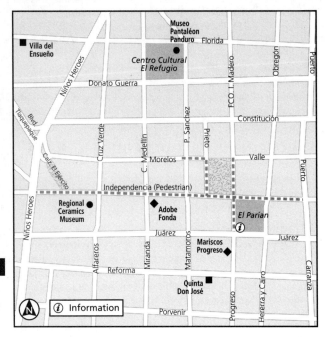

The **Tlaquepaque Tourism Office** (© **33/3562-7050,** ext. 2320; turismotlaquepaque@yahoo.com.mx) has an information booth in the town's main square by El Parián. It's staffed from 10am to 8pm daily.

If you are interested in pottery and ceramics, make sure to see the Pantaleón Panduro Museum, listed above. Another is the **Regional Ceramics Museum,** Independencia 237 (© **33/3635-5404**), which displays several aspects of traditional Jalisco pottery as produced in Tlaquepaque and Tonalá. The examples date back several generations and are grouped according to the technique used to produce them. Note the crosshatch design known as *petatillo* on some of the pieces; it's one of the region's oldest traditional motifs and is, like so many other motifs, a real pain to produce. Look for the wonderful old kitchen and dining room, complete with pots, utensils, and dishes. The museum is open Tuesday through Saturday from 10am to 6pm, Sunday from 10am to 3pm; admission is free.

The following list of Tlaquepaque shops will give you an idea of what to expect. This is just a small fraction of what you'll find; the best approach might be to just follow your nose. The main shopping is along **Independencia,** a pedestrians-only street that starts at El Parián. It was recently resurfaced in stone and looks pretty sharp. You can go door-to-door visiting the shops until the street ends, then work your way back on **Calle Juárez,** the next street over, south of Independencia.

Agustín Parra So you bought an old hacienda and are trying to restore its chapel—where do you go to find traditional baroque sculpture, religious art, gold-leafed objects, and even entire *retablos* (altar pieces)? Parra is famous for exactly this kind of work, and the store is lovely. It's open Monday through Saturday from 10am to 7pm. Independencia 158. ✆ **33/3657-8530.**

Bazar Hecht One of the village's longtime favorites. Here you'll find wood objects, handmade furniture, and a few antiques. It's open Monday through Saturday from 10am to 2:30pm and 3:30 to 7pm. Juárez 162. ✆ **33/3657-0316.**

Sergio Bustamante Sergio Bustamante's imaginative, original bronze, ceramic, and papier-mâché sculptures are among the most sought-after in Mexico—as well as the most copied. He also designs silver jewelry. This exquisite gallery showcases his work. It's open Monday through Saturday from 10am to 7pm, Sunday from noon to 4pm. Independencia 238 at Cruz Verde. ✆ **33/3639-5519.**

Teté Arte y Diseño Architectural decorative objects—especially hand-wrought-iron hardware for the "Old Mexico" look—are the specialty here. The store also has a large collection of wrought-iron chandeliers. It's open Monday through Saturday from 10am to 7:30pm. Juárez 173. ✆ **33/3635-7347.**

Tonala: A Tradition of Pottery Making

Tonalá ★★ is a pleasant town 5 minutes from Tlaquepaque. The streets were paved only recently, and there aren't fancy shops here. The village has been a center of pottery making since pre-Hispanic times; half of the more than 400 workshops produce a wide variety of high- and low-temperature pottery. Other local artists work with forged iron, cantera stone, brass and copper, marble, miniatures, papier-mâché, textiles, blown glass, and gesso. This is a good place to look for custom work in any of these materials; you can locate a large pool of craftspeople by asking around a little.

Market days are Thursday and Sunday. Expect large crowds and blocks and blocks of stalls displaying locally made pottery and glassware, as well as cheap manufactured goods, food, and all kinds of bric-a-brac. "Herb men" sell a rainbow selection of dried medicinal herbs from wheelbarrows, magicians entertain crowds with sleight-of-hand, and craftspeople spread their colorful wares on the plaza's sidewalks. I prefer to visit Tonalá on non–market days, when it's much easier to get around and see the stores and workshops. This is the place for buying sets of margarita glasses, the widely seen blue-rimmed hand-blown glassware, finely painted *petatillo* ware, and the pottery typically associated with Mexico.

The **Tonalá Tourism Office** (*©* **33/3284-3092**) is in the Artesanos building, set back from the road at Atonaltecas 140 Sur (the main street leading into Tonalá) at Matamoros. There is an information booth in front. Hours are Monday through Friday from 9am to 3pm, Saturday from 9am to 1pm. The office offers **free walking tours** on Monday, Tuesday, Wednesday, and Friday at 9am and 2pm, Saturday you'll see ceramics, stoneware, blown glass, papier-mâché, and the like). Tours last 3 to 4 hours and require a minimum of five people. Visitors can request an English-speaking guide. Also in Tonalá, cater-cornered from the church, you'll see a small tourism information kiosk that's staffed on market days and provides maps and useful information.

Tonalá is also the home of the **Museo Nacional de Cerámica,** Constitución 104, between Hidalgo and Morelos (© **33/3284-3000,** ext. 1194). The museum occupies a two-story mansion and displays work from Jalisco and all over the country. There's a large shop in the front on the right as you enter. The museum is open Tuesday through Friday from 10am to 5pm, Saturday and Sunday from 10am to 2pm. Admission is free; the fee for using a video or still camera is 85 pesos per camera.

3 GUADALAJARA AFTER DARK

MARIACHIS

You can't go far in Guadalajara without coming across some maria-chis, but seeing really talented performers takes some effort. Try **Casa Bariachi,** Av. Vallarta 2221 (© **33/3615-0029**). In Tlaquepaque, go to **El Parián,** the building on the town square where mariachis sere-nade diners under the archways.

THE CLUB & MUSIC SCENE

Guadalajara, as you might expect, has a lot of variety in entertain-ment. For the most extensive listing of clubs and performances, get your hands on a copy of *Ocio,* the weekly insert of *Público.* You'll find listings in the back, categorized by type of music. For good mariachis, you should go to Casa Bariachi, mentioned above. Across the street from that club is another called **La Bodeguita del Medio** (© **33/ 3630-1620**), at Av. Vallarta 2320. It offers live old-school Cuban son. The groups come from Cuba and rotate every few months. The last night I visited the place, a small combo was playing in a little corner, partly mixing in with the crowd. The place is small, but people were making room to dance. Another thing to do is track down a Cuban diva, named **Rosalia,** who lives in Guadalajara. She's a great talent and always has a tight band playing with her as she belts out salsa and merengue tunes. The last time I was in Guadalajara, she was singing weekends at the bar at the Hotel Presidente InterContinental.

Tequila: The Name Says It All

Tequila is an entertaining (and intoxicating) town, well worth a day trip from Guadalajara. Several taxi drivers charge about 650 pesos to drive you to the town, get you into a tour of a distillery, take you to a restaurant, and haul you back to Guadalajara. A few of them speak English. One recommended driver is José Gabriel Gómez (© **33/3649-0791;** jgabriel-taxi@hotmail.com); he has a new car and drives carefully. Call him in the evening. Tour companies also arrange bus trips to Tequila; ask at the ticket kiosk of Tranvías Turísticos, mentioned above. That company has started a weekend tour to Tequila, taking people to the Cofradía distillery.

Tequila has many distilleries, including the famous brands **Sauza** and **José Cuervo.** All the distilleries—the big, modern ones and the small, more traditional ones—offer tours. If you're on your own, a good place to hook up with a tour is at the little booth outside the city hall on the main square; two young English-speaking women run tours to any of the local factories. Tours cost only 50 pesos and last about 2 hours. All tours show how tequila is made, what traditions the process follows, and what differences exist between tequilas; they end, of course, with a tasting. Avenida Vallarta runs straight to the highway to Tequila, which is about an hour outside of Guadalajara.

Another approach is to take the **Tequila Express** to the town of Amatitán, home of the Herradura distillery. This excursion is more about having a good time and enjoying some of the things this area is known for than it is about sampling tequila. Serious tequila enthusiasts will be disappointed. There's a nice tour of the distillery, but most of the time is spent watching mariachis and Mexican cowboys perform. The tequila tastings are limited. Everyone has a good time and drinks a fair share, but a trip to the town proper is more informative and offers a greater opportunity for trying different tequilas.

The Tequila Express leaves from the train station on Friday and Saturday, and sometimes on Sunday during vacation and holiday season. It's well organized. You need to be there by 10am. The Guadalajara Chamber of Commerce (Cámara de Comercio), at Vallarta and Niño Obrero (© **33/3880-9099**), organizes this trip. Buy tickets ahead of time at the main office; at the small office in the Centro Histórico at Morelos 395; at Calle Colón (no phone); or through Ticketmaster (© **33/3818-3800**). Office hours are Monday through Friday from 9am to 2pm and 4 to 6pm. Tickets cost 850 pesos for adults, 500 for children 6 to 12. The tour includes food and drink. It returns to Guadalajara at about 8pm. Travel time is 1$^3/_4$ hours each way. For more information, see **www.tequila express.com.mx**.

Fast Facts

1 FAST FACTS: MID-PACIFIC MEXICO

AREA CODES   See "Staying Connected," p. 35.

BUSINESS HOURS   Most businesses in larger cities are open between 9am and 7pm; in smaller towns many close between 2 and 4pm. Most close on Sunday. In resort areas stores commonly open in the mornings on Sunday, and shops stay open late, until 8 or even 10pm. Bank hours are Monday through Friday from 9 or 9:30am to anywhere between 3 and 7pm. Banks open on Saturday for at least a half-day.

DRINKING LAWS   The legal drinking age in Mexico is 18; however, asking for ID or denying purchase is extremely rare. Grocery stores sell everything from beer and wine to national and imported liquors. You can buy liquor 24 hours a day, but during major elections, dry laws often are enacted by as much as 72 hours in advance of the election—and they apply to tourists as well as local residents. Mexico does not have laws that apply to transporting liquor in cars, but authorities are beginning to target drunk drivers more aggressively. It's a good idea to drive defensively.

It's illegal to drink in the street; but many tourists do. If you are getting drunk, you shouldn't drink in the street, because you are more likely to get stopped by the police.

DRIVING RULES   See "Getting There and Getting Around," p. 11.

ELECTRICITY   The electrical system in Mexico is 110 volts AC (60 cycles), as in the United States and Canada. In reality, however, it may cycle more slowly and overheat your appliances. To compensate, select a medium or low speed on hair dryers. Many older hotels still have electrical outlets for flat two-prong plugs; you'll need an adapter for any plug with an enlarged end on one prong or with three prongs. Many better hotels have three-hole outlets (*trifásicos* in Spanish). Those that don't may have loan adapters, but to be sure, it's always better to carry your own.

EMBASSIES & CONSULATES Embassies and consulates provide valuable lists of doctors and lawyers, as well as regulations concerning marriages in Mexico. Contrary to popular belief, your embassy cannot get you out of jail, provide postal or banking services, or fly you home when you run out of money. Consular officers can provide advice on most matters and problems, however. Most countries have an embassy in Mexico City, and many have consular offices or representatives in the provinces.

The Embassy of the **United States** in Mexico City is at Paseo de la Reforma 305, next to the Hotel María Isabel Sheraton at the corner of Río Danubio (© **55/5080-2000**); hours are Monday through Friday from 8:30am to 5:30pm. Visit **http://www.usembassy-mexico. gov** for information related to U.S. Embassy services. In mid-Pacific Mexico, there is a U.S. Consulates at Progreso 175, Col. Americana, Guadalajara (© **333/268-2100**); in addition, there are consular agencies in Mazatlán (© **669/916-5889**) and Puerto Vallarta (© **322/ 222-0069**).

The Embassy of **Australia** in Mexico City is at Rubén Darío 55, Col. Polanco (© **55/1101-2200;** www.mexico.embassy.gov.au). It's open Monday through Thursday from 9:30am to noon.

The Embassy of **Canada** in Mexico City is at Schiller 529, Col. Polanco (© **55/5724-7900** or for emergencies 01-800/706-2900); it's open Monday through Friday from 9am to 1pm and 2 to 5pm. Visit www.dfait-maeci.gc.ca or www.canada.org.mx for addresses of consular agencies in Mexico. In mid-Pacific Mexico, there are Canadian consulates in Guadalajara (© **333/671-4740**); Mazatlán (© **669/ 913-7320**); and Puerto Vallarta (© **322/293-0098**).

The Embassy of **New Zealand** in Mexico City is at Jaime Balmes 8, 4th floor, Col. Los Morales, Polanco (© **55/5283-9460;** www. nzembassy.com/home.cfm?c=50). It's open Monday through Thursday from 8:30am to 2pm and 3 to 5:30pm, and Friday from 8:30am to 2pm.

The Embassy of the **United Kingdom** in Mexico City is at Río Lerma 71, Col. Cuauhtémoc (© **55/5207-2089** or 5242-8500; http://ukinmexico.fco.gov.uk/en). It's open Monday through Thursday from 8am to 4pm and Friday from 8am to 1:30pm.

The Embassy of **Ireland** in Mexico City is at Cda. Boulevard Manuel Avila Camacho 76, 3rd Floor, Col. Lomas de Chapultepec (© **55/5520-5803;** www.irishembassy.com.mx). It's open Monday through Friday from 9am to 5pm.

The **South African** Embassy in Mexico City is at Andrés Bello 10, Edificio Fórum, 9th Floor, Col. Polanco (© **55/5282-9260**). It's open Monday through Friday from 8am to 4pm.

EMERGENCIES In case of emergency, dial © **065** from any phone within Mexico. For police emergency numbers, turn to the "Fast Facts" sections in each of the individual chapters.

GASOLINE (PETROL) There's one government-owned brand of gas and one gasoline station name throughout the country—**Pemex** (Petroleras Mexicanas). There are two types of gas in Mexico: *magna,* 87-octane unleaded gas, and *premio,* which is 93-octane. In Mexico, fuel and oil are sold by the liter, which is slightly more than a quart (1 gal. equals about 3.8L). Many franchise Pemex stations have restroom facilities and convenience stores—a great improvement over the old ones. Gas stations accept both credit and debit cards for gas purchases.

HOLIDAYS For schedules, see "Calendar of Events," in chapter 1.

INSURANCE For information on traveler's insurance, trip cancellation insurance, and medical insurance while traveling, please visit www.frommers.com/planning.

LANGUAGE Spanish is the official language in Mexico. English is spoken and understood to some degree in most tourist areas. Mexicans are very accommodating with foreigners who try to speak Spanish, even in broken sentences. See chapter 9 for a glossary of simple phrases for expressing basic needs.

LEGAL AID Travelers who find themselves in legal trouble in Mexico should contact their respective embassy or consulate, which may be able to offer limited legal assistance, including information concerning Mexico's legal system, a possible list of attorneys, jail visits, and monitoring of your situation.

MAIL Postage for a postcard or letter is 11 pesos; it may arrive anywhere from 1 to 6 weeks later. The price for registered letters and packages depends on the weight, and unreliable delivery time can take 2 to 6 weeks. The recommended way to send a package or important mail is through FedEx, DHL, UPS, or another reputable international mail service.

NEWSPAPERS & MAGAZINES The English-language newspaper, the *Miami Herald,* is published in conjunction with *El Universal.* You can find it at most newsstands. The *News*—a new English-language daily with Mexico-specific news, published in Mexico City—launched in late 2007. Newspaper kiosks in larger cities also carry a selection of English-language magazines.

PASSPORTS See www.frommers.com/planning for information on how to obtain a passport.

For Residents of Australia Contact the **Australian Passport Infor-** **mation Service** at © 131-232, or visit the government website at www.passports.gov.au.

For Residents of Canada Contact the central **Passport Office,** Department of Foreign Affairs and International Trade, Ottawa, ON K1A 0G3 (© 800/567-6868; www.ppt.gc.ca).

For Residents of Ireland Contact the **Passport Office,** Setanta Centre, Molesworth Street, Dublin 2 (© 01/671-1633; www.irlgov. ie/iveagh).

For Residents of New Zealand Contact the **Passports Office** at © 0800/225-050 in New Zealand or 04/474-8100, or log on to www.passports.govt.nz.

For Residents of the United Kingdom Visit your nearest passport office, major post office, or travel agency or contact the **United Kingdom Passport Service** at © 0870/521-0410 or search its website at www.ukpa.gov.uk.

For Residents of the United States To find your regional passport office, either check the U.S. State Department website or call the **National Passport Information Center** toll-free number (© 877/ 487-2778) for automated information.

POLICE Several cities have a special corps of English-speaking Tourist Police to assist with directions, guidance, and more. In case of emergency, dial © 065 from any phone within Mexico. For police emergency numbers, turn to "Fast Facts," in the individual chapters.

SMOKING See p. 25 in chapter 1.

TAXES The 15% IVA (value-added) tax applies on goods and services in most of Mexico, and it's supposed to be included in the posted price. This tax is 10% in Cancún, Cozumel, and Los Cabos. There is a 5% tax on food and drinks consumed in restaurants that sell alcoholic beverages with an alcohol content of more than 10%; this tax applies whether you drink alcohol or not. Tequila is subject to a 25% tax. Mexico imposes an exit tax on every foreigner leaving the country by plane.

TELEPHONES See "Staying Connected," p. 35 in chapter 1.

TIME Central Time prevails throughout Mexico's mid-Pacific region, except in Mazatlán which is on Mountain Time. All of Mexico observes **daylight saving time.**

TIPPING   Most service employees in Mexico count on tips for the majority of their income, and this is especially true for bellboys and waiters. Bellboys should receive the equivalent of 50¢ to $1 per bag; waiters generally receive 10% to 15%, depending on the level of service. It is not customary to tip taxi drivers, unless they are hired by the hour or provide touring or other special services.

TOILETS   Public toilets are not common in Mexico, but an increasing number are available, especially at fast-food restaurants and Pemex gas stations. These facilities and restaurant and club restrooms commonly have attendants, who expect a small tip (about 50¢).

VISAS   Citizens of Australia, Canada, the U.K., the U.S., and New Zealand do not require visas to visit Mexico; however, they must have a tourist card. For detailed information regarding visas to Mexico, visit the **National Immigration Institute** at www.inm.gob.mx. For more information on visas and tourist cards, see p. 8 in chapter 1.

VISITOR INFORMATION   The **Mexico Tourism Board** (© 800/ 446-3942; www.visitmexico.com) is an excellent source for general information; you can request brochures and get answers to the most common questions from the exceptionally well-trained, knowledgeable staff. More information (15,000 pages' worth) about Mexico is available on the official site of Mexico's Tourism Board, **www.visit mexico.com**.

The **Mexican Government Tourist Board**'s main office is in Mexico City (© 55/5278-4200). Satellite offices are in the U.S., Canada, and the U.K. In the **United States:** Chicago (© 312/228-0517), Houston (© 713/772-2581), Los Angeles (© 310/282-9112), Miami (© 786/621-2909), and New York (© 212/308-2110). In **Canada:** Toronto (© 416/925-0704). In the **United Kingdom:** London (© 020/7488-9392).

The **Jalisco Tourism Board** is at Morelos No. 102, Plaza Tapatia, CP 44100 Guadalajara, Jalisco (© 33/613-1196). The **Nayarit Tourism Board** is at Calz. del Ejército and Av. México s/n, Ex-Convento de la Cruz de Zacate, CP 63168 Tepic, Nayarit (© 311/214-8071). The **Sinaloa Tourism Board** is at Av. Camarón Sabalo and Tiburon, Edificio Banrural 4th Floor, CP 82100 Mazatlán, Sinaloa (© 667/916-5160).

WATER   Tap water in Mexico is generally not potable and it is safest to drink purified bottled water. Some hotels and restaurants purify their water, but you should ask rather than assume this is the case. Ice may also come from tap water and should be used with caution.

2 AIRLINE, HOTEL & CAR-RENTAL WEBSITES

MAJOR AIRLINES

Aeroméxico
www.aeromexico.com

Air France
www.airfrance.com

Alaska Airlines/Horizon Air
www.alaskaair.com

American Airlines
www.aa.com

Aviacsa
www.aviacsa.com.mx

Continental Airlines
www.continental.com

Delta Air Lines
www.delta.com

Frontier Airlines
www.frontierairlines.com

Mexicana
www.mexicana.com

Northwest Airlines
www.nwa.com

TACA
www.taca.com

United Airlines
www.united.com

US Airways
www.usairways.com

BUDGET AIRLINES

Click Mexicana
www.clickmx.com

Frontier Airlines
www.frontierairlines.com

Interjet
www.interjet.com.mx

jetBlue Airways
www.jetblue.com

Volaris
www.volaris.com.mx

MAJOR HOTEL & MOTEL CHAINS

Best Western International
www.bestwestern.com

Courtyard by Marriott
www.marriott.com/courtyard

Crowne Plaza Hotels
www.ichotelsgroup.com/crowneplaza

Embassy Suites
www.embassysuites.com

Four Seasons
www.fourseasons.com

Hilton Hotels
www.hilton.com

Holiday Inn
www.holidayinn.com

Hyatt
www.hyatt.com

InterContinental Hotels & Resorts
www.ichotelsgroup.com

Marriott
www.marriott.com

Omni Hotels
www.omnihotels.com

Radisson Hotels & Resorts
www.radisson.com

Ramada Worldwide
www.ramada.com

Renaissance
www.renaissancehotels.com

Sheraton Hotels & Resorts
www.starwoodhotels.com/sheraton

Westin Hotels & Resorts
www.starwoodhotels.com/westin

Wyndham Hotels & Resorts
www.wyndham.com

Advantage
www.advantage.com

Alamo
www.alamo.com

Auto Europe
www.autoeurope.com

Avis
www.avis.com

Budget
www.budget.com

Dollar
www.dollar.com

Enterprise
www.enterprise.com

Hertz
www.hertz.com

Kemwel (KHA)
www.kemwel.com

National
www.nationalcar.com

Thrifty
www.thrifty.com

Useful Terms & Phrases

Most Mexicans are very patient with foreigners who try to speak their language; it helps a lot to know a few basic phrases. Included in this appendix are simple phrases for expressing basic needs, followed by some common menu items.

1 BASIC VOCABULARY

ENGLISH-SPANISH PHRASES

English	Spanish	Pronunciation
Good day	**Buen día**	bwehn *dee*-ah
Good morning	**Buenos días**	*bweh*-nohss *dee*-ahss
How are you?	**¿Cómo está?**	*koh*-moh ehss-*tah?*
Very well	**Muy bien**	mwee byehn
Thank you	**Gracias**	*grah*-syahss
You're welcome	**De nada**	deh *nah*-dah
Good-bye	**Adiós**	ah-*dyohss*
Please	**Por favor**	pohr fah-*vohr*
Yes	**Sí**	see
No	**No**	noh
Excuse me	**Perdóneme**	pehr-*doh*-neh-meh
Give me	**Déme**	*deh*-meh
Where is . . . ?	**¿Dónde está . . . ?**	*dohn*-deh ehss-*tah?*
the station	**la estación**	lah ehss-tah-*syohn*
a hotel	**un hotel**	oon oh-*tehl*
a gas station	**una gasolinera**	*oo*-nah gah-soh-lee-*neh*-rah
a restaurant	**un restaurante**	oon res-tow-*rahn*-teh
the toilet	**el baño**	el *bah*-nyoh

English	Spanish	Pronunciation
a good doctor	**un buen médico**	oon bwehn *meh*-dee-coh
the road to . . .	**el camino a/hacia . . .**	el cah-*mee*-noh ah/*ah*-syah
To the right	**A la derecha**	ah lah deh-*reh*-chah
To the left	**A la izquierda**	ah lah ees-*kyehr*-dah
Straight ahead	**Derecho**	deh-*reh*-choh
I would like	**Quisiera**	key-*syeh*-rah
I want	**Quiero**	*kyeh*-roh
to eat	**comer**	koh-*mehr*
a room	**una habitación**	*oo*-nah ah-bee-tah-*syohn*
Do you have . . . ?	**¿Tiene usted . . . ?**	tyeh-neh oo-*sted*?
a book	**un libro**	oon *lee*-broh
a dictionary	**un diccionario**	oon deek-syow-*nah*-ryo
How much is it?	**¿Cuánto cuesta?**	*kwahn*-toh *kwehss*-tah?
When?	**¿Cuándo?**	*kwahn*-doh?
What?	**¿Qué?**	keh?
There is (Is there . . . ?)	**(¿)Hay (. . . ?)**	eye?
What is there?	**¿Qué hay?**	keh eye?
Yesterday	**Ayer**	ah-*yer*
Today	**Hoy**	oy
Tomorrow	**Mañana**	mah-*nyah*-nah
Good	**Bueno**	*bweh*-noh
Bad	**Malo**	*mah*-loh
Better (best)	**(Lo) Mejor**	(loh) meh-*hohr*
More	**Más**	mahs
Less	**Menos**	*meh*-nohss
No smoking	**Se prohibe fumar**	seh proh-*ee*-beh foo-*mahr*
Postcard	**Tarjeta postal**	tar-*heh*-ta pohs-*tahl*
Insect repellent	**Repelente contra insectos**	reh-peh-*lehn*-te *cohn*-trah een-*sehk*-tos

USEFUL TERMS & PHRASES

9

BASIC VOCABULARY

English	Spanish	Pronunciation
Do you speak English?	¿Habla usted inglés?	*ah*-blah oo-*sted* een-*glehs*?
Is there anyone here who speaks English?	¿Hay alguien aquí que hable inglés?	eye *ahl*-gyehn ah-*kee* keh *ah*-bleh een-*glehs*?
I speak a little Spanish.	Hablo un poco de español.	*ah*-bloh oon *poh*-koh deh ehss-pah-*nyohl*
I don't understand Spanish very well.	No (lo) entiendo muy bien el español.	noh (loh) ehn-*tyehn*-doh mwee byehn el ehss-pah-*nyohl*
The meal is good.	Me gusta la comida.	meh *goo*-stah lah koh-*mee*-dah
What time is it?	¿Qué hora es?	keh *oh*-rah ehss?
May I see your menu?	¿Puedo ver el menú (la carta)?	*pueh*-do vehr el meh-*noo* (lah *car*-tah)?
The check, please.	La cuenta, por favor.	lah *quehn*-tah pohr fa-*vorh*
What do I owe you?	¿Cuánto le debo?	*kwahn*-toh leh *deh*-boh?
What did you say?	¿Mande? (formal)	*mahn*-deh?
	¿Cómo? (informal)	*koh*-moh?
I want (to see) . . .	Quiero (ver) . . .	*kyeh*-roh (vehr)
a room	un cuarto or una habitación	oon *kwar*-toh, oo-nah ah-bee-tah-*syohn*
for two persons	para dos personas	*pah*-rah dohss pehr-*soh*-nahs
with (without) bathroom	con (sin) baño	kohn (seen) *bah*-nyoh
We are staying here only . . .	Nos quedamos aquí solamente . . .	nohs keh-*dah*-mohss ah-*kee* soh-lah-*mehn*-teh
one night.	una noche.	oo-nah *noh*-cheh
one week.	una semana.	oo-nah seh-*mah*-nah

English	Spanish	Pronunciation
We are leaving . . .	**Partimos (Salimos) . . .**	pahr-*tee*-mohss (sah-*lee*-mohss)
tomorrow.	**mañana.**	mah-*nya*-nah
Do you accept . . . ?	**¿Acepta usted . . . ?**	ah-*sehp*-tah oo-*sted*
traveler's checks?	**cheques de viajero?**	*cheh*-kehss deh byah-*heh*-roh?
Is there a	**¿Hay una**	eye *oo*-nah lah-*vahn*-
laundromat . . . ?	**lavandería . . . ?**	deh-*ree*-ah
near here?	**cerca de aquí?**	*sehr*-kah deh ah-*kee*
Please send these clothes to the laundry.	**Hágame el favor de mandar esta ropa a la lavandería.**	*ah*-gah-meh el fah-*vohr* deh mahn-*dahr* ehss-tah *roh*-pah a lah lah-*vahn*-deh-*ree*-ah

NUMBERS

1	**uno** (*ooh*-noh)	17	**diecisiete** (dyess-ee-*syeh*-teh)
2	**dos** (dohss)	18	**dieciocho** (dyess-ee-*oh*-choh)
3	**tres** (trehss)	19	**diecinueve** (dyess-ee-*nweh*-beh)
4	**uatro** (*kwah*-troh)	20	**veinte** (*bayn*-teh)
5	**cinco** (*seen*-koh)	30	**treinta** (*trayn*-tah)
6	**seis** (sayss)	40	**cuarenta** (kwah-*ren*-tah)
7	**siete** (*syeh*-teh)	50	**cincuenta** (seen-*kwen*-tah)
8	**ocho** (*oh*-choh)	60	**sesenta** (seh-*sehn*-tah)
9	**nueve** (*nweh*-beh)	70	**setenta** (seh-*tehn*-tah)
10	**diez** (dyess)	80	**ochenta** (oh-*chehn*-tah)
11	**once** (*ohn*-seh)	90	**noventa** (noh-*behn*-tah)
12	**doce** (*doh*-seh)	100	**cien** (syehn)
13	**trece** (*treh*-seh)	200	**doscientos** (do-*syehn*-tohs)
14	**catorce** (kah-*tohr*-seh)	500	**quinientos** (kee-*nyehn*-tohs)
15	**quince** (*keen*-seh)	1,000	**mil** (meal)
16	**dieciseis** (dyess-ee-*sayss*)		

TRANSPORTATION TERMS

English	Spanish	Pronunciation
Airport	**Aeropuerto**	ah-eh-roh-*pwehr*-toh
Flight	**Vuelo**	*bweh*-loh
Rental car	**Arrendadora de autos**	ah-rehn-da-doh-rah deh ow-tohs
Bus	**Autobús**	ow-toh-*boos*

English   **Spanish**   **Pronunciation**

English	Spanish	Pronunciation
Bus or truck	**Camión**	ka-*myohn*
Lane	**Carril**	kah-*reel*
Nonstop (bus)	**Directo**	dee-*rehk*-toh
Baggage (claim area)	**Equipajes**	eh-kee-*pah*-hehss
Intercity	**Foraneo**	foh-rah-*neh*-oh
Luggage storage area	**Guarda equipaje**	gwar-dah eh-kee-*pah*-heh
Arrival gates	**Llegadas**	yeh-*gah*-dahss
Originates at this station	**Local**	loh-*kahl*
Originates elsewhere	**De paso**	deh *pah*-soh
Stops if seats available	**Para si hay lugares**	*pah*-rah see eye loo-*gah*-rehs
First class	**Primera**	pree-*meh*-rah
Second class	**Segunda**	seh-*goon*-dah
Nonstop (flight)	**Sin escala**	seen ess-*kah*-lah
Baggage claim area	**Recibo de equipajes**	reh-see-boh deh eh-kee-*pah*-hehss
Waiting room	**Sala de espera**	*sah*-lah deh ehss-*peh*-rah
Toilets	**Sanitarios**	sah-nee-*tah*-ryohss
Ticket window	**Taquilla**	tah-*kee*-yah

---

2 MENU TERMS

Achiote Small red seed of the *annatto* tree.

Achiote preparado A Yucatecan prepared paste made of ground *achiote,* wheat and corn flour, cumin, cinnamon, salt, onion, garlic, and oregano.

Agua fresca Fruit-flavored water, usually watermelon, cantaloupe, chia seed with lemon, hibiscus flour, rice, or ground melon-seed mixture.

Antojito Typical Mexican supper foods, usually made with *masa* or tortillas and having a filling or topping such as sausage, cheese, beans, and onions; includes such things as *tacos, tostadas, sopes,* and *garnachas.*

Atole   A thick, lightly sweet, hot drink made with finely ground corn and usually flavored with vanilla, pecan, strawberry, pineapple, or chocolate.

Botana   An appetizer.

Buñuelos   Round, thin, deep-fried crispy fritters dipped in sugar.

Carnitas   Pork deep-cooked (not fried) in lard, and then simmered and served with corn tortillas for tacos.

Ceviche   Fresh raw seafood marinated in fresh lime juice and garnished with chopped tomatoes, onions, chiles, and sometimes cilantro.

Chayote   A vegetable pear or mirliton, a type of spiny squash boiled and served as an accompaniment to meat dishes.

Chiles en nogada   Poblano peppers stuffed with a mixture of ground pork and beef, spices, fruits, raisins, and almonds. Can be served either warm—fried in a light batter—or cold, sans the batter. Either way, it is then covered in walnut-and-cream sauce.

Chiles rellenos   Usually poblano peppers stuffed with cheese or spicy ground meat with raisins, rolled in a batter, and fried.

Churro   Tube-shaped, breadlike fritter, dipped in sugar and sometimes filled with *cajeta* (milk-based caramel) or chocolate.

Cochinita pibil   Pork wrapped in banana leaves, pit-baked in a *pibil* sauce of *achiote,* sour orange, and spices; common in the Yucatán.

Enchilada   A tortilla dipped in sauce, usually filled with chicken or white cheese, and sometimes topped with *mole* (*enchiladas rojas* or *de mole*), or with tomato sauce and sour cream (*enchiladas suizas*—Swiss enchiladas), or covered in a green sauce *(enchiladas verdes),* or topped with onions, sour cream, and guacamole *(enchiladas potosinas).*

Escabeche   A lightly pickled sauce used in Yucatecan chicken stew.

Frijoles refritos   Pinto beans mashed and cooked with lard.

Garnachas   A thickish small circle of fried *masa* with pinched sides, topped with pork or chicken, onions, and avocado, or sometimes chopped potatoes and tomatoes, typical as a *botana* in Veracruz and Yucatán.

Gorditas   Thick, fried corn tortillas, slit and stuffed with choice of cheese, beans, beef, chicken, with or without lettuce, tomato, and onion garnish.

Horchata   Refreshing drink made of ground rice or melon seeds, ground almonds, cinnamon, and lightly sweetened.

Huevos mexicanos   Scrambled eggs with chopped onions, hot green peppers, and tomatoes.

Huitlacoche   Sometimes spelled "cuitlacoche." A mushroom-flavored black fungus that appears on corn in the rainy season; considered a delicacy.

Manchamantel   Translated, means "tablecloth stainer." A stew of chicken or pork with chiles, tomatoes, pineapple, bananas, and jicama.

Masa   Ground corn soaked in lime; the basis for tamales, corn tortillas, and soups.

Mixiote   Rabbit, lamb, or chicken cooked in a mild chile sauce (usually chile *ancho* or *pasilla*), and then wrapped like a tamal and steamed. It is generally served with tortillas for tacos, with traditional garnishes of pickled onions, hot sauce, chopped cilantro, and lime wedges.

Pan de muerto   Sweet bread made around the Days of the Dead (Nov 1–2), in the form of mummies or dolls, or round with bone designs.

Pan dulce   Lightly sweetened bread in many configurations, usually served at breakfast or bought in any bakery.

Papadzules   Tortillas stuffed with hard-boiled eggs and seeds (pumpkin or sunflower) in a tomato sauce.

Pibil   Pit-baked pork or chicken in a sauce of tomato, onion, mild red pepper, cilantro, and vinegar.

Pipián   A sauce made with ground pumpkin seeds, nuts, and mild peppers.

Poc chuc   Slices of pork with onion marinated in a tangy sour orange sauce and charcoal-broiled; a Yucatecan specialty.

Pozole   A soup made with hominy in either chicken or pork broth.

Pulque   A drink made of fermented juice of the maguey plant; best in the state of Hidalgo and around Mexico City.

Quesadilla   Corn or flour tortillas stuffed with melted white cheese and lightly fried.

Queso relleno   "Stuffed cheese," a mild yellow cheese stuffed with minced meat and spices; a Yucatecan specialty.

Rompope   Delicious Mexican eggnog, invented in Puebla, made with eggs, vanilla, sugar, and rum.

Salsa verde   An uncooked sauce using the green tomatillo and puréed with spicy or mild hot peppers, onions, garlic, and cilantro; on tables countrywide.

Sopa de flor de calabaza   A soup made of chopped squash or pumpkin blossoms.

Sopa de lima   A tangy soup made with chicken broth and accented with fresh lime; popular in Yucatán.

Sopa de tortilla   A traditional chicken broth–based soup, seasoned with chiles, tomatoes, onion, and garlic, served with crispy fried strips of corn tortillas.

Sopa tlalpeña (or *caldo tlalpeño*)   A hearty soup made with chicken, carrots, zucchini, corn, onions, garlic, and cilantro.

Sopa tlaxcalteca   A hearty tomato-based soup filled with cooked nopal cactus, cheese, cream, and avocado, with crispy tortilla strips floating on top.

Sope   Pronounced "*soh*-peh." An *antojito* similar to a *garnacha,* except topped with refried beans, crumbled cheese and onions.

Tacos al pastor   Thin slices of flavored pork roasted on a revolving cylinder dripping with onion slices and juice of fresh pineapple slices. Served in small corn tortillas, topped with chopped onion and cilantro.

Tamal   Incorrectly called a tamale (*tamal* singular, *tamales* plural). A meat or sweet filling rolled with fresh *masa,* wrapped in a corn husk or banana leaf, and steamed.

Tikin xic   Also seen on menus as "tik-n-xic" and "tikik chick." Charbroiled fish brushed with *achiote* sauce.

Torta   A sandwich, usually on *bolillo* bread, typically with sliced avocado, onions, tomatoes, with a choice of meat and often cheese.

Xtabentun   Pronounced "shtah-behn-*toon.*" A Yucatecan liquor made of fermented honey and flavored with anise. It comes *seco* (dry) or *crema* (sweet).

Zacahuil   Pork leg tamal, packed in thick *masa,* wrapped in banana leaves, and pit-baked, sometimes pot-made with tomato and *masa;* a specialty of mid- to upper Veracruz.

INDEX

See also Accommodations and Restaurant indexes, below.

RESTAURANTS